Dead from the Waist Down

Dead
from
the
Waist
Down

Scholars and Scholarship
in Literature and the
Popular Imagination

A. D. Nuttall

Yale University Press
New Haven & London

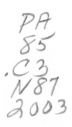

PA
85
.C3
N87
2003

Published with assistance from the Mary Cady Tew Memorial Fund.

Designed by Mary Valencia
Set in Cochin type by Binghamton Valley Composition.
Printed in the United States of America by Vail-Ballou Press.

Library of Congress Cataloging-in-Publication Data

Nuttall, A. D. (Anthony David)
  Dead from the waist down : scholars and scholarship in literature and
the popular imagination / A.D. Nuttall.
    p. cm.
Includes bibliographical references and index.
  ISBN 0-300-09840-5 (cloth : alk. paper)
  1. Casaubon, Isaac, 1559–1614. 2. Learning and scholarship—Moral and
ethical aspects. 3. Browning, Robert, 1812–1889. Grammarian's funeral.
4. Eliot, George, 1819–1880—Characters—Scholars. 5. Great
Britain—Intellectual life—19th century. 6. Eliot, George, 1819–1880.
Middlemarch. 7. Classicists—Great Britain—Biography. 8. Learning and
scholarship in literature. 9. Scholars—Great Britain—Biography. 10.
Pattison, Mark, 1813–1884. 11. Scholars in literature. I. Title.
  PA85.C3N87 2004
  809'.93352—dc21

A catalogue record for this book is available from the British Library.

The paper in this book meets the guidelines for permanence and durability of the
Committee on Production Guidelines for Book Longevity of the Council on
Library Resources.

10 9 8 7 6 5 4 3 2 1

To Oxford

Towery city and branchy between towers . . .

Contents

Preface   ix

Introduction:
Desiccation and Descent — Browning's Confusion   1

1
Mr. Casaubon in *Middlemarch*   26

2
Mark Pattison   72

3
Isaac Casaubon:
The Real Thing   123

Conclusion:
The Other Sexuality and the Morality of Scholarship   171

Notes   207

Index   222

Preface

Scholars are deathly, sexless, tedious; scholars are passionate, devoted heroes of the invisible life, the life of the mind. They are despised and they are to be feared. All who love fiction and poetry owe them a great deal. This book is about scholarship as it was perceived in the nineteenth century, when George Eliot wrote *Middlemarch* and Mark Pattison stalked through the streets of Oxford, and as it was when the sixteenth century gave way to the seventeenth.

At one time, indeed, scholarship was seen as magical. Shortly before his death in 1637 Nicholas Ferrar, the friend of George Herbert, made a bonfire of all his classical texts, comedies, tragedies, epic poems, love poetry. His reasons were religious; a good Protestant must, at the last, turn his back on secular things. So great was the smoke that men came running from the fields "and within a few days it was by rumour spread at Market Townes all the country over that Mr Nic. Ferrar lay a dying, but could not dye until he had burned all his Conjuring-Bookes." To the villagers the lettered man is a magician; the dying Ferrar is seen as a Faustus who repented in time. The story is often told as a humorous example of simple-minded misunderstanding. Of course the villagers were wrong; Nicholas Ferrar was not, nor had he ever been, a magician. But the distance between his conception of the matter and that of the unlettered is less than one is led to expect. Ferrar, too, thinks his deep reading is touched with devilry. Today the Knower, in the popular imagination, is no longer a figure of terror. Rather, in films and soap operas we have come to expect that the intellectual of the group will be shorter, thinner, and weaker than the others and have less immediate pull for the opposite sex. Within the academy, however, among the intellectuals themselves, there has been a paradoxical rejection of the notion of cold intellectual neutrality (which fed the cruder idea of "the sexless scholar") and a sudden obsession with sexuality.

Anyone who writes about scholars and scholarship between these dates will find that the study of Latin and Greek is central. I wondered, when I began this book, whether I would be able to meet the needs of the modern reader by excluding Latin and Greek from my own text. I found in the end that this was impossible. If I had stuck to my original idea, one of two things would have followed. Either the book would have become hopelessly superficial, offering personalities and characters but simply giving up on the heart of its subject — what scholars do, how scholars think — or it would have recorded comments and editorial decisions without disclosing the matter treated; for the reader, the experience would be like listening to one end of a telephone conversation. Neither Robert Browning, when he wrote his poem about a grammarian for Greekless readers in the nineteenth century, nor Tom Stoppard, when he wrote his play about A. E. Housman for an audience presumably innocent of both Greek and Latin at the end of the twentieth, could keep the ancient languages out of the text. So I let them in — but I translate everything.

The background changes — a country town, Oxford, Geneva,

Montpellier, Cambridge, Oxford again. People in other countries see the two ancient universities of England as substantially similar, and it is true, of course, that they have much in common. The British, meanwhile, sense difference: "cool, rational, sober, scientific Cambridge . . . aesthetic, literary, playful, dreaming Oxford," as Sheldon Rothblatt puts it in his *Revolution of the Dons: Cambridge and Society in Victorian England*. The Oxford of this book is the Oxford encoded in Lewis Carroll's *Alice in Wonderland* and *Alice Through the Looking Glass* (and partly decoded in Jonathan Miller's brilliant television film, in which Carroll's genial, logic-chopping monsters are, quite visibly, well-known academic figures of the time). Or it is the systematically repressed Oxford of the film *American Friends*, a world of brittle learned conversation alternating with furtive assignations, in a damp, obscure cottage, a mile or two down river, in the grey-green, misty countryside.

It soon became clear to me that I was describing a vanished — or a vanishing — world. The experience of the schoolroom for several centuries, the pupils laboriously construing the surviving words of an alien civilisation, peremptorily checked and rebuked from moment to moment by the teacher — the scene wonderfully conjured by Rudyard Kipling in his short story "Regulus" — is now a memory for only a few. I remember it myself vividly. I decided that this personal experience was one of the few advantages I had in trying to explore so difficult a subject, and that I would therefore allow myself something which may look a little unprofessional to the more austere reader, the occasional reminiscence.

I am grateful to John Barnard, John Batchelor, Terence Cave, Eric Christiansen, Laura Jones Dooley, Anthony Grafton, Wojciech Jajdelski, Robin Lane Fox, Hermione Lee, Adam Thirlwell, and George Watson for many positive suggestions and for saving me from some bad mistakes. I know that there is a special demon who lies in wait for people who make a thing of accuracy as I do in this book. This means that certain errors — all mine — will have survived. The demon will have his victim.

Part of my "Introduction" is a revised version of an essay, "Browning's Grammarian: Accents Uncertain?" which appeared in

Essays in Criticism 51, no. 1 (2001): 86–100. Part of my final chapter appeared in an essay, "Scholarship and Morality," in *Studies in English Literature* (Tokyo: English Literary Society of Japan, 1995), 1–13. Quotations in the final chapter from Tom Stoppard's play *The Invention of Love* (1997) are reproduced with permission from the publisher, Faber and Faber, Ltd.

Introduction

Desiccation and Descent — Browning's Confusion

This book is about three men, two of them real, one fictitious. It is also about a great change which crept over the idea of the Knower (or the intellectual, or the scholar . . .) between the early modern period and the nineteenth century. The three men are Isaac Casaubon (1559–1614), Mark Pattison (1813–84), and Mr. Edward Casaubon in George Eliot's *Middlemarch* (1871–72). The change in the idea of the Knower is a movement away from electric danger, Faustian glamour, commerce with the devil, towards a sexless deathliness. For the rest of this book "Casaubon" will mean "Isaac Casaubon" and "Mr. Casaubon" will mean the Casaubon in *Middlemarch*.

The division between reality and fiction may seem — in a way is — absolute, but, for all that, our three figures are intimately and intricately related. The relation can even resolve itself at moments into mere identity. It is as if we have before us one of Francis Galton's

1

"composite photographs." Galton delighted in superimposing successive photographic images of members of a class or group, producing at last an image that somehow "covered" all the members and yet retained an appearance of individuality. In this way he arrived at an image of the archetypal British Soldier and the archetypal Violent Criminal.[1] Here is Mr. Casaubon, seemingly solid, but this figure is really — was originally — three distinct persons. Obviously Mr. Casaubon is the odd man out in so far as he is the invention of a novelist. But it has long been suggested that he is actually made, at least in part, out of memories of Mark Pattison. Mark Pattison meanwhile is the author of a marvellous book — still the standard work — on Isaac Casaubon. The book is meticulously attentive to its project, yet one senses as one reads that it is simultaneously about someone else. It is in fact, as Hugh Lloyd-Jones said, concealed autobiography.[2] It is further clear that Pattison actively constructed himself according to the pattern laid down by Casaubon. All three are Knowers, scholars.

This study is a kind of coda to my book *The Alternative Trinity* (1999). There I explored at length what may be termed the preliminary, Faustian phase. The Bible tells in its opening pages how Adam and Eve fell because they ate the fruit from the forbidden tree of knowledge. This mind-setting story ensured that for the Renaissance the sudden sense of an ascent in knowledge carried with it a smell of brimstone. This new adventure of the mind was hell-brink stuff. It is important to remember that science and magic were as yet almost inextricable. The Renaissance as everyone knows began in Italy, so it is perhaps not surprising that one of the earliest passages in which the peculiar juxtaposition of intellectual excitement with damnation can be found is in Dante's *Commedia*. Dante's Ulisse (unlike Homer's, who in the *Odyssey* wants above all to get home) has in old age an unappeasable yearning to sail again over unknown seas. This he links explicitly with the appetite for knowledge:

> *"O frati," dissi "che per cento milia*
> *perigli siete giunti all'occidente,*
> *a questa tanto picciola vigilia*
> *de' nostri sensi ch'è del rimanente,*

non vogliate negar l'esperïenza,
di retro al sol, del mondo sanza gente.
Considerate la vostra semenza:
fatti non foste a viver come bruti,
ma per seguir virtute e canoscenza."

[*Inferno* 26.112–20]

"My brothers," he said, who through a hundred thousand dangers have made landfall in the west, do not willingly withhold, from the time — so brief — left to us of waking sense, the experience of the unpeopled world, in the track of the sun. Consider the seed from which you grew. You were not created to live like brute beasts, but to pursue virtue and knowledge."

In joining the physical errancy of the voyager to the spiritual exploration of the Knower, Dante makes a fundamental move. The germ perhaps was always there in Homer. The word "knew" (*egnō*) appears at the very beginning of the Odyssey, at 1.3. "He saw the cities of many men and *knew* their minds." When the sirens tempt Odysseus / Ulysses with their song, the temptation is gnostic: those who linger to listen, they tell him, will go on their way afterwards "*knowing more things*" (12.188).

The Italian words are stirring, but they are uttered by a spirit in hell. Ulisse set out on his last voyage, heading down into the southern hemisphere and sailed until he saw, dim in the distance, the hugest of all mountains, Mount Purgatory. Here it pleased another — one infinitely stronger than Ulisse — to plunge his ship in the sea and to damn its master for all eternity. A couple of generations later, in a more northerly clime, John Gower described Ulysses as a "clerk knowende of everything." He continues excitedly,

He was a gret magicien;
Of Tullus the rethorique,
Of King Zorastes the magique,
Of Tholome thastronomie,
Of Plato the Philosophie . . .
Of Salamon and the proverbes,
Of Macer al the strengthe of herbes,

3

Introduction

And the Phisique of Ypocras
And lick unto Pictagoras . . .
Through Sorcerie his lust he wan,
Through Sorcerie his wo began,
Through Sorcerie his love he ches,
Through Sorcerie his lif he les.[3]

We are still in the fourteenth century, but the sense of the Renaissance *uomo universale,* "universal man," is strong. This Ulysses has the mathematical powers of a Pythagoras ("Pictagoras"), the philosophical insight of a Plato, the medical knowledge of Hippocrates ("Ypocras"), and the astronomy of Ptolemy ("Tholome"), but, above all, he is, like Faustus, a magician. God said to Adam, "Of the tree of knowledge of good and evil, thou shalt not eat of it: for in the day thou eatest therof thou shalt surely die" (Gn 2.17). As with Adam, so with Ulysses. They make their choice and, by God's will, die. The centuries that followed Gower saw the rise of philosophic magicians: followers of Hermes Trismegistus, the Egyptian sage, supposedly of pre-biblical antiquity, who left behind in the Hermetic treatises a store of primal learning, followers of Plato, men seeking the Philosopher's Stone, alchemists, sorcerers, conjurers. It was not a case of science rising while religion decayed. Rather, step for step, the rise of the Hermetists was matched by the rise of Protestantism, with its unremitting Calvinist insistence on damnation. One party taught that human capacity was limitless, the other that it was zero. Christopher Marlowe's Faustus was not "a Renaissance man who paid a medieval price." He was a Renaissance man paying a Renaissance price—the old sense of a hell in waiting now revived by the contemporary Reformation. No figure is so vividly alive as that which is doomed even as it ventures. These daredevils in the life of the mind crackle with energy. Touch them, and you may be burned. Move later still in time and you will meet the words.

who would lose,
Though full of pain, this intellectual being,
Those thoughts that wander through Eternity
[Paradise Lost 2.146–48]

We have reached John Milton. These inescapably stirring words are, like those of the voyager Ulisse in Dante, spoken by one already in hell. Belial himself is speaking.

There are puzzles in the story. Why is the *earlier* rationalist movement of medieval Scholasticism virtually untouched by this sense of danger? Admittedly, when Peter Abelard, about 1119 or 1120 embarked upon a quasi-rationalist theology, his work was in due course attacked by Bernard of Clairvaux, on the ground that he applied reason to divinity[4] (*theo-logia* as a term, "God-reasoning," appears to be Abelard's invention). When Dante calls Aristotle "the master of those who know" (*Inferno* 4.131), we cannot help being aware, as with Ulisse, that this hero of the mind is damned, but somehow the intuition of evil is much fainter in the case of Aristotle. We are within earshot, somehow, of the unproblematic admiration felt for Aristotle by Thomas Aquinas. Aquinas, writing a little later than Abelard, calls him "the Philosopher," in simple deference. The medieval theologian would of course understand the arguments against supposing that any pagan, however great, could be saved, but he seems wholly unshaken by the special memory of the tree of knowledge and all that it entailed. He seems not to have considered that intelligence itself might be something which God hates and punishes.

All of this gradually cools. Francis Bacon was obviously an agent of the cooling. He removes from science the element of unsocial, exciting (Hermetic) mystery, the lonely individualism of the astronomer in his tower by night, invents the scientific committee, recommends pooling of information. In his *Redargutio Philosophiarum* the new philosopher bears himself modestly, in contrast with the conscious grandeur of the assembled sages of Paris, who *vultu ipso dignitatem cum probitate singuli prae se ferrent*, "to a man declared dignity and righteousness combined, in their very looks." The new man, when he enters, proves to be *aspectus . . . admodum placidi et sereni; nisi quod oris compositio erat tanquam miserantis*, "of an aspect rather peaceable and serene — unless it was that the cast of his features was that of one feeling pity." There is, then, an immediate contrast at the level of body language. Still greater is the implied contrast — not with comfortable establishment figures but with the off-stage, dangerously analogous magician-scientists. As we watch, the extreme arrogance of such as Cornelius Agrippa or Paracelsus is being displaced by the second generation. That Bacon's hackles rose instinctively at this grandiosity is clear in *Temporis Partus Masculus* when he speaks of "the gang of chemists, among whom Paracelsus boasted of his supremacy, and deserved solitary confinement for his braggart air." When the learned men rise at the entrance of the new man and invite him to take the seat of honour, he smiles gently and takes instead a seat level with the rest. He then begins his speech: "homines estis: hoc est, ut ego existimo, non animantes erecti, sed Divi mortales. Deus, mundi conditor et vestrum animas vobis donavit mundi ipsius capaces." "You are men. That means, I reckon, not animals walking on two legs but mortal divinities. God who made the world and you, gave your souls which can comprehend that world." What is happening? We have suddenly returned to the words of Ulisse in the *Commedia*. "You were not created to live like brute beasts, but to pursue virtue and knowledge." He goes on to tell the assembled dignitaries that their wealth is poverty, their power imbecility. When he has finished, his auditors murmur together, like men who have passed suddenly from darkness and shadows into light, and see less than before.[5] So ends, wrote E. A. Abbott, "one of the most rhetorical, aggressive, and negative of all Bacon's philosophical treatises."[6]

Bacon may have begun the "cooling" of the Faustian "Knower" and set in motion the process that will lead in due course to the barren dryness of Mr. Casaubon in *Middlemarch*, but there is nothing sterile about the natural philosopher in the *Redargutio*. In fact a fascinating doubleness runs through the episode as Bacon presents it. This man is modest, we sense, because he can afford to be. His unaggressive smile may indeed have been as Bacon half-discloses, a smile of pity, *de haut en bas*. This man holds all the cards. It is easy to imagine a twenty-first-century equivalent. A Nobel Prize–winner from MIT arrives, tie-less, at a conference in an old European city where the assembled professors are all wearing gowns, refuses the seat at the head of the table, and urges everyone to call him "Ed." Meanwhile the real hierarchy, in which Ed rules and the rest serve, is utterly clear.

Behind the social paradox of intimidating modesty lies a similarly structured paradox of Baconian epistemology. We are to put our notions by and go to the things themselves. Here too one must begin by acknowledging the humility of the stance adopted: the arrogant human intelligence is to lay down its arms and submit to mere fact, itself always prior to any theory. But—at the same time—all this forms part of a plan to acquire power, "the empire of man over things."[7] In the famous Baconian tag, *Natura enim non nisi parendo vincitur*, "It is only by obeying nature that we shall conquer her,"[8] it is a nice question which is more fundamental, the submission or the conquest. This means that the Faustian buzz is still to be felt, behind the new, cooler manner. When Bacon echoed Dante, there was one point of difference. Dante says nothing about human beings as divinities. But the supposedly anti-magical natural philosopher, with the word *divi*, does just that. Applied as it is to seekers after knowledge, it reawakens the dangerous Hermetical aspiration and can even take us to the serpent's promise in Eden—that once Adam and Eve have eaten the fruit from the tree of knowledge, they will be "as gods" (Gn 3.5). Of course we are dealing here with a form of knowing already distinguishable from learning or scholarship. We are looking at early science, now differentiated as such. Neither the nineteenth nor the twentieth century will ever come to see the scientist as dead from the waist down. Eccentric? Certainly. Mad? Perhaps. Powerful? Yes, yes. It is no absurdity to suppose, in 2003, that these are people who could destroy the whole world. The scholars are a good deal safer.

The awkward word "knower," it may be said, covers a number of quite distinct things. There are magician-scientists, theologians, jurists, philosophers, and there are Humanist *grammatici*, experts on Greek and Latin language. To speak of a transition from devilish energy to deathliness is misleading, principally because the devilish party become the scientists, and they, as we have seen, never look deathly exactly (though, when they come up with the nuclear bomb, they will be seen as bringers of death, a rather different thing). The "deathly" party, by contrast, derives from the grammarians. Faustus, in the famous syllogism at the beginning of Marlowe's play, speaks of himself as moving towards "an everlasting death" (1.1.47), but this death is damnation. The deathliness of Mr. Casaubon in *Middle-*

march is not eschatological but mundane. It has nothing — or very little — grand about it. It is indeed a kind of *footling* deathliness, involved in a cloud of insubstantial minutiae. All of this however is clearly present and forms the matter of hilarious comedy in Shakespeare's *Love's Labour's Lost*. Of course Shakespeare was not the first to see scholars as futile (comic) persons. About 1430 Leon Battista Alberti was already descanting on the feebleness of scholars,[9] but Shakespeare has a knack of becoming, immediately, "central."

The country schoolmaster Holofernes, called "the Pedant" in the Folio text stage directions, exists in a state of tremulous enthusiasm, largely directed at points of Latin usage: "*Facile, precor gelida quando pecus omne sub umbra ruminat* and so forth. Ah, good old Mantuan!" . . . "*Bone? Bone* for *bene*, Priscian a little scratched, 'twill serve" (4.2.93, 5.1.28–29). I remember, as I read these words, the face of the kindly old man who taught me Greek, bobbing up from the huge dictionary in which it had been buried with the words, "Don't you feel *the thrill of the chase?!*" Holofernes is innocently drunk on linguistic niceties. Shakespeare loves him, as is clear when the great people make fun of the show put on by Holofernes and his friends and Holofernes is given a moment of great natural dignity: "This is not generous, not gentle, not humble" (5.2.629). Yet when all is said and done Holofernes is undoubtedly a figure of fun. We cannot say that he is *not* footling.

At the same time, however, despite the growing distinction between scholarship and natural philosophy or science, it still makes sense to keep up the general category, "life of the mind," in which various stands are merged. Prospero in *The Tempest* is obviously a magician-scientist of the new kind, but, equally obviously, he is a bookish man ("Burn but his books" cries his enemy, Caliban, at 3.2.95; Prospero himself speaks of "volumes that I prize above my dukedom," at 1.2.167–68, and the act in which he sacrifices and abjures his dangerous knowledge is the drowning of a book, at 5.1.57). *Love's Labour's Lost* gives us not only the narrow pedant, Holofernes, but also, at the centre of the comic plot, the "academe" planned by the young king (1.1.13). Dumaine refers to the scheme as "living in philosophy," a term that covers the whole field, but

8

Shakespeare's emphasis from the beginning is on reading, books, and (mere) words in books. It is clear, first, that these young men are opting for the life of the mind and, second, that this choice entails a repudiation of sex. Shakespeare is not, indeed, interested here in the sin of Adam and Faustus, but he is interested in sinning against love and life.

We began with the idea of a transition to a sexless deathliness. Robert Browning's phrase in "A Grammarian's Funeral," "Dead from the waist down" (l. 132), goes to the heart of the matter.[10] In *Doctor Faustus* there is no antithesis between sex and the life of the mind. In *Love's Labour's Lost* and in *Middlemarch* the antithesis is central. With the schoolmaster Holofernes it is done very lightly. When the vividly (almost grossly) female Jaquenetta approaches, cheerfully wishing him good day, Holofernes says (perhaps raising one hand as he does so to command attention), "A soul feminine saluteth us" (4.2.81). Earthling meets Martian (or vice versa). But with the king and his noble companions the conflict of learning with sex is absolute and profound. Of course, because we are in a comedy, the conflict is not long sustained. As soon as the young women arrive the plans for deep, celibate reading are out of the window. It is curious that Shakespeare touches on an idea which will figure powerfully in *Middlemarch*, the idea of the blind reader, or of the human being blinded by reading. Berowne, who was sceptical from the start, observes that too much reading can make you go blind: "Light, seeking light, doth light of light beguile" (1.2.77). In *Middlemarch* Mr. Brooke observes, of Mr. Casaubon's eyes, "I think he has hurt them a little with too much reading."[11] But the main burden of Berowne's speech against the "academe" is that it is an act of treason against youth itself: truth to these proposed vows to abjure all society for the sake of learning involves, at the deepest level, a hideous untruth to one's own nature and to love (4.3.259, 358–61). We are clearly set upon a path that will lead in time to such modern lyrics as that of W. B. Yeats:

> *Bald heads forgetful of their sins,*
> *Old, learned, respectable bald heads*
> *Edit and annotate the lines*

That young men, tossing on their beds,
Rhymed out in love's despair
To flatter beauty's ignorant ear.

All shuffle there; all cough in ink;
All wear the carpet with their shoes;
All think what other people think;
All know the man their neighbour knows.
Lord, what would they say
Did their Catullus walk that way?[12]

It is interesting to see by what sort of person the life of the mind is deemed to be best represented. Is it by the Dangerous Voyager or by Dryasdust? Certainly the tendency is to move away from the former, towards the latter. Shakespeare, as so often, is ahead of the field, but Bacon, by banishing demons, plays an important part.

"Dead from the waist down" remains the single most powerful phrase, the lethal weapon in the anti-intellectual arsenal, and it belongs to Browning. But the poem in which it is found is not, as a whole, a confident assertion. It is rather a protracted spasm of anxiety—an anxiety that smells strongly of the nineteenth century but is projected by the writer back upon an earlier period. Conceived in the century of Mr. Casaubon, it meditates—and is baffled by—the age of Isaac Casaubon. "A Grammarian's Funeral" needs to be taken slowly, step by step. It is a poem that raises in an acute form a certain question of principle: the difference between ambiguity and confusion. In poetry, we are told, ambiguity is good but confusion is (still) bad. Everyone knows how some of the best poems are balanced between, say, admiration and condemnation—Andrew Marvell's "Horatian Ode," for example. Is "A Grammarian's Funeral" a poem of this kind, or is it simply confused? And, more generally, how in critical reading are we to tell the virtue from the vice?

The tone at the outset of the poem is hearty. A chorus of strong young voices, like something in a Wagner opera, exhorts to action: "Let us begin," "Singing together" (ll. 1, 2). But the action to which they rally one another is the carrying of a corpse to its place of burial; youth and energy are thus in immediate contrast with death. Browning knew, even if the first-time reader does not yet know, that his theme would be paradoxical, the half-discovery of a kind of glory in negation, abstinence, and withdrawal from life, in the celebration not of a soldier or a lover but of a scholar. The poet, famous in his own day for obscurity, was at the same time naturally drawn to rollicking verses, and this indeed might seem to be appropriate in a poem of celebration. But then this style is not easily applicable, somehow, to the life of the mind. The jollity of "Marching along, fifty-score strong, / Great-hearted gentlemen, singing this song" ("Marching Along," ll. 12–13) will do for hard-drinking Cavaliers, but hardly for the present case. But then scholars, in real life, have students. What had begun to look like a literary difficulty is, after all, neatly objectified in a plausible picture of full-throated youth carrying their professor shoulder-high (even if the professor is now dead and, moreover, was never, perhaps, fully alive). The first person plural imperative, "Let us begin," is already instinct with esprit de corps. German students sing "Gaudeamus igitur": these sing "Incipiamus igitur." Nevertheless, in the opening lines of the poem the reader experiences a mild vertigo. The voices are young but the occasion is desolate — and yet there may, for all that, be matter here for celebration. So far, so skilful. This is not confusion.

The sing-along mode is reasserted at intervals: "Step to a tune, square chests, erect each head," "Singing together," "Hearten our chorus," "Step two abreast" (ll. 25, 32, 76, 91) — the last is rallentando, as the bearers adapt their pace to the narrowing path. This tone, however, is not continuously sustained. No significant composer, as far as I know, has ever set this poem to music, despite what might seem to be a strenuous invitation from Browning to do so. The poem in fact resists — is far too quirky for — a musical setting.

As it moves towards daybreak over the high rocks the procession leaves behind "the common crofts, the vulgar thorpes / Each in its tether . . . / Cared-for till cock-crow" (ll. 3–4, 6). A world of nursery-tale villages, where children are frightened or comforted before they fall asleep with stories of ghosts who troop home at cockcrow is broken in upon by light from a higher region. When Marvell wrote his poem of precarious balance, his "Horatian Ode," he punned on an invisible Latin word: "With his keener Eye / The Axes edge did try" (ll. 59–60) is built secretly upon the Latin *acies*, which means both "edge" and "sight." Browning, instead, employs unstated key-terms of intellectual history: "liberal arts," "humanism," "renais-sance." "Each in its tether" (l. 4) immediately implies that the gram-marian and his students are untethered, which takes us easily to "liberal" (that which belongs to a free man, not to a slave). This notion is reinforced by "the common crofts, the vulgar thorpes" (l. 3), where, indeed, there may be a further allusion to the ostentatious exclusiveness of Hermetical humanists (Bacon has yet to invent the scientific committee for pooling information.) Then "man's thought" (l. 9) can take us to *humanitas*, the humanist study of the literature and philosophy of Greece and Rome, in implicit contradistinction to theology, hitherto queen of the sciences. The reference to daybreak (l. 7) is a transparent code for the dawn of new knowledge. "En-lightenment" belongs properly to a later phase, but is easily projected back upon the earlier movement. Meanwhile "day again" (l. 7) can now easily hint rebirth, renaissance. Petrarch in his *Africa* (9.454 f.) speaks of darkness breaking, poetry turning green with new life as the splendour of ancient times is recovered.[13] It is often said that the Middle Ages did not know they were the Middle Ages but the Re-naissance was vividly aware that it was the Renaissance. Indeed it was a self-announcing enterprise. Lorenzo Valla wrote excitedly of the coming to life again (*reviviscant*) of those arts closest to the liberal arts.[14] Huldrichus Coccius in his dedicatory epistle to the works of Vives (1555) writes of lamplit work (*lucubratio*) bringing the ancients back from the dead,[15] Vasari of a second birth (*rinascita*) in the Proe-mio to his *Lives of the Most Eminent Painters*.[16] It would be easy to extend the list of quotations, to Vives himself, to Giovanni Boccaccio on Giotto, Joseph Justus Scaliger on Petrarch. The Renaissance was, then, a conscious movement — almost a movement of conscious-ness. By this point in the poem the reader is clear that we are in the Renaissance period, not the nineteenth century, as regards, that is, the matter presented. It is often said that Browning is distinguished from Alfred, Lord Tennyson by having a genuinely historical imag-ination, that while Tennyson's Arthurian knights are Victorians in Pre-Raphaelite armour, Browning's Renaissance men and women are just that — Renaissance men and women. Even so, in reading a Browning poem we never leave the Victorian world completely, never become indigenous inhabitants in the imagined other time. Browning's decision to present his poem in the form of a song sung in funeral procession by manly youths is discernibly Victorian, the literary equivalent of paintings of pageants and the like, such as Lord Leighton's "Cimabue's celebrated Madonna is carried in procession through the streets of Florence." One senses that (for all that Browning's own very brief student career was at London University) Oxford undergraduates are modelling for these conscientiously imagined pre-Victorians. What Browning has done, however, with what swiftly became a commonplace notion of life emerging from death, is to relocate, within his poem, the element of death. The grammarian, the agent of rebirth, is himself a corpse, and was deathly before he died. This, again, is not confusion.

The choice of burial on the mountain, rather than in, say, the churchyard, also entails deft allusion to humanist values. Lucan's words *Caelo tegitur qui non habet urnam*, "He is covered by the sky, who has no funeral urn" (*De Bello Civili* 7.819), was the favourite proverb of humanist Thomas More's traveller, Hythloday.[17] The sentiment relegates religious ritual to the province of priestcraft and benighted superstition. It is a kind of Deism before the Deists. The mountain itself, we should note, is no Hebraic wilderness but is "citied to the top" (l. 15) — "civic," "civilised" — an Italian hill-town such as might be seen in the background of a painting by Andrea Mantegna.

The key elements of "the Revival of Learning in Europe" are swiftly assembled. But then we become aware of a different strain, oddly close to comedy. "Vulgar" and "unlettered" ("the vulgar thorpes," "the unlettered plain" (ll. 3, 13), while they may evoke an exalted Hermeticism, also lead us naturally back into Shakespeare's comedy about learning pursued in defiance of life's imperatives, *Love's Labour's Lost*. There the "fantastical Spaniard," Armado calls the clown, Costard, "that unlettered small-knowing soul" (1.1.250–51). Similarly it is Armado who writes in a letter, "which to annothanize in the vulgar — O base and obscure vulgar" (4.1.68–69). "Vulgar" here means "vernacular," but there is a strong social connotation. When the page Moth says, in response to Armado's "It doth amount to one more than two," "Which the base vulgar do call three," the word refers directly to persons. As the poem unfolds the grammarian will in due course be revealed as conceivably magnificent, but in the meantime he is also absurd—desiccated, sickly, a Burtonian pantaloon.

Perhaps the first moment where we can say the poet's grip is uncertain comes with the suddenly soaring lines, "He was a man born with thy face and throat, / Lyric Apollo!" (ll. 33–34). The mild linguistic oddity of "face and throat," in a poem about arcane learning, may alert us to the possibility of interference from another, older language. I strongly suspect that the name "Chrysostom" ("Golden Mouth") was at the back of Browning's mind. Just conceivably, meanwhile, behind Chrysostom there may lurk the ghostly figure of Didymus Chalcenteros ("Brazen-guts"), the most industrious and craziest of the ancient *grammatici*.[18] Browning's mingling of exaltation with a simultaneous absurdity, elsewhere in the poem, is masterly. The false note, here, is "Lyric Apollo." One is tempted to say, "It is just one of Browning's bad, rhyme-led, choices." This, after all, is the poet of "Replies to Challenges to Rhyme," who brings off the circus trick of rhyming on "fabric" (with "dab brick") elsewhere in "A Grammarian's Funeral," at lines 70 and 72. But "follow," the word rhymed by "Apollo," is scarcely in this special league of difficulty. One is left simply unpersuaded, unimpressed. Whatever the grammarian may be, we are clear that he was not an inspired poet.

But there is a way to meet this difficulty—to save the consistency of the picture. If we remind ourselves that these words belong not to Browning but to the students who carry the dead man—or else (because Browning obviously is not confining himself to the actual words of their song, but is allowing associated thoughts to enter) suppose that these ideas belong to contemporaries of the grammarian, we can say that the confusion is theirs, not Browning's: "This is the kind of wild chatter that was in the air." A still stronger point can be made by carefully emphasizing the word "born." This poem, after all, is concerned to exhibit a dreadful sequence in time; it is about a person who began with great capacities but terminated in futility. So is all well? Not quite. There remains an excess of energy in the words chosen. To say "He might have been a poet" is one thing. To say he was "born with thy face and throat, lyric Apollo!"

is another. The ear registers it as an odd explosion, as faintly crazy, as if some extra enthusiasm is somehow escaping the satiric-ironic framework of the poem.

Lines 35 to 50 indeed describe a failed sequence, a life that is incapable of developing as lives normally do. The grammarian lives obscure, unaware that old age will seize him. He finds that he has become weak and ill, that there are no "New measures, other feet anon" for him (l. 39). This, we perceive is not the young Milton, who looked forward, unsubduably, to fresh woods and pastures new after the death of a learned friend. The sad words "My dance is finished?" (l. 40) are, however, followed at once by an experience analogous to that of conversion. At line 43 the grammarian is given a "signal." He is in fact being conducted to a new species (not the monastic kind) of *contemptus mundi*. He proudly disdains the pitying glances of the worldly — indeed, he despises the world — but he turns away, not to contemplate eternal Christian verities, but to pursue learning. Given this, the words "grappled with the world" (l. 45) are disconcerting, but the phrase may connote mere antagonism, as distinct from participation; "grappled with the world," after all, is immediately followed by "Bent on escaping." No radiant vision is vouchsafed to him. Instead he seems for a moment to be confronted by a sinister figure whose message is too terrible to be disclosed. "What's in the scroll . . . thou keepest furled?" he cries, for all the world like Charles Dickens's Scrooge, confronted by the Ghost of Christmas Yet to Come (the spirit whose face is hidden, who points to the grave which awaits Scrooge). *A Christmas Carol* came out in 1843. "A Grammarian's Funeral" was first published in *Men and Women* in 1855. It is entirely possible that Dickens was in Browning's mind.[19] Others will wish to insist that Shakespeare is a likelier source: "A carrion Death, within whose empty eye / There is a written scroll! I'll read the writing!" (*Merchant of Venice* 2.7.63–64). Either way, there is a momentary sense of the macabre: death in a grotesque mode. But for the grammarian the scroll at once becomes a humanist codex, a counter-universe to be entered and heroically explored.

Browning, we sense, is developing, behind the major satiric thrust of a poem about a man who chose not to live and was punished with weakness and futility, a paradox. The grammarian is, physically, a pathetic wreck, but mentally he may have been in some way a Hercules. To be sure, the phrase "to taste life" (l. 55), a notion receiving warm support elsewhere in Browning's work, is disdained by the grammarian. At the same time, however, he is himself a voluptuary in the world of scholarship. Strong gustatory imagery returns, this time on the scholar's side of the equation, with "eat up the feast" (l. 63) and "(soul-hydroptic with sacred thirst) / Sucked at the flagon" (ll. 95–96). John Donne is obviously behind "hydroptic," but John Keats with his "purple-stainèd mouth" is there too.[20] Still, we partly think, this man has a mess of shadows for his meat. The question is: Does one half of the antinomy undermine the other? Does the application of (glorious) Keatsian gluttony to books instead of food or sex render the glutton palpably absurd? It is hard to be confident, now, that the answer is an unequivocal "Yes." The deathliness, the pathos, and the splendour are given simultaneously; all seem real.

The scholar's sickness ("*Calculus* racked him . . . / *Tussis* attacked him," ll. 86, 88) is itself a topos. "Wee that are university men," says the lean and slippered Robert Burton, ". . . wither away as a flowre ungathered in a garden, and are never used." He lists the various ills with relish: "gouts, catarrhes, rhumes, *cacexia, bradiopepsia,* bad eyes, stone and collick, crudities, oppilations, vertigo, windes, crampes, consumptions." Scholars, he continues, "are most part leane, dry, ill coloured"; they lose their wits and many times their lives, and all through immoderate pains and extraordinary studies.[21] Erasmus's list is only a little less exuberant: "Paleness, Leaness, Crasiness, sore Eyes and an Old-age and Death contracted before their time (though yet what matter is it, when he dye that never lived?)."[22] In calling the scholars' infirmities a topos, I do not mean to imply that it is confined to the realm of literature. The entirely historical Renaissance scholar, Isaac Casaubon, was afflicted in his last years by *calculus,* the stone, and by a hacking cough (*tussis*), just like Browning's grammarian.[23]

The scholar is at odds with life. Also, more disquietingly and more risibly perhaps, he is at odds with — cut off from — sex. But this too is part of the inherited picture. Burton (here thinking, we must allow, of monasteries) speaks of "fearfull maladies, ferall diseases," which stem from choosing "to suppress the vigor of youth," "against the lawes of nature."[24] The celibacy of Browning's grammarian is not monastic but, distinctively, scholarly. It is true that we are told at line 123 that he resembles the unworldly man who "throws himself on God" (though as we shall see, there may be problems with the identification), but Browning at once reminds us that his hero was toiling away at intricacies of grammar (l. 126). In *Love's Labour's Lost* the posture of celibacy adopted by the young men is, quite clearly, a humanist, Renaissance celibacy. The king's plan is not for the religious life but for study. Yet it still entails a turning away from sex. Browning's "dead from the waist down" must, as a mere phrase, be on the edge of comedy. If one keeps up the fiction of the singing students, the words could be heard as a rumble of ribaldry within the paean, like the bawdy inserted in the celebratory singing at a Roman triumph.[25] Remember the glassy circumspection with which Holofernes marked the appearance within his field of vision of a woman — Jaquenetta. Meanwhile, as we saw, Berowne, the sexually switched-on sceptic of the comedy, tells the would-be scholars, at 1.1.77, that if they read day and night they will not only miss out on sex, they will ruin their eyesight so that reading itself will become impossible for them: "Light seeking light doth light of light beguile" is perhaps the most brilliantly mannered line Shakespeare ever wrote. With this ultimate futility, it might seem, the scholar's dream is finally destroyed. But the same absurdity attaches itself to Browning's grammarian — yet here an intuition of strange heroism survives.

As the poem nears its conclusion both the absurdity and the glory are intensified. The coarse, damning words, "Dead from the waist down," near the end, are juxtaposed with the description of the mountaintop where the scholar finds his proper resting place.

But what did the grammarian do?

> *He settled* Hoti's business . . .
> *Properly based* Oun —
> *Gave us the doctrine of the enclitic* De . . .
>   [ll. 129–31]

Do these lines belong in the comic register or the heroic? More comic than heroic, I would guess, because of the *littleness* of the examples offered. It is possible that these lines were begotten in the poet's mind, in the process of composition, by the phrase "Accents uncertain," earlier (l. 54). In context these words refer to the faltering speech of the grammarian, but the same words must have been written countless times by nineteenth-century schoolmasters on Greek proses submitted by their pupils. Greek accents, "perispomenon," "paroxytone," and the rest, are notoriously difficult to get right. The grammarian, who might have assailed such grand Greek terms as *psyche* or *logos*, works instead on "that" and "so." George Monteiro's attempt to discern a sequence here—first engagement with the world, then a movement to a different approach (on the ground that *hoti* connotes the world of fact, *oun* brings in consequence, and enclitic *de* means motion towards)[26] is profoundly unpersuasive. The grammarian himself would surely wish to point out that enclitic *de* does not in any case always imply motion towards; if, instead of being appended to place-names, it is joined to a word like *toios*, "such," it merely implies emphasis: "Such as one as *he*." There is no metaphysical progression here. The grammarian's work has been about as dry as it is possible for work to be. Erasmus described a man he knew (probably Thomas Linacre) as having abruptly turned at the age of sixty from a notable master of many arts—Erasmus drops into Greek for this: *polytechnotaton*—a classicist, mathematician, philosopher, physician, to the task of settling, exactly, the eight parts of speech. These words to be sure are spoken by "Folly," but, as often, there is every sign that Erasmus agrees with her. When we are told that his man reached the point at which he considered it a matter to be settled by the sword whether a particular expression belonged properly with the conjunctions or with the adverbs, the hapless subject has become, clearly, a figure of fun.[27]

Erasmus has introduced subdivisions within the general category "life of the mind." The study of grammar no longer merely equals "mental life" but involves, in this case, a clear diminution, a falling away. The effect of Erasmus's words is to make one vividly aware of all that Browning's grammarian is *not*. He is not a philosopher, not a scientist. Virgil's great line about the blessedness of knowledge, *Felix qui potuit rerum cognoscere causas* (*Georgics* 2.490), "Happy the man who could learn the causes of things," is simply inapplicable to the grammarian. He will never learn the causes of things as the early atomists, Epicurus and Lucretius, did.

By this time, however, anyone who really knows about language will want to say, "But the little words are the hardest!" If we think of Browning's scholar as writing J. D. Denniston's *Greek Particles*, centuries before, the grandeur of the achievement is suddenly apparent. Oddly enough, the question posed in Erasmus about conjunctions and adverbs reappears in Denniston's great book when he argues that many of the Greek particles (little words like *oun*) were originally other parts of speech.[28] Again, the grammarian himself would wish me to point out that *hoti* is in fact not a particle, though the Penguin editors think it is.[29] But is Browning as clear as Erasmus is on the difference between the grammar and philosophy, the difference between a steady, piecemeal analysis of linguistic mechanisms and a comprehensive understanding? "Show me their shaping, / Theirs who most studied man, the bard and sage" (ll. 48–49). Here the grammarian turns to the poets, not it would seem, in order to check their linguistic usage, but rather to glean humane wisdom. Yet at line 57 we find,

> *"Actual life comes next?*
>   *Patience a moment!*
> *Grant I have mastered learning's crabbed text,*
>   *Still there's the comment.*
> *Let me know all!"*

The wisdom of the poet is now a crabbed *text*, with a commentary subjoined. We appear to be moving away from philosophy towards detailed scholarship. But then, with the words "Let me know all!" the picture suddenly expands again. "Image the whole . . . / Fancy the fabric" (ll. 69–70) continues the dream of universal understanding. In like manner the most natural sense of "before living he'd learn how to live" (l. 77) is ethical, philosophy rather than grammar. "Man has Forever" (l. 84), is, again, majestic in a manner that sits uneasily with the figure who, when all his feats were summed, had settled *hoti*'s business and properly based *oun*. Instead we imagine someone like Spinoza, who wrote, *Sentimus experimurque nos aeternos esse*, "We feel and know by experience that we are eternal."[30] The slow satiric undoing of the grammarian is here strangely fractured.

The suggestion is that Browning intends us to have in mind, generally, a downward progression: that the grammarian begins, like Erasmus's friend, with high philosophical ambitions but ends locked in a desperate struggle with linguistic detail, here runs into problems. As we have seen, "crabbed text" and "comment" do not follow but precede "learn how to live," and settling "*Hoti's* business" is in its turn *followed* by the majestically open-ended "not to Live, but Know" (l. 139). Could this be real—mere—confusion? Even if we are confident that Browning (unlike the author of this book) unequivocally despises settling *hoti's* business, a vein of splendour, a thread of mental heroism, seems to survive the ironic reduction. Does Browning, now, not know what he means, what he thinks?

The lines that might seem to promise a resolution of our difficulties are these:

> *That low man seeks a little thing to do,*
> > *Sees it and does it:*
> *This high man, with a great thing to pursue,*
> > *Dies ere he knows it.*
> *That low man goes on adding one to one,*
> > *His hundred's soon hit:*
> *This high man, aiming at a million,*
> > *Misses an unit.*
> *That, has the world here—should he need the next,*
> > *Let the world mind him!*
> *This, throws himself on God, and unperplexed*
> > *Seeking shall find him.*

[ll. 113–24]

We then move straight from the unperplexed man throwing himself on God to the scholar, grinding at grammar (l. 126). This makes it hard for us to be sure whether the grammarian is to be identified with "the high man" or "the low man." Is he engaged in great designs or is he humbly concerned with steady, cumulative work? Most of the signals we are given suggest that the grammarian is "the high man." But this idea is fractured—not enriched—by everything we are told about what the grammarian actually did. Grinding at grammar must fall, most naturally, on "the low man" side.

Certainly lines 113 to 124 read, until we reach "throws himself on God," as an attack on "the high man." Some may say, however, that even "throws himself on God" is thoroughly consistent with the general undermining of the grammarian because in the end these words are simply bitter; to say that this absurd person throws himself on God and then finds him means — brutally — that the grammarian will die, no more, no less. But, if the reference to "Lyric Apollo" betrayed an unassimilated excess of heroic energy, surely it is still clearer that these words carry a like excess. People who know nothing else about Browning know the lines, "Ah, but a man's reach should exceed his grasp / Or what's a heaven for?" ("Andrea del Sarto," ll. 97–98). This poem, like "A Grammarian's Funeral," was first published in the two-volume *Men and Women*, in 1855. Andrea, the speaker in the poem, is an "achiever"; he is "the faultless painter," with a string of finished masterworks to his name. But this "finished" quality, this highly successful finitude, is precisely what troubles Andrea. Suddenly, the person who essays the infinite and fails is by implication a finer figure than the person who works progressively and successfully with manageable quantities. Of course in the case of the grammarian the folly of biting off more than one can chew is made very evident, but the ringingly positive note in "throws himself on God" and "shall find him" is, equally, inescapable. If the grammarian is after all to be seen as, at some level, a hero of the mind in line with the pattern in the lines from "Andrea del Sarto," even the fact that his visible achievement shrinks to a few dry philological demonstrations is actually in full accord with the idea that the dream was itself *essentially* unrealisable; settling *hoti*'s business is now, in a curious manner, less discreditable than the bland perfection of Andrea's finished paintings. But it is far from certain that Browning has actually pursued this line of thought to the end. A last-ditch attempt might still be made to argue "artful tension," as distinct from confusion on the grounds that the singing students may well acknowledge the futility, in worldly terms, of the scholar before they discover his splendour. But there is now a tremor, an uncertainty in the writing that does not accord with the natural speech or thoughts of imagined students. For example, the phrase "Misses an unit," is too strong. These words cannot, as a matter of mere English, mean, "misses by only a unit," as the commentary in the Penguin edition says.[31] They must mean "gets nowhere." It seems wrong to claim that the man who settled *hoti*'s business accomplished nothing, in the way of detailed work. So the impression grows stronger: the poet does not know what he means.

The difference between (good) ambiguity and (bad) confusion comes down, then, to this. A poetically strong ambiguity may well present a formal contradiction but will always turn out to be intelligible and coherent, when the context, literary or referential, is taken into account. In Shakespeare's *Othello* the status of the protagonist is ambiguous. We feel that Othello is both noble and ignoble. But the Venetian context makes this entirely intelligible; Othello is noble in his warlike prowess, ignoble in his incomprehension of things. This is not contradiction but strong coherence. On the other hand, it looks as if Thomas Hardy, when he wrote *Tess of the D'Urbervilles* was actually confused; was Tess innocent because she was the passive victim of rape or was her innocence the innocence of a natural, finally compliant sexuality?[32] That a secular apostle of the rebirth of learning — this grammarian — should be dead to the joys of the flesh is formally paradoxical but entirely credible. The collision between the minute scholar and the Great Explainer, on the other hand, will not resolve itself, shake free and form a richer, intelligible unit. The differing terms remain unfruitfully at war.

In fact Browning is fully in command as long as he is proposing a simple contrast between a life of vivid engagement with the physical world and the life of the mind. When, however, the second term of the antithesis, the life of the mind, begins to resolve itself into different elements, the poet falters. Critics have tried to deal with the difficulty by supposing that the grammarian's career is ultimately involved in — or implies — some philosophy or faith. Martin J. Svaglic finds, reasonably, a twinge of Platonism in "Hence with life's pale lure!" (l. 112).[33] But Platonism and grammar are poles apart, simply refuse to join in the reader's mind (quasi-Platonist grammarians like Chomsky are still in the womb of time). Robert C. Schweik finds a progression from seeking knowledge as a guide to life ("learn how to live," l. 77) to seeking knowledge for its own sake.[34] Here, one senses, is a horse that might run. The question whether that-which-is-known-for-its-own-sake is a set of grammatical analyses or an understanding of the whole remains. Earlier, apropos of "Man has Forever," I quoted Spinoza's "We feel and know by experience that we are eternal." The next proposition in Spinoza's *Ethics* reads, "The more we understand particular things, the more we understand God."[35] But this almost Blakean notion of minute particulars conducting us to God does not work as a strong resolving agent in Browning's poem. Spinoza is in command of an antinomy that in Browning remains at the level of incoherence. It may be suggested that it is a mistake to judge the poet as if he were describing a progression in time; rather Browning has in mind a straight contrast between a dream of exhaustive knowledge and painful toil. But this too comes to pieces in our hands. One half of our (new) antithesis, the "dream," turns out to be, at one point, emphatically the study of man and at another to be throwing oneself on God.

"Confused" is a harsh word—a pedagogue's word. But this is a poem about pedantry. Browning is not alone in his difficulty over the clash between comprehensiveness and detail. Indeed it seems in some strange way to be a property of the nineteenth century. When George Eliot drew her most elaborate portrait of a scholar, Mr. Casaubon in *Middlemarch*, she clearly had trouble reconciling the evident sense that Mr. Casaubon's dried-up mind could never rise above detail with the simultaneous need to contrast day-to-day concrete living (including sex) with vast intellectual designs. Many readers of *Middlemarch* have been surprised—it is a point to which we shall return—to find that Mr. Casaubon is writing, not flinty little pieces for learned journals, but "The Key to All Mythologies" (if Browning's grammarian is writing Denniston's *Particles*, Mr. Casaubon is writing *The Golden Bough*). But a difficulty shared is not really a difficulty halved. When Browning is in command of his antithesis the poem is strong; when he cannot decide what kind of knower we are to wonder at it is weak. An immediate consequence is that the reader is less moved than he or she would otherwise have been. I think Browning knew that something was wrong. It shows in the strange violence of the ending:

Here — here's his place, where meteors shoot, clouds form,
    Lightnings are loosened,
Stars come and go! Let joy break with the storm,
    Peace let the dew send!
Lofty designs must close in like effects:
    Loftily lying,
Leave him — still loftier than the world suspects,
    Living and dying.

[ll. 141–48]

This crash of thunder, blaze of lightning should mean glory breaking through at the end, the proper apotheosis of the grammarian. But we sense instead that the poet is shouting to cover his uncertainty. There is, within the grandeur, a batsqueak of hysteria. "My case is weak so I will overstate it." Naturally the fanfare (because the triumph is inwardly frail) cannot sustain itself and in the last four lines of the poem the register drops again, to a modest prosiness. First the word "effects" may hint, behind the main sense, "results," the other sense referring to aesthetic or artistic rather than practical efficacy. Have we, as readers, just been given an "effect" of this kind — something more theatrical than real? Then we are asked to concede, now that all has become quiet and the tone is conversational, that the grammarian may really have been a greater man than was generally suspected. After that, the very last line, "Living and dying," is, though sonorous, interestingly not triumphant in its cadence. Had the upward surge of "Lightnings are loosened" been sustained, the last word of the poem should have been "living." As it is the binary phrase rocks back, into ordinary sadness. This life was followed not by a larger existence but by death. For those who think the poem is primarily satiric — exposing the ultimate futility of the grammarian — this movement back from life to ordinary death will be, so to speak, no surprise; it will be read as authorising their reading of the whole. But even here the lines twitch, listlessly, at the very last moment, with the words "still loftier than the world suspects." The greyness of this, its limp prosiness amid the thunder and lightning, betrays much. These are not the accents of "Lyric Apollo" but the residual rumination of a confused human being, living in the nineteenth century. Here the poet's doubts and confusions are half-confessed. Browning translated Aeschylus and "transcribed" Euripides; he never produced a "Browning version" of Sophocles. For the Greeks the great "knower" was Oedipus, "who solved the famous riddle and was the wisest of men" (*Oedipus Rex* 1525). At the end of Sophocles' *Oedipus Coloneus*, after the thunder and lightning Oedipus is received by unseen powers and vanishes from human sight. Browning's great "knower" is left behind, abandoned by his vision, on the cold hillside.

At this point I propose to reverse the natural order of history and to enter the world of *Middlemarch* and the rector of Lincoln College before I consider Isaac Casaubon. This is partly because I require the advantage of hindsight in treating the most complex of my specimens, and partly because I know that he will be strong enough, when the time comes, to shake himself free of later accreted myths and presuppositions. Bacon would certainly not approve of my way of proceeding. Cicero, alluding to such chronological wantonness in a letter to his friend Atticus, used the Greek phrase *husteron proteron Homērikōs* "backwards-forwards, in Homer's way."[36] Cicero, note, with a truer intellectual modesty than will ever be found in Bacon, has smuggled in a reference to the majestic achievement of *the* "pre-learned" poet, to the "writer" who may have been unable to write or read, to Homer. Homer began his *Iliad* with "the wrath" itself, that wrath of Achilles whose slow genesis in the unfolding of the Trojan War will be afterwards gradually discovered by those listening to the poem. Had he done otherwise we would not have understood what it was that was unfolding before our eyes. So here we begin, not with wrath indeed nor with tenderness, but with the very antithesis of all such energies: with Mr. Casaubon.

1

Mr. Casaubon in *Middlemarch*

The Death's Head

Mr. Casaubon, the desiccated walking corpse to whom the ardent Dorothea Brooke is joined in indissoluble wedlock, is actually in his forties (somewhere between forty-six and forty-nine). People say, "Ah, but forty-something in the twenty-first century is very different from forty-something in the nineteenth," or else suppose that George Eliot has made a strange mistake. It is however likely that the novelist knew very well what she was about. Vain people commonly pretend to be younger than they are, but these surely are the amateurs in vanity. Your more expertly vain person will pretend to be older. Suppose that James, fifty years old and looking fifty, says, "I'm forty"; one thinks at once, "He's not doing very well." But if James lies in the opposite direction and says, "I'm sixty," the response is, "He's a wonderful sixty." So here Mr. Casaubon is actually younger than he appears to be. Therefore he is losing the battle of life. Old age has seized him prematurely. The hold of senescence upon him is proved, by his chronological age, to be abnormally strong, at the very beginning of the book.

We meet the gentleman himself in the second chapter. Before we meet face to face, however, George Eliot employs the usual novelistic technique: Mr. Casaubon is talked about and thought about before he appears.

> Sir James Chettam was going to dine at the Grange today with another gentleman whom the girls had never seen, and about whom Dorothea felt some venerating expectation. This was the Reverend Edward Casaubon, noted in the county as a man of profound learning, understood for many years to be engaged on a great work concerning religious history; also as a man of wealth enough to give lustre to his piety, and having views of his own which were to be more clearly ascertained on the publication of his book. His very name carried an impressiveness hardly to be measured without a precise chronology of scholarship. [1.1:11]

This, it may be thought, is not especially artful. It is a thinly disguised programme-note, conveying simple information. Mr. Casaubon is a scholar, writing a great book, comfortably off. The paragraph is however a little subtler than this summary would suggest. The whole picture is presented half inside and half outside the expectant imagination of Dorothea. We are told at the beginning about her anticipatory reverence for Mr. Casaubon. The reader cannot then be quite certain whether the following sentences represent simply the general account which Middlemarch society and "the county" is giving of him or whether they incorporate, more sharply and idiosyncratically, Dorothea's own response to the common talk—the general opinion filtered through her selective memory? The reference to his "views," which will be ascertained when the book is published, presumably carries no immediate, sinister charge for the first-time reader. It is only as the story unfolds that we discover the futility of the enterprise, that the work is hollow, without a thesis to demonstrate. Then indeed these words, if recalled, will have become savagely ironic. It is as if the novelist is secretly goading her victim, before the reader can be fully aware that she is doing so. Modern editors usually explain the concluding reference to the impressiveness of the name as a reference to Isaac Casaubon and at the same time, perhaps, to his son Meric, also a scholar. But there is a luminous protective vagueness about the wording here which actually suggests that we are indeed in Dorothea's mind. Dorothea, I would guess, cannot actually remember anything specific about earlier Casaubons but probably has heard their names. All that is left is a tantalising sense: this is *scholarship*. The thought is more energising in its unclarified form. Meanwhile of course George Eliot's mind is also working. For her (though, once more, not for the ordinary reader) the evocation of a "chronology of scholarship," another kind of history to answer the religious history essayed by Mr. Casaubon (the former perhaps having the power to provide a pathology of the latter), may in its turn have evoked thoughts of the rector of Lincoln, Mark Pattison, who dreamed of writing just such a book.

In chapter 2 we suddenly find ourselves in the middle of the promised dinner party and Mr. Casaubon is here. But he is as silent as a *kōphon prosōpon*, the "unspeaking mask" in a Greek play. All the talking is being done by Mr. Brooke, Dorothea's uncle. Mr. Brooke is reminiscing about the time when he had dinner with Sir Humphrey Davy, a dinner also attended by the poet Wordsworth. One cannot be sure, but it looks as if this opening speech is loosely based on the "Gloucestershire scenes" in Shakespeare's *Henry IV,* Part 2 — old men reminiscing, losing the thread as life slips away. Mr. Brooke remembers how he was at Cambridge just as Justice Shallow remembers how he was at Clement's Inn (*2 Henry IV* 3.2.14). The little word "there," the word for past-presence, is important in both. "I dined with him at Cartwright's and Wordsworth was there. . . . But Davy was there" (*Middlemarch* 1.2:16); and now Justice Shallow: "There was I, and little John Doit of Staffordshire, and black George Barnes" (3.2.19–20). Davy is on hand in the *Middlemarch* passage to represent science, no doubt, but another Davy walks in and out of the Gloucestershire scenes — Shallow's servant. The name rings out repeatedly in both places. It is not inconceivable that the Shakespearean Davy came first in George Eliot's conception. When Mr. Brooke suddenly says, of Wordsworth in his Cambridge years, "I never met him," we have a faint echo of the wonderful effect of Shallow's words at 3.2.39, "By my troth, I was not there" ("there," again!). The marvellous discontinuous dialogue of the Gloucestershire scenes, where Shakespeare showed how he could if he wished write like Anton Chekhov, is in Mr. Brooke confined to a staccato monologue, the speaker continually losing and recovering the thread of his own discourse. Both, throughout, are all about time.

The analogy cannot be pressed too hard. One might be tempted to say that if Mr. Brooke is Justice Shallow, Sir James Chettam must be Falstaff (Falstaff, oddly enough is almost the "straight man" in these scenes), and the aptly named Silence would then become Mr. Casaubon. But of course Mr. Brooke is too robust to be Justice Shallow, it would take at least three Sir James Chettams to make a Falstaff, and the unspeaking Mr. Casaubon meanwhile is himself alone. Yet the visual contrast George Eliot is setting up here between rosy abundance and pallid age is in the Shakespeare scenes too.

Before Mr. Casaubon speaks we are told how he looks like the philosopher John Locke, with his deep eye sockets and his iron-grey hair (1.2:16). Clearly George Eliot has seen a portrait of Locke, perhaps the one in the hall of Christ Church College, Oxford. Locke's prose style, unchecked by any visual information about the writer, would of itself suggest a solid sort of person; the picture shows a wraith, pallid and ghostly. This is what Dorothea, who perhaps unconsciously avoids focussing her eyes, sees. It is her sister Celia who adds the terrible detail, "two white moles with hairs on them" (1.2:20). Meanwhile Mr. Brooke rattles on about Adam Smith, Robert Southey, and what not, and at last appeals to Mr. Casaubon for an opinion. "You know Southey?" he asks. Mr. Casaubon answers,

No. I have little leisure for such literature just now. I have been using up my eyesight on old characters lately; the fact is, I want a reader for my evenings; but I am fastidious in voices, and I cannot endure listening to an imperfect reader. It is a misfortune, in some senses: I feed too much on the inward sources; I live too much with the dead. My mind is something like the ghost of an ancient, wandering about the world, and trying mentally to construct it as it used to be, in spite of ruin and confusing changes. But I find it necessary to use the utmost caution about my eyesight. [1.2:17]

These are his first words in the novel. The speech is loaded to the gunwales with thematic indicators. First, on the knowledge theme, Eliot swiftly establishes Brooke as superficial, having a smattering of this and that, so that Mr. Casaubon can then enter as representing, conversely, depth of knowledge, true research. Then, within the contrast so established, she must plant an opposite suggestion: that Mr. Casaubon's "depth" is as much a matter of ignorance or incapacity as of knowledge. His very first syllable, "No," is a statement of ignorance, not knowledge. He has not read Southey's *History of the Peninsular War*. Then what may be called the Milton theme is evoked. The reader has already been told in the first chapter how Dorothea would have liked to be married to the blinded Milton.

The allusion is highly charged. Milton is learning, genius, greatness of mind; at the same time his harshness to the daughters who read to him was notorious, from Samuel Johnson's account in his *Life of Milton*. Mr. Casaubon shows no sympathy with the difficulty of the reader but speaks only of his own techy impatience with imperfect pronunciation. Johnson in fact divides his sympathies. He plainly feels for the hapless reader but at the same time endorses John Phillips's judgement that listening to a person reading without comprehension of what they read must be a trial of patience almost beyond endurance.[1] George Eliot also, as grows clear before the book has ended, has strong sympathy with the unlovable Mr. Casaubon. From the first Dorothea is shown to be shying away from her own sexuality. She says that she is looking for a "father" in her husband (1.1:10). Her devout eagerness to subordinate herself to a great male intelligence is poignantly mitigated by one contrary note. A "truly delightful" husband, she says, is one who "could teach you even Hebrew, if you wished it" (1.1:10). Here for a moment the imagined husband is not simply a superior being to be humbly assisted but a potential giver of knowledge. Add to all this the mythical resonance of blindness, anciently associated, as in Sophocles' *Oedipus Rex*, with knowledge, and the account is almost complete. One must say "almost" because it is just possible that blinding carries a further sexual implication of emasculation. By blinding her imagined husband Dorothea has unmanned him. The notion of emasculation haunts Milton's *Samson Agonistes* (Samson has always seemed, with his blindness, his great powers, and his imprudent marriage, a clear projection of Milton himself) in both the cutting of the hero's hair and the blinding. The more fugitive associations of "hung it in my hair" (l. 59), "tender ball" (l. 94), to say nothing of that strangest of synecdoches, "A thousand foreskins fell" (l. 144), when linked to the booming word "effeminacy," referring to the condition of being unmanned (ll. 410, 1133) plant the idea at the back of the mind. Behind Samson stands the Greek Hercules, and behind Hercules the bleeding Attis of the Phrygians.[2] It may be said that George Eliot could never have had these thoughts when reading *Samson Agonistes*. This I would counter with a simple denial. She could have.

Finally there is the theme of death: Mr. Casaubon is himself a ghost, conversing more with dead people than with living. Indeed the loading of so many strong instructions, so many pointers, creates a technical problem. The speech is a thematic programme. George Eliot is anxious to get A, B, C, D, and, yes, E into our heads as early as possible. The result is that Mr. Casaubon, in saying so many deep things about his own nature, almost falls out of character. He is not, after all, supposed to be strong on self-knowledge. It is one thing for George Eliot to speak as she does of the "chilling ideal audience which crowded his laborious uncreative hours with the vaporous pressure of Tartarean shades" (1.10:84); it is quite another for Mr. Casaubon to say, himself, "I live too much with the dead." At a certain level the words are thoroughly appropriate. Mr. Casaubon is perhaps — ahead of the game — establishing the difference between himself and the genially this-worldly, un-intellectual Sir James Chettam, who is a potential rival. Certainly he is happy with the picture presented. A sort of mild self-congratulation is going on. So far, we must grant that the words are thoroughly "in character." But there is an extra power in the language — in the word "ghost" and in the stark simplicity of "the dead." With this accession of power the novelist crosses the line between character-bound utterance and the more resonant enunciation of a deep underlying theme. The words say, in effect, "I am a ghost." Within the story, *he* is not supposed to know that he is death-in-life. As it is the speech is almost disarming with its apparent degree of intelligent insight, seems on the edge of humour with a touch of self-deprecating charm. This, I fancy, George Eliot did not intend.

The central message, that Mr. Casaubon is antagonistic to life, is hammered home in a dozen ways. Even when something approaching a real interest in another human being is kindled in him, as at the time of his courtship of Dorothea, his face is lit up only by a "pale wintry sunshine" (1.3:25–26). Here the seasonal imagery may cause thoughts of January and May, the ill-matched couple of Chaucer's *Merchant's Tale*, to arise in the reader's mind. The "deep eye-sockets" (1.2:16), already noticed as carrying a resemblance to the philosopher Locke, are at the same time reminders of "the skull beneath the skin." Mrs. Cadwallader, the outspoken older woman of the book, says that beside Sir James Chettam, Mr. Casaubon "looks like a death's head skinned over for the occasion" (1.10:89). When Sir James himself hears that Dorothea, whom he had hoped to marry, is now engaged to Mr. Casaubon, he cries out, "Good God! It is horrible! He is no better than a mummy! . . . He has one foot in the grave" (1.6:56–57). Earlier Sir James had summed up Mr. Casaubon as "a dried bookworm" (1.2:22). Much later Will Ladislaw sees Dorothea's marriage, in terms borrowed from the lush iconography of baroque churches in southern Italy, as "beautiful lips kissing holy skulls" (4.32:360). When Celia hears of the engagement she fears that there may be something "funeral" in the whole affair and adds, fascinatingly, that it is as if Mr. Casaubon were the officiating clergyman rather than the bridegroom (1.5:48). Later Will Ladislaw says that Dorothea's life with her husband at Lowick Manor will be like being "buried alive" (2.22:218). In book 5—the book itself is called "The Dead Hand"—Dorothea, married and now living at Lowick, sees her existence as living more and more in "a virtual tomb, where there was the apparatus of a ghastly labour producing what would never see the light" (5.48:468). Here the notion of death is, by a kind of hypallage, extended from Mr. Casaubon to his book on religious history, "The Key to All Mythologies," thus neatly dovetailing with Mr. Casaubon's words at the very beginning, "I live too much with the dead" (1.2:17). When Mr. Casaubon, who is the one major character who is literally dead before the conclusion of the novel,[3] is nearing his end and crushes Dorothea by asking her in effect to continue his work after he is gone, she, now thoroughly aware of the futility of it all, sees the labour imposed as an archaeology of Cadavers, "sorting what might be called the shattered mummies and fragments of a tradition" (5.48:472). Here Eliot's language takes on an almost Dickensian intensity, but quite without the demonic humour which recurrently informs such moments in Dickens: the theory of Mr. Casaubon's book is "withered in the birth like an elfin child" (5.48:472). There are some moments when the death imagery of *Middlemarch* really does border on Dickensian comedy. For example, Will Ladislaw's mental picture of Mr. Casaubon as one who "chose to grow grey crunching bones in a cavern" (4.37:356) has unsubdued humorous gusto. Compare Dickens's description of that emblem of female learning, Miss Blimber: "There was no light nonsense about Miss Blimber . . . she was dry and sandy with working in the graves of deceased languages. None of your live languages for Miss Blimber. They must be dead — stone dead — and then Miss Blimber dug them up like a Ghoul" (*Dombey and Son* ch. 11). At important moments in *Middlemarch*, the language of death is used with serious imaginative power. When she is widowed, Dorothea feels committed to the construction of a tomb (5.1:486). The book is the tomb, but whose tomb is it? Who is inside? Not only its author but, by a kind of implied suttee of the intellect, the widow also.

We are dealing here with the formation of a stereotype and it should therefore not be surprising if the writing, while strong (because at this period in history the stereotype is coming to life, is not yet cliché), is a little crude. There is however one point in the book where the theme of death suddenly explodes, in a passage that is simultaneously profound and complex, a moment of radical originality. Eliot has brought her heroine, for her dreadful honeymoon, to Rome. She is discovered, at the beginning of 2.20, weeping in her boudoir in the via Sestina. She has been seeing the sights of Rome and something strange is happening to her mind.

Forms both pale and glowing took possession of her young sense, and fixed themselves in her memory even when she was not thinking of them, preparing strange associations which remained through her after-years. Our moods are apt to bring with them images which succeed each other like the magic lantern pictures of a doze; and in certain states of dull forlornness Dorothea all her life continued to see the vastness of St Peter's, the huge bronze canopy, the excited intention in the attitudes and garments of the prophets and evangelists in the mosaics above, and the red drapery which was being hung for Christmas spreading itself everywhere like a disease of the retina. [2.20:191]

The last sentence is a moment of genius, but before we reach it we sense that the imagining is no longer stereotypical. Energies are quickened perhaps by the proto-Freudian character of the moment. Dorothea is weeping, we surmise, partly from sexual disappointment, but this is something she cannot herself comprehend. She "had no distinctly shapen grievance that she could state even to herself" (2.20:190). She struggles, trying to blame her own *spiritual* poverty. In all of this it is possible to discern a Freudian doubling of the psyche. There is a Dorothea who desires and is frustrated and another Dorothea who is genuinely unaware of the nature of her own need. This produces a strange *aporia*, which itself energises the imagination.

It is curious how, again and again, if we look for examples of unconscious motivation before Freud, these turn out to be female. Chaucer famously hesitates at *Troilus and Criseyde*, 3.575, and tells his reader that his "authority," Lollius (almost certainly a spoof) has let him down by failing to make it clear whether Criseyde did or did not know that her lover would be waiting for her at the house of Pandarus. The Freudian vocabulary is not available to him, yet he has somehow reached the point of wishing the reader to hold two possibilities in mind: Criseyde knows and yet innocently does not know. With a brilliance born, we may guess, of obscure desperation, Chaucer projects the doubleness of motivation as an equivocation in the pretended literary source. The effect, in a prolix medieval narrative, is that ten minutes later the reader or auditor will retain the vague thought: "She knew and yet she didn't." Centuries later Hardy, as we saw, hesitated in a similar manner over the character of Tess's innocence in *Tess of the D'Urbervilles*. She was raped and yet, seemingly, at some level she consented. Are women really more subject to unconscious motivation because they are subjected to a greater degree of repression and censorship (the Freudian Unconscious, after all, is actually made of repressed matter)? A brisker response might be to say that the whole affair is a characteristically male self-deception: it suits male interests to pretend that "No" does not mean "No." This works well enough for Hardy and Chaucer; but George Eliot was a woman.

Eliot disconcertingly says that Dorothea's Protestantism made her see the sensuous forms of Italian art as involved with spiritual degeneracy and therefore as themselves deathly: "long vistas of white forms whose marble eyes seemed to hold the monotonous light of an alien world," a "vast wreck" (2.20:191). One wonders whether the novelist herself may be losing control of her governing imaginative antithesis. A running agalmatophilia, together with a frightened recoil therefrom, can be traced in the nineteenth-century novel. Dorothea finds the ancient casts that her uncle has brought home from his travels discomfiting: "To poor Dorothea these severe classical nudities and smirking Renaissance-Corregiosities were painfully inexplicable, staring into the midst of her Puritanic conceptions"(1.9: 72). Set against this Hardy's excited enthusiasm, as Car Darch strips off her bodice to fight in *Tess of the D'Urbervilles* (ch. 10): "She had bared her plump neck, shoulders, and arms to the moonshine, under which they looked as luminous and beautiful as some Praxitelean creation, in their possession of the faultless rotundities of a lusty country girl." Somewhere between these two passages we might place sad Sue Bridehead in *Jude the Obscure*, extending a finger to touch the nude figures of Venus and Apollo, as she enquires the price (book 2, ch. 3). Sue has reacted intellectually against Christianity, but, herein differing sharply—we may guess—from Dorothea, lacks a strong inner sexual drive; she half-fears the statues not simply because they are too inflammatory but because she is incipiently aware that she herself is not flammable enough. Once more, we might expect this kind of thing to be confined to male writers, but

George Eliot is female, and she has it too. There is a touch of it in the "sleeping Ariadne" passage in *Middlemarch*.

Eliot tells us, in effect, how Dorothea's breasts are even more beautiful than those of the sculpture (on the actual statue one breast is exposed); her "form," she says, is "not shamed by the Ariadne" (2.19:186). "Form" is here, as often in nineteenth-century writing, a mildly titillating euphemism. Eliot is seeing Dorothea through the eyes of Ladislaw and she actually wants Ladislaw to see her as, among other things, a sex object here. Twenty-first-century readers may well think that "soft porn" is too strong an expression even for Hardy's description of Car Darch, but one must remember that law which says, the shorter the supply the stronger the effect. The episode in the Vatican gallery is tense. Ladislaw catches sight of Dorothea, beside the statue. Eliot describes the statue (which, she observes, was then known as "the Cleopatra") in sensuous language, "marble voluptuousness" (2.19:186). Again it is likely that this happens because she is looking through male eyes, but the strong response of the male is here in its turn exciting to the woman novelist. The alternative would be to find a lesbian interest in the passage, but that I believe would be a mistake. Ladislaw's friend Naumann develops the comparison, begun by the novelist, of the *Ariadne* with the living Dorothea: "What do you think of that for a fine bit of antithesis? . . . There lies antique beauty, not corpse-like even in death, but arrested in the complete contentment of its sensuous perfection: and there stands beauty in its breathing life, with the consciousness of Christian centuries in its bosom. But she should be dressed as a nun; I think she looks almost what you call a Quaker; I would dress her as a nun in my picture. However, she is married" (2.19:187). Here the play of Protestant against Roman Catholic becomes less important than the larger contrast between Christian and pagan. Dorothea is either a nun or a Quaker, yet these are not antithetical but offered as virtual equivalents. Richard Jenkyns in his discussion of this passage stresses the Hellenic side, Dorothea as a Greek heroine,[4] but in fact George Eliot carefully maintains a double reference: to Christianity as well as to paganism. Naumann calls her "a sort of *Christian* Antigone" (2.19:188, my italics). At the end of the novel she is once more likened to Antigone, but also to Saint

Theresa (Finale:821). Indeed the affinity of Dorothea to pagan sensuousness is at least as important as the contrast noted by Naumann, whose perceptions fall well short of the truth. "Voluptuousness" remains an important word. The entire passage is a fascinating novelist's *ecphrasis*, the work of art described, as in Keats's "Ode on a Grecian Urn," within another work of art. As is usual with ecphrasis, there is a poignant tension between the stillness of the stone and the warm life depicted. But the real brilliance of the passage lies in the way George Eliot then doubles the ecphrastic effect. Dorothea too is strangely arrested; in her moment of abstraction in the gallery, in her marriage, in her misguided and misguiding piety. It is all-important that Eliot chooses a *sleeping* statue. Ariadne, beautiful in her sleep, is waiting perhaps for her Theseus. Dorothea is the sleeping beauty of fairy tale. Sleep is here a metaphor of the Unconscious.

Roman art celebrates the nude, glows with vitality, and would seem therefore naturally and immediately antithetical to Mr. Casaubon. But Rome is ruined, peopled by the ghosts of history, a sort of echo to Mr. Casaubon's dreamed-of great work, a visible "Key to All Mythologies," and this intuition suddenly transfers the weight of the complex image of the huge, ancient city into the scale of death, not life. It is time that we returned to the image of the red draperies in Saint Peter's, spreading "like a disease of the retina." The truth is that there are two Romes as there are two Dorotheas. In relation to Dorothea the deathly Rome is the perverse product of her distorted and distorting religion; that this should generate a sudden *coincidence* with the ghostly imagery elsewhere associated with Dorothea's opposite, Mr. Casaubon, is, at the deepest level, not strange at all. There is that in the conscious Dorothea—religion—which is indeed anti-life, is destructive of her essential ardour within just as Mr. Casaubon is destructive from the outside. Things are now moving very fast and I am not sure that Eliot (in this a little like the bewildered Dorothea) fully understands the movement of her own mind. The result, which is not rationally channelled, is that death itself, elsewhere a matter of grey negation, becomes charged with energy. Death turns red. The drapery in Saint Peter's is the colour of blood. The blood is spreading everywhere, is violently spilled, across the consciousness of the principal character, suffusing her eyes with sickness. Religion has allied itself with sensuality—with that sensuality which should accompany sexuality and life but is here perverted by the northern spirituality of Dorothea into disease and terror. At the beginning Dorothea says how much she would have liked to marry Milton "when his blindness had come on" (1.1:10). The blindness that took hold of Milton and frightens Mr. Casaubon here threatens to engulf Dorothea herself.[5] It is the best thing in the book.

Religion and Sexual Desire

We have reached a place where the death motif is joined to the running reference in *Middlemarch* to religion. The elementary tension between false theory and sexuality in Dorothea is now partly expressed in terms of a second antithesis, within the field of religion, between the vividness of Roman Catholicism and the austerity of Protestantism. Of course George Eliot will never endorse Catholicism as she will sexuality. Catholic sensuality will always carry for her as for her heroine a hint of the distorted or perverse. Eliot may at one level attack Dorothea's Protestant shrillness but, when Italian art is in question, the novelist herself is an aesthetic Protestant. Dorothea within the story knows nothing of the ardent Catholic saint with whom the author compares her at the beginning of the book. It is tempting to suppose that, as Dorothea paused before the statue of the sleeping Ariadne in the Vatican, George Eliot must have paused before Gian Lorenzo Bernini's *Rapture of Saint Theresa* in the chapel of Santa Maria della Vittoria.

Dorothea, Eliot tells us, was not attending to the statue, though the statue has much to tell us, the readers, about Dorothea. But George Eliot had to know. She, one guesses, would have looked very hard at Bernini's *Theresa*. It is true that George Eliot's Roman journal makes no mention of this work (though Bernini's architecture, the colonnade outside Saint Peter's, is mentioned). Eliot in her journal exhibits the taste of the time, which favoured the antique and generally condemned the baroque. There is no reason to suppose that there is anything insincere about Eliot's conformity to this set of values. It is indeed probable that she was disgusted by baroque art rather than merely indifferent to it, and disgust, unlike indifference, is an aesthetic *response*. George Eliot was an indefatigable sightseer.

It is overwhelmingly probable that she would have stood before Bernini's statue and looked at it.

The historical Theresa to whom Eliot explicitly directs our attention was famous for combining religious ardour with hard practical work. Obviously this is relevant to the character of Dorothea as it unfolds. At the same time, however, the real Theresa wrote a famous account of an occasion on which she was visited by an angel, who offered to pierce her with his loving dart. The account is in some ways like a narrative of a sex dream and Bernini's wonderful fluid marble statue, depicting this very occasion in the life of the spiritually orgiastic saint, famously borders on the erotic. Theresa wrote, "In his hands I saw a great golden spear, and at the iron tip there appeared to be a point of fire. This he plunged into my heart several times so that it penetrated to my entrails. When he pulled it out, I felt that he took them with it, and left me utterly consumed by the great love of God. The pain was so severe that it made me utter several moans. The sweetness caused by this intense pain is so extreme that one cannot possibly wish it to cease."[6] What seems obvious to a post-Freudian reader would be obscure to a nineteenth-century intellectual novelist, but it could still be perceptible. Indeed it may be that our too-easy acceptance of a libidinal meaning makes us, in a way, bad readers of nineteenth-century fiction, bad appraisers of baroque religious sculpture. We make the implicit explicit and to do this is, in a manner, to falsify. The implicit carries a charge of imaginative energy which can make the explicit look, by contrast, inertly bland. It is entirely possible that George Eliot picked up the sexual resonance of the Bernini as just that — an undermeaning. Eliot never refers to sexual rapture in any of her allusions to Theresa, though the word "passionate" is applied to her in the "Prelude," where it is immediately followed by an allusion to "the common yearning of womanhood" (3). The idea of a sexual component in Theresa's ecstasy may well be operating, behind the surface of the writing.

Dorothea herself, consciously and by education, is clearly and emphatically Protestant. That, as we have seen, causes her to recoil from the sensuous splendour of Rome. Mrs. Cadwallader, when breaking the news of Dorothea's engagement, refers to "a flighty sort of Methodistical stuff" (1.6:56) and then adds that girls grow out of this. She is here ascribing the engagement very precisely to something other than sexuality. Sir James Chettam is at once alarmed by the fear that Miss Brooke may have run away to join "the Moravian Brethren, or some preposterous sect unknown to good society" (1.6: 56). The first Moravians have strong associations with Lutheranism. Later they became famous as Protestant missionaries in faraway places (this may be part of what is worrying Sir James). There is a link with English Methodism; the Moravian Peter Boehler, who set up a community at Fetter Lane in London, had a great influence on John Wesley. The word "methodistical" is later applied by Mr. Hawley, the jolly hard-riding lawyer and town clerk of Middlemarch, to persons who bother the poor with too much praying and preaching (2.18:182). Mrs. Cadwallader herself reverts to the term, in thought, after her conversation with Sir James, "Methodistical whims" (1.6: 59), but then shifts the analogy in the direction of pre-Reformation extravagance with "I wish her joy of her hair shirt."

When Dorothea is first introduced the reader is told that, though "the hereditary strain of Puritan energy . . . glowed" in her, she "had strange whims of fasting, like a Papist" (1.1:9). She reads Protestant Jeremy Taylor far into the night, and Anglican Richard Hooker also figures in her misguided girlish dreams of an ideal husband (1.1:10), but at the same time she reads Catholic Pascal (1.1:8). Pascal, to be sure, was a very Protestant sort of Catholic, who never shed the effects of his Jansenist education and loved to attack Jesuits. When Dorothea is talking to Sir James Chettam about her scheme for providing labourers with new cottages, she says "energetically" (George Eliot's intruded adverb), "I think we deserve to be beaten out of our beautiful houses with a scourge of small cords" (1.3:31). Suddenly the language of political and social zeal is invaded by that of medieval flagellation. The interesting thing is the unlooked-for precision — the strong focus and close knowledge — in the phrase, "of strong cords." Dorothea, we abruptly realise, has been imagining this intently upon some other occasion. Of course the tone is partly facetious. In Protestant culture Roman Catholic extremism becomes simultaneously picturesque and comic. One can watch the process beginning with John Donne's saints and relics of the erotic. Dorothea as a matter of general culture is heir to all this. Her Saint Bernard dog, the constant companion of her walks, is called "Monk" (1.3:26). We may think for a moment of the "discipline" kept by Molière's Tartuffe in his closet (3.2.1) — that is, we may think of hypocrisy — but we shall do better perhaps to remember the extraordinary words used by Isabella, Shakespeare's glowing devotee, in *Measure for Measure:*

> *Th'impression of keen whips I'd wear as rubies*
> *And strip myself to death as to a bed*
> *That longing had been sick for, ere I'd yield*
> *My body up to shame*

> [2.4.101–4]

Here Isabella, all but committed to the life of a religious sect, but set, by Shakespeare, to be married at the end of the comedy to the duke, verbally lashes the deathly intellectual, Angelo. As with Dorothea, but much more strongly, there is a sense that the speaker has, as it were, thought too vividly about whipping.

Dorothea is a personality stretched, in a rich awareness, between Protestant and Catholic worlds. Mr. Casaubon is then seen, through the eyes of this same divided Dorothea, as himself compounded of both elements. Again, it is the mildly facetious writing that can be oddly revealing. Because it is uncommitted, imagery that would elsewhere be censored as dangerous is here allowed to pass. Dorothea before her marriage is presented (at 1.5:49) as metaphorically kissing Mr. Casaubon's unfashionable shoe-ties as if he were a Protestant pope. The faint, jarring oxymoron, "Protestant pope," is in its context brilliant. It reinforces Celia's sense, expressed just before, that Mr. Casaubon is more like the officiating clergyman than a bridegroom. There is an implication of self-immolation, which is culturally Papist; Dorothea's self-dedication to Mr. Casaubon is analogous, by this logic, to her whimsical fasting like a Papist (1.6:57). At the same time however this is not the Vicar of God in Rome but, in simple, English bourgeois-Protestant terms, "the vicar" — the Reverend Edward Casaubon in fact. Celia's sense that Dorothea is yoking herself to the wrong figure in the wedding scene is important, but important too is the reminder that Mr. Casaubon belongs properly to the northern form of Christianity.

The strong iconography surrounding Mr. Casaubon places him very firmly as a Protestant. His physical resemblance to Locke and still more his association with Puritan Milton keeps this before our minds. These allusions are heavily made, but there are lighter allusions on the other side of the equation. Dorothea also says that life with Mr. Casaubon would be like being married to Blaise Pascal (1.3:28), but Pascal, as we saw, is an equivocal figure.[7] Her mental description of him as "a modern Augustine" (1.3:24), on the other hand, may seem more straightforwardly Catholic, though Augustine is early enough — patristic enough — to transcend the Protestant-Catholic divide. He was after all the principal doctor not only of the Jansenists but also of the Calvinists. But in the same sentence that mentions Augustine we are given, in parallel, the phrase, " a living Bossuet." Jacques-Bénigne Bossuet is centrally, indeed polemically Roman Catholic. This burns in the superb, complex rhetoric of his sermons and, more materially, in his brilliant *Histoire des variations* (1688), in which he pitilessly exposed the crazed, fissiparating sects of Protestantism. Why Bossuet? The answer may be disappointingly simple: Bossuet is there to represent the strand of learning and that is that. A similar explanation may be given for the stiller odder idea which Ladislaw's friend Naumann has of painting Mr. Casaubon as Thomas Aquinas, the central Roman Catholic theologian (2.22:212). Does Naumann not know that Thomas, "the dumb ox of Aquino," was a huge, fat man, that a semi-circular section had to be cut out of his worktable to accommodate his great belly? Does George Eliot, dare we suggest, not know this? The truth is that there is simply no precision in the allusion. Aquinas was brainy and Mr. Casaubon has a brainy look.

The playing off of religion against sexuality, if analysed and presented in the early twenty-first century, can hardly avoid the appearance of cliché. We are all post-Freudians now and Freud's originally alarming propositions have been thoroughly tamed. They are now the matter of innumerable jokes. But when George Eliot discerns a strange alliance of spiritual and sexual energies in her heroine, this is live material.

Take the description of Dorothea's love of riding: "Most men thought her bewitching when she was on horseback. She loved the fresh air and the various aspects of the country, and when her eyes and cheeks glowed with mingled pleasures she looked very little like a devotee. Riding was an indulgence which she allowed herself in spite of conscientious qualms; she felt that she enjoyed it in a pagan sensuous way, and always looked forward to renouncing it" (1.1:10). In some degree this is saved from cliché by its humorous lightness. The last phrase about looking forward to renunciation ("God make me good, but not yet") is really quite funny. In Euripides' *Hippolytus* the protagonist loves hunting while his stepmother, Phaedra, is locked inside the prison of incestuous desire yet, from within that prison, has dreams of drinking from springs in open country, of hunting the stag and galloping on horseback over the levels (ll. 209–10, 218, 231–32). Here riding and sexuality are antithetical. In the George Eliot passage they are profoundly allied. Behind this manifest contrast between the ancient writer and the Victorian, however, there are after all deeper affinities. Dorothea is not only the Saint Theresa of a bourgeois society, she is also a kind of female Hippolytus, hot-cheeked, ardently virtuous, yet fated to fall under the sway of the scorned goddess of sexual love. But then, at the end of our comparison, we are confronted by a final difference. The ultimate victory of Aphrodite-Venus, which in Euripides — and in Jean Racine's *Phèdre* — is seen as dreadful, is in *Middlemarch* ostensibly happy.

The first words quoted, "Most men thought her bewitching," belong to a strain in *Middlemarch* that is counter-feminist. One running thesis, easily discoverable in the novel, is "Dorothea Brooke — dear girl! — has all sorts of nonsensical notions about the life of the mind but all that she really needs to put her right is some good strong sex from a man." Simultaneously the novel enforces another, more elevated thesis about the proper intellectual development of women. Here Eliot opens the subject very cunningly by seeing Dorothea (once more) through the sexually anticipatory gaze of the male. It is, as we saw, a commonplace of feminism that males "detect" signals where none were willingly sent. It is a further commonplace that men think "In women's mouths, in case of love, 'No' no negative will prove."[8] The light cadence of Eliot's opening phrase takes the male, non-feminist side in the game: the implicit logic is that Dorothea is unconsciously emitting strong positive sexual signals and that *these are real,* that is, that they convey her real though unacknowledged wishes, as a woman. It follows that "No" is indeed no negative, in the case of this particular woman. She is saying "No" to sensuality in the asserted conduct of her life, but this "No" masks a secret "Yes." She "glowed with mingled pleasures." "Mingled" is here a tantalising word. What are the components in the mixture? Simple pleasure in exercise, certainly, will no longer serve. "Glowed," meanwhile, obviously suggests a state close to sexual fulfilment. "Very little like a devotee," which roughly means "most un-nun-like," reinforces the point. The wonderfully vague word "qualms" then continues the implication of an imperfectly acknowledged sexuality. Dorothea suspects that it is wrong but does not quite know why. She gets as far as "pagan and sensuous."

Both sides of Dorothea, the conscious religious side eager for renunciation and the sensuous side, are real. She is not pretending to desire sacrifice. One perfectly authentic element in her is seeking a husband who is as un-husband-like as the equestrian Dorothea was un-nun-like. She wants, as we have seen, to marry a blinded Milton and thinks the "really delightful" marriage must be that where your husband was a sort of father (1.1:10). She really is asking here for marriage not only to wisdom and learning but to age and incapacity. Blindness, we saw, may carry a faint implication of emasculation. Throughout humour exercises a redeeming effect, saving the novel from portentousness. Take, for example, the miniature domestic comedy in which Dorothea induces in her sister Celia an understandable state of irritation by remarking that jewellery may be all right for Celia, but she, Dorothea, scorns it; yet then she responds to the beauty of jewels, observing how the deep colours "seem to penetrate one," struggling the while to baptise her pleasure by associating it with Saint John of the Cross (1.1:13–14). Theresa and the angels with the dart that "penetrated" her heart cannot, one feels, be far away. Note also that Celia, like her namesake in Shakespeare's *As you Like It,* is marginalised by the more brilliant sister.

I have suggested that there are in *Middlemarch* moments of coincidence with a certain coarsely anti-feminist view. In 3.28 we find

Mr. and Mrs. Casaubon home from their honeymoon, installed at Lowick Manor. The house with its pictures and furniture echoes the deathly appearance of Mr. Casaubon. Dorothea, contrariwise, appears from her morning toilette, "glowing . . . as only healthful youth can glow: there was a gem-like brightness on her coiled hair and in her hazel eyes; there was a warm red life in her lips; her throat had a breathing whiteness above the differing white of the fur which itself seemed to wind about her neck and cling down her blue-grey pelisse with a tenderness gathered from her own, a sentient commingled innocence which kept its loveliness against the crystalline purity of the outdoor snow" (3.28:271). This is erotically excited writing. The "breathing whiteness" of the throat and neck are charged with a feeling that is almost Keatsian. Madeline in *The Eve of St. Agnes* "unclasps her warmèd jewels, one by one" (l. 228). Nothing can equal the tender intimacy of Keats's word "warmèd"; the jewels on this cold winter night are warm where they have just been touching the living throat of Madeline. But for all that, the sense of physicality is similar. The fur winding itself around Dorothea's neck is itself erotically personified; it cannot help embracing her, in a manner that is now not so much Keatsian as Renaissance. So we may think, instead, of Cleopatra on the Cydnus, of the amorous winds and the coloured fans which "did seem / To glow the delicate cheeks which they did cool" (*Antony and Cleopatra* 2.2:203–4). Remember that George Eliot tells us that the sleeping Ariadne, whose beauty was outmatched by Dorothea, was then known as the "Cleopatra" (2.19:186). "Commingled" is a suggestive term here, as "mingled" was earlier. The very painterly play with the idea of "white-on-white," Dorothea's white innocence set "against" the purity of the snow is a chromatic equivalence for the central ambiguity of a nature that is both austere and sensual. Purity set beside purity should produce an unbroken field of whiteness. But here, because of a latent complexity in Dorothea, whose innocence, unlike the "crystalline" snow, is mysteriously "commingled," we find instead an enchanting line of difference.

It is slightly surprising, in terms of the general imaginative economy of the novel, that Dorothea should "glow" both after the sensuous experience of riding and after a honeymoon with Dr. Death. Later we are told how Dorothea recovers her beauty rapidly after the death of Mr. Casaubon; this is in line with what we expect. It is likely that here, in the description of the bride returned, Eliot simply wants a vivid contrast between the blooming young wife and the desiccated bridegroom. Whatever the reason, Eliot proceeds at once to a straight piece of standard nineteenth-century feminism, an attack on the sterile, suffocating existence imposed by society on the sort of middle-class lady who is not permitted any action approximating to work. This produces a brief deflection from the sexual story to a more generalised social message, but the sterility of the marriage as marriage is maintained in the reader's mind. The narrative momentum of the novel seems momentarily arrested, and in the stillness Dorothea's eye falls on a portrait of the Casaubon's Aunt Julia, Will Ladislaw's grandmother, the lady who made an "unfortunate marriage" (3.28:272). Dorothea responds to the picture with a sudden intense sympathy: "She felt a new companionship" (3.28: 273). But, as she gazes, something odd happens to the object of her vision: "The colours deepened, the lips and chin seemed to get larger, the hair and eyes seemed to be sending out light, the face was masculine and beamed on her with that full gaze which tells her on whom it falls that she is too interesting for the slightest movement of her eyelid to pass unnoticed and uninterpreted. The vivid presentation came like a pleasant glow to Dorothea: She felt herself smiling" (3.28:273). The idea of a living eye, trained on an inanimate object, a picture, of itself suggests a wholly passionless experience. Instead, this expected state of affairs is overtaken by something dynamic, a tense relationship at first suggesting narcissism but then a full encounter with a lover of the opposite sex; the face within the frame is now actively gazing, is deemed to be keenly interested in the viewer, will notice if Dorothea's eyelid moves. All this is set in motion, we know, by a family resemblance. Julia looks like her grandson.

In this passage George Eliot may have learned from the brilliant manipulation of a glancingly perceived family resemblance in a portrait, which is to be found in Dickens's *Bleak House* (1852–53). The initial rapport between Dorothea and Julia is an effect of circumstance. One unhappy wife is looking at another. Dorothea wonders if Julia's marriage may not really have been unhappy at all (a potentially erotic thought). Then, however, she reverts to the intuition of a shared unhappiness. This is enough to generate in the reader a sense that Dorothea is in some way looking at herself, yet this time not with the self-immolating asceticism of the religious enthusiast but with simple sympathy, "sympathy" here having some reference to the sexual life. Then, presumably because of family likeness, the miniature permits infiltration by another face, the face of Will Ladislaw. I called this the face of a lover. Ladislaw has made no such declaration as yet, though he as called Dorothea "a poem" (2.22:221). Nevertheless, by a clairvoyance of the heart, that is what he is here. Much later (4.37:359), when Will is very close indeed to declaring his love for Dorothea, the light falls on his face, with "its defiant curves of lip and chin," as in the picture. This time it is the female gaze that is anticipatory. The foregrounding of Dorothea's sexuality is no longer conducted in an anti-feminist mode. Rather Dorothea learns humanely to value herself, including herself as woman, in a manner which feminism can welcome or actively encourage. Nora in act 2 of Henrik Ibsen's *A Doll's House* suddenly questions the ordinary ethical requirement of automatic altruism by speaking of her duty to herself. The warmth of this new sympathy in Dorothea, which is also self-sympathy, then modulates into an imagined heterosexual love. This sexuality is in immediate contrast not with Dorothea's intellectual pretensions but with the oppressive nature of her servitude to her husband and to her social class. The persisting ethical problem — that the liberation may seem to border on mere egoism — is mitigated in the present case by the division of Dorothea's psyche into conscious and half-conscious. When Gerard Manley Hopkins wrote, "Mine own heart let me more have pity on. / Let me live to my sad self hereafter kind" ("Mine Own Heart," ll. 1–2), the reader could not be sure whether the poet's real nature, hereafter to be treated with humanity, does or does not include his sexual yearnings. With Dorothea there are many signs that this is exactly what is intended. Self *A* being kind to Self *B* can seem a degree less egoistic than self-loving, *simpliciter*.

It is obvious that Eliot vastly prefers the half-absurd, psychologically charged, contradictory asceticism of Dorothea to the effortless sexlessness of Mr. Casaubon. Mr. Casaubon's letter of proposal is a minor masterpiece. In it he ends by explaining that he can offer "an affection hitherto unwasted, and the faithful consecration of a life which, however short in the sequel, has no backward pages whereon, if you choose to turn them, you will find records such as might justly cause you bitterness or shame" (1.5:42). "Unwasted" is a remarkable word. Mr. Casaubon is evidently proud that he has not been lavishing his affections with a loose freedom on all and sundry, and George Eliot, equally clearly, hates him for it. This time, while information is being conveyed to the reader, Mr. Casaubon remains thoroughly in character. He has no idea how his words will sound in a mind unlike his own. When he says his life will withstand any scrutiny he presumably means that there are no earlier love affairs. Here again one catches an altered echo of Angelo in *Measure for Measure*. Angelo, espoused to Mariana by a *de futuro* contract (roughly equivalent to engagement), is able to cast her off quite legally because her reputation was "disvalued / In levity" (5.1.221–22). Mr. Casaubon, an Angelo from whom all power has been withdrawn, presents *himself* as an unsullied bride. "Some rise by sin and some by virtue fall" (*Measure for Measure* 2.1.38). The icy chastity that Mr. Casaubon thinks will commend him, in the new value-system ruins him. It is noticeable that fictional dream-men, wish-fulfilment heroes in books written by women, are again and again endowed by their authors with a previous erotic life. Lord Peter Wimsey has even employed prostitutes (Dorothy L. Sayers, the writer, seems to find this obscurely thrilling).[9] Rochester in *Jane Eyre* has a continental past. And Maxim de Winter, poor fellow, had Rebecca.

I used to argue that the reticence conventionally imposed on nineteenth-century writers was no real impediment to communication, that without a word anywhere which could bring a blush to the cheek of a young person, George Eliot was easily able to make her reader keenly aware that the marriage between Dorothea and Mr. Casaubon was sexually disastrous. While I still think that reticence can be a source of power (the reader who is spurred to make guesses is more active imaginatively than one who passively receives full information), I find that I would like to know more than George Eliot is prepared to tell us about what happened in bed between these unhappy persons, in Rome and at Lowick Manor. It is possible that nothing sexual happened at all. That is one story. Or it is possible that Mr. Casaubon tried, incompetently, to have sexual relations with his wife. That is another story. Incidentally Wilkie Collins, who clearly wished the reader to understand that sexual intercourse never took place between Sir Percival Glyde and his wife, Laura, in *The Woman in White,* solves the problem, neatly and easily, by having Sir Percival affirm, with obvious truth and sincerity, that there is absolutely no chance of Laura's becoming pregnant (part 2, ch. 8). Something similar could have been done in *Middlemarch.* Mr. Casaubon's inability to write a book is set beside the fact that he has not begotten a son (3.29:276). Eliot tells us that he has determined to meet, at least, the second requirement, which may seem to settle my question, until we meet the words, "to leave behind him that copy of himself which seem so urgently required of a man — *to the sonneteers of the sixteenth century.*" We are left wondering if Mr. Casaubon's ideas about reproduction are after all wholly theoretical.

As one struggles to answer the unanswerable question, one grasps at straws. A learned husband who shrinks from sexual contact — a honeymoon in Italy, with much visiting of art galleries — these at the time when *Middlemarch* appeared would immediately call to mind the notorious fiasco of John Ruskin's marriage to Effie Chalmers Gray. Ruskin was said to have been repelled by the sight of his wife's naked body to the point of sexual paralysis. Mary Lutyens guessed in 1965 that the repellent factor may have been pubic hair (the ladies in the works of art had never had pubic hair).[10] In a statement dated 27 April 1854, giving his own account of the marriage but, in the event, never used by the lawyers, Ruskin said, "Though her face was beautiful, her person was not formed to excite passion. On the contrary there were certain circumstances in her person which completely checked it."[11] Mary Lutyens later hedged her bets and suggested that the explanation could have lain as easily in some personal smell,[12] but this seems improbable in the light of the pointed use of the word "saw" in a letter Effie herself wrote to her father when it was all over (7 March 1854): "He had imagined women were quite different to what he saw I was. . . . He was disgusted with my person the first evening."[13] John Batchelor argues powerfully that Ruskin would in fact have known that women had pubic hair because of the lubricious pictures of "naked bawds" passed round by the young gentlemen of Christ Church, Ruskin's Oxford college.[14] Mary Lutyens's initial guess could still be right. It is easy to imagine Ruskin not caring to look too closely at the naughty pictures, as it were preserving the crowded art gallery of his mind intact. George Eliot refers in *Middlemarch* to a "brilliant English critic" who "mistook the flower-flushed tomb of the ascended Virgin for an ornamental vase" (2.19:186). We may think for a moment that we are in Ruskin territory, but the allusion, it turns out, is to William Hazlitt. But there is really no problem here. John Batchelor says that George Eliot would certainly have heard the story about Effie and Ruskin: "Everyone knew!"[15] Ruskin and Effie were married for seven years, a lot longer than the Casaubons. The divorce with all its attendant publicity came in 1854, seventeen years before the publication of *Middlemarch*. The Ruskin marriage terminated in a law court, an environment that licenses or even commands an unsparing presentation of physical detail forbidden in the world of the novel. But Mr. Casaubon is no Ruskin. The aesthetic revulsion of the great art critic (if it ever happened) seems, for all its negative character, still too strong, too vivid for Mr. Casaubon.

The Mind of Mr. Casaubon

Mr. Casaubon, as Celia shatteringly observed at the beginning of the novel, is not physically attractive. But if his body is defective, does his great mind make good the deficiency? Famously the novel remorselessly exposes the fact that Mr. Casaubon has neither a pleasing body nor a great mind.

His scholarship is, as scholarship, unskilful, unintelligent, uninformed, barren. As we saw, he enters the novel complacently affirming that he has *not* read a book mentioned by Mr. Brooke. Brooke says of him, "I never got anything out of him — any ideas, you know" (1.4:38). It is as if he is best described by a series of negations. With the character of Mr. Brooke George Eliot adopts the manner of Jane Austen. He is a mildly comic character, as Mr. Bennett is in *Pride and Prejudice*. In *Middlemarch*, however, the miniature Austenian comedy has been transposed to a very different context. George Eliot is writing about knowledge. The comedy of Mr.

Bennett is a comedy of familial moral relations. The comedy of Mr. Brooke is a comedy of intellection, that is to say, of mildly scatty intellection. The humour indeed is very gentle. There is a tendency in writing about *Middlemarch* to exaggerate the foolishness of Mr. Brooke just as there is a tendency in writing about *Hamlet* to exaggerate the foolishness of Polonius. Mr. Brooke's wide-ranging unretentive brain is viewed by the writer with a degree of affection. Beside the black nescience of Mr. Casaubon, Mr. Brooke's intelligence is positively luminous. Therefore when Mr. Brooke says he could never get anything in the way of ideas out of Mr. Casaubon, this is far more damaging to Mr. Casaubon than it is to Mr. Brooke. We may think for a moment that the failure is all on Mr. Brooke's side, that he is simply not up to the level of Mr. Casaubon and naturally could not understand the great man's work, but this thought is at once crushed by a darker intuition: Mr. Brooke could get no ideas because no ideas were there.

Later, when Dorothea asks Mr. Casaubon when he is going to embark on the actual writing of the great work, Mr. Casaubon is very upset (2.20:197–200). In the following chapter Will Ladislaw calls on Dorothea. He is at this point in the story a feckless, charming youth who cannot settle to a career, and Dorothea talks to him *de haut en bas*, like the vicar's wife she in fact is. It is here that Ladislaw, effortlessly and casually, puts his foot through the paper screen of Mr. Casaubon's jealously guarded learning. Dorothea, sternly but kindly, points to the contrast between Ladislaw's happy-go-lucky existence and Mr. Casaubon's steady, persevering labour. Will is stung by the comparison: "It is a pity that it should be thrown away, as so much English scholarship is, for want of knowing what is being done by the rest of the world. If Mr. Casaubon read German, he would save himself a great deal of trouble" (2.21:205). Dorothea, who has already implicitly questioned her husband's work but without any distinct criticism, is at once anxious and says she does not understand. "I merely mean," Will continues, "that the Germans have taken the lead in historical inquiries, and they laugh at results which are got by groping about in woods with a pocket-compass while they have made good roads. When I was with Mr. Casaubon I saw that he deafened himself in that direction: it was almost against his will that he read a Latin treatise written by a German." Mr. Casaubon's incipient blindness, insisted on earlier, is here replaced by a deafness, which is willed, self-induced. In a way this passage is a rerun of the earlier one in which even scatty Mr. Brooke could expose Mr. Casaubon. Now any agreeable, footloose young man can, it seems, overturn the huge projected edifice. Of course Ladislaw is intellectually more serious than this summary implies, but we do not know that until the end of the story. What we have been told is that Mr. Casaubon has in fact been funding Ladislaw's slightly shoddy indecision for some time (1.9:79). Our sense of Will's nature actually changes as we read these words about scholarship. His manner remains offhand but the shaft is plainly well aimed. What we are seeing is not perhaps the way things ought to be, but it is the way things are. All those with experience of research and academic affairs will know exactly how dogged Dr. X can toil for years and be suddenly refuted by Mr. Y, who has never toiled at all but has kept his eye on current periodicals and has an instinct for spotting the critical argument when it comes along. As Ladislaw speaks, the relation between him and Dorothea is subtly reversed. When his sentence ends she can no longer patronise him ("matronise" would be a better word, but, alas, it does not exist).

The sudden sense of a cultural inferiority to Germany is confined to a select but important circle at this date. The more culturally alert classical scholars such as Mark Pattison, to whom we shall come, were vividly aware of a new German pre-eminence, first in classical philology and then in history. Eliot is here thinking of historiography, and the implicit point is to do with secularisation, the ousting of a predetermined Christian view of historical development by a non-Christian view. Eliot's own work on David Friedrich Strauss's *Leben Jesu* (1835–36), a book which got its author dismissed from his post at Tübingen, and Ludwig Andreas Feuerbach's openly anti-Christian *Wesen des Christentums* (1841) probably motivates the passage, from below. The unstated implication is that Mr. Casaubon's uncritical Christianity probably unfits him for research. In fact *Middlemarch* is a "loss of faith" or "de-conversion" novel, but all this is perhaps too well buried. *Robert Elsmere* (1888) does all this explicitly. Many readers of Mrs. Humphry Ward's novel, though properly grateful to its author, have wished that George Eliot had written it instead.

It remains mildly puzzling that Mr. Casaubon should have had the spirit to have imagined so vast an enterprise. The work he hopes to complete is "The Key to All Mythologies." I have already suggested, in connection with Browning's grammarian, that one would expect such a dryasdust pedant to be either editing a text by another, more creative hand or else, at best, producing a series of small-scale nitpicking articles on points of fact. But he is writing *The Golden Bough!* In the brief time of frail hope before the wedding, he explains to Dorothea how he had undertaken to show (what indeed had been attempted before, but not with that thoroughness, justice of comparison, and effectiveness of arrangement at which Mr. Casaubon aimed) that "all the mythical systems or erratic mythical fragments in the world were corruptions of a tradition originally revealed" (1.3: 23). The idea is stupendous in its scope and in the essayed explanatory power.

There is a real technical problem here. Eliot needs the vast enterprise because she needs the nightmare of the labyrinth, of an endlessly recessive labour. But that a mind as lifeless as that of Mr. Casaubon should so much as conceive of such a task is wholly implausible. If, nevertheless, we accept that he really is trying to understand the aetiology of all myth-systems and to discern a unitary principle behind them, he becomes at once a different person. This dried-up insect of a man can dream of adventures of the intellect that never impinge on the consciousness of most human beings.

It may be said that this is precisely the paradox which Eliot wished to present in her construction of Mr. Casaubon, that she fully intended the mitigating factor of intellectual imagination as part of a complex picture. She writes, "Mr. Casaubon had an intense consciousness within him, and was spiritually a-hungered like the rest of us" (3.29:275). Here, it may be said, George Eliot has intervened personally to make sure that the reader understands that the power to envisage great designs — that power which I have been denying to the poor failed scholar — really was latent in him. Yet it is not I but George Eliot herself who has already consolidated the picture of a personality without any trace of such a capacity to dream, to think of explaining all the mythologies of the world. To suddenly assert that he knew spiritual hunger will not of itself remove the difficulty. There are signs in the writing here — qualifications and hesitations — which show that the author is aware that she is in difficulties. She adds the words "like the rest of us," one suspects, in order to make believable that which she knows is at first sight not believable at all. She is saying in effect, "Well he *was* a human being, and we all have these feelings, don't we?" If Mr. Casaubon had only as much spiritual hunger as the average human being (and all the signs are that he actually had rather less than average) this manifestly will not account for the Great Design. Most people do not form a plan to explain historically the mythic culture of *Homo sapiens*. Hesitations continue in the clever, convoluted paragraphs that follow. First she qualifies her own term, "intense consciousness," in the direction of a nervous self-regard, away from cognitive, intelligent awareness of what lies outside the circle of self: "His soul was sensitive without being enthusiastic; it was too languid to thrill out of self-consciousness into passionate delight" (3.29:277). Then, as if uneasy that Mr. Casaubon-the-Dreamer-of-a-Great-Dream is once more slipping through her fingers, she endeavours to hold the conception together with a series of mild oxymorons: "scholarly and uninspired, ambitious and timid, scrupulous and dim-sighted" (3.29: 278). "Uninspired" actually works against the idea of the dreamer of dreams; "scholarly," in the other scale, does nothing to redress this. Nor does "scrupulous," when set against the pejorative "dim-sighted." Indeed we can easily believe that Mr. Casaubon was scholarly (in his old-fashioned way) and that he was scrupulous. *That* is not the problem. "Ambitious," set against "timid," may seem however to meet the case. The trouble is that we have already been given to understand that Mr. Casaubon's ambition will be like his sensitivity — self-regarding rather than intellectual. Had she essayed a bolder oxymoron — say, "incompetently pedantic but inspired" — this would indeed cover the problem, and the reader (George Eliot would know) simply would not swallow it. Mr. Casaubon is palpably unimaginative, without courage of the spirit. The problem remains. George Eliot, like Robert Browning, is confused.

The notion of the labyrinth meanwhile has, of course, its own effectiveness. At this point in the story Dorothea is described as looking "deep into the ungauged reservoir of Mr. Casaubon's mind" and as "finding reflected there in vague labyrinthine extension every quality she herself brought" (1.3:23). Here the image of a reservoir (of life-sustaining water?) is usurped by the image of the maze. "Ungauged" is cunningly planted, as a warning that her hopes of drinking deep may possibly be ill-founded. Just as earlier we noted an element of narcissism in Dorothea's passionate response to the portrait of Ladislaw's grandmother Julia, so here there is a poignant, transient narcissism involving, this time, Dorothea's *intellectual* energies. She sees in the mere surface of the Casaubon reservoir — what lies beneath now forgotten — a shimmering, mazy echo of her own dream of really understanding the world. "Reservoir," incidentally, with its connotation of "reserve," is an especially well-chosen word. The reticence of Mr. Casaubon will prove in due course to be a pusillanimous secrecy, covering utter incapacity. The labyrinth becomes, once more, an image of Mr. Casaubon's mind and not of Dorothea's: "the scope of his great work, also of attractively labyrinthine extent" (1.3:23). There is here a growing sense of threatening darkness and sterile confusion. "Attractively" signals that Dorothea is actually being drawn in, actively wishes to enter the maze. But a labyrinth no more suggests freedom or opening horizons than it suggests life-giving water. At the deepest level, however, there could be a seed of hope. The first labyrinth was the labyrinth of Crete, which Theseus entered. For Theseus it was an essentially solvable puzzle. Nothing in the book implies that Dorothea is Theseus, but we have seen that at a certain level she is Ariadne. It was Ariadne who supplied the solution to the puzzle of the labyrinth.

Meanwhile Mr. Casaubon's notion of a comprehensive corruption and fragmentation of an original revelation may be intended to suggest a wrong-headed biblical centralism. "Revealed" is a difficult term here. Is it or is it not supposed to imply "Revelation," "Revealed Religion," that biblical line which the Deists had laboured to set aside, a century earlier? The answer is not clear. It looks like authorial hesitation. The labyrinths of medieval Europe, such as that on the floor of Chartres Cathedral, were unicursal. The route twists to and fro but never divides. The person in the labyrinth is confused but never lost. He follows the path this way and that and eventually reaches the centre. He is safe in the hands of God. But Mr. Casaubon finds himself in a post-Renaissance labyrinth where the paths branch and branch again, presenting him with choices he had never expected and with which he is not equipped to deal.

If we think of a primary revelation subsequently corrupted, in less narrowly biblical terms, the Hermetists of the sixteenth century come to mind. The writings of Hermes Trismegistus were thought to be at least as old as Moses and to contain an original, untainted philosophical and theological truth. This was distorted by later ages. This was the doctrine spectacularly refuted at the beginning of the seventeenth century by the other Casaubon, Isaac. The irony is indeed profound. The nineteenth-century figure espouses an essentially irrational doctrine of gradually adulterated purity that his namesake had already destroyed, seemingly for all time. Mr. Casaubon is the primitive, Isaac Casaubon the sophisticated scholar. The contrast indeed, can and should be qualified. Isaac Casaubon was a devout Christian; Mr. Casaubon's faith seems in comparison a gutless thing. "He held himself to be, with some private scholarly reservations, a believing Christian" (4.41:419). But it remains true that it was Isaac Casaubon who, as Mark Pattison put it, turned the tables and "set up 'Antiquity' as canon of religious truth."[16] It appears that Mr. Casaubon, conversely, while believing far less than his great namesake, is setting up a species of revelation as the canon of antique truth. In this way George Eliot cunningly contrives an anti-Enlightenment narrowness in the central design of Mr. Casaubon's book and this does, in some degree, mitigate the difficulty of allowing him, initially, so grand a conception.

The Book That Explains Everything

Sir James Frazer's *Golden Bough*, with its dying gods, solar deities, and year spirits, comes after the time of *Middlemarch*. So do Gilbert Murray and Jane Harrison, the author of *Themis*. But diachronic total explanation was already in the air, some time before Frazer or, indeed, George Eliot, got to work. In July 1856 Eliot reviewed Heinrich von Riehl's *Natural History of the People, or the Foundation of a German Sociopolitical System*, a ground-breaking work in what was to become the field of social anthropology.[17] Sigmund Freud wrote in a letter to his fiancée, "What we once were," we "in part still remain."[18] The sense that the key to our own identity and nature as human beings, living now, lies in our historical aetiology, was suddenly strong. The great synchronic explanatory enterprise of the eighteenth-century philosophers had terminated paralysingly in David Hume. It may be said that the wheel had come full circle, for if we go still further back, to the seventeenth century, the Great Explanation is, again, diachronic. John Milton in *Paradise Lost* sought to explain everything by telling the old, Christian story of the Fall of Man. Milton began his biblical epic with the proud hope that he would "justify the ways of God to men" (1.26). More than half a century later Alexander Pope wrote *An Essay on Man.* The eighteenth-century poet consciously matches himself with Milton, saying that he in his turn will "Vindicate the ways of God to man" (1.16). But Pope does not tell the old story; instead he tackles the problem of evil head on, arguing in a quasi-Leibnizian manner, that imperfection is necessarily inherent in any graduated scheme of creation. This at least is true of the greater part of *An Essay on Man,* but it must be conceded that in the third epistle a kind of "fall-narrative" reappears; but now the fall is not from Paradise but from a naturalistically, politically, socially conceived "state of nature." When narrative returns in the nineteenth century, it is soon clear that there is no longer an inner, prior requirement that the story must be the story of a fall. A certain Whiggish cheerfulness begins to break in. The story might even be the story of a rise. This change is continually thwarted and complicated by counter-movements and qualifications, but it is nevertheless discernible. It is neatly illustrated by the semantic history of the word *primitive,* once a term of praise (as in "primitive Christianity"), later a pejorative word. At the same time, however, there is a new sophistication. We no longer naively repeat the Great Story; rather, having noticed a host of more or less parallel Great Stories in different times and places, we set ourselves the task of telling the story of storytelling. "Mythology" becomes a separate category, as it never was for Milton. The new narrative is meta-narrative.

Frazer's key to all mythologies, although often described as the beginning of modern anthropology, is better understood as the last flowering of this nineteenth-century tradition. We see *The Golden Bough* today as it is transmitted through the glass of T. S. Eliot's *Waste Land*. This means that we see it as resonating with primal religious significance. But, as I have argued elsewhere, there is an irony in this situation.[19] Eliot reaching maturity amid the dry scepticism of the early twentieth century found in *The Golden Bough* a succession of voices all speaking of one thing: resurrection. Eliot was not a Christian when he wrote *The Waste Land*, but one can smell it coming, in the dying-god-who-lives-again of Frazerian myth. But Frazer did not see his own work in this way. He saw himself as a scientific historian, exposing barbarous materials to the cold light of scepticism. He can indeed sound oddly like Edward Gibbon, as when he remarks that "the good taste and humanity of the Greeks must have recoiled form the more violent rites of the Magna Mater."[20] Eliot in a curious way is restoring the conceptual order favoured by Mr. Casaubon: the idea of a deep original truth that is to prove consonant with Christianity. Again, this was something "in the air" in the 1920s. The word *primitive*, predictably, begins once more to take on a positive connotation. The primitive cult effigy is good art, the Enlightenment marble figure, bad. Now, however, paradoxically in 1922, all the life, all the fire is with the religious conception. Eliot, who likes to play the lean and slippered pantaloon, may in his more antic Prufrockian moments have taken on the look and air of dry-asdust Mr. Casaubon, but he had genius, which Mr. Casaubon had not. Strangest of all, we can sense in the world-weary, Jazz Age *Waste Land* that the intuition of a disenchanting multiplicity in mythology, with its implications of cultural relativism, has somehow gone into reverse, that all these stories of dying gods are really one story, the story of the God who really did die.

Meanwhile the nineteenth-century historians of competing mythologies have their own overarching story to tell, and this overarching story has the status of a deep, explanatory myth. When I say that, while we see Frazer as a richly imaginative mythmaker, he saw himself as a myth-analyst, I do not wish to imply that either view has a monopoly of the truth. The case of Freud is analogous. Where we today see an excitingly murky imagination he presented —

and saw—himself as a scientist, a pourer of cold water on treasured, beautiful illusions. Then is truth in both pictures.

Before Frazer we have, as will by this time be predictable, the Germans. The Sanskrit scholar Friedrich Max Müller was the son of the poet Wilhelm Müller. He grew up in Germany but was made a British subject in the 1820s. He became a prominent Oxford figure. His *Lectures on the Science of Language,* given at the Royal Institution in 1861–64, is a fundamental text. Müller resembles Mr. Casaubon in so far as he believed in an original, pure religious intuition, but instead of interpreting myth syncretically, as "lisping" the great truths (T. S. Eliot's way) he saw it—myth itself—as an obscuring, corrupting agent. Myth misplaced the notion of substance, ascribing to it names that were really wholly fictitious, merely poetical, hiding the primal insight under a woven fabric of glittering deceit. Myth, he said, was "a disease of language."[21] One may compare with this Matthew Arnold's idea, set out in *Literature and Dogma,* of an invading *Aberglaube,* or "Extra-belief," obscuring an original moral intuition. Meanwhile Müller's "original truth" hypothesis is presented in a way that smells of eighteenth-century Deism. The distinctively cultural (not racial) anti-Semitism that permeates English sceptical Deism is there. He saw his task as being to discover the first seeds of "the language, religion, and mythology of our forefathers, the wisdom of Him who is not the God of the Jews only."[22] It is precisely this willingness to consider the extra-Christian East that divides him from Mr. Casaubon. Ladislaw adds to Mr. Casaubon's ignorance of German a second ignorance of Eastern religion. "He is not an Orientalist" (2.22:218). George Eliot called the first series of Müller's *Lectures* "a delightful book."[23] She made copious notes.[24] Frank M. Turner allows one significant exception on the English side of the scholarly divide: Edward Pococke's *India in Greece or Truth in Mythology* (1852).[25] Pococke's book is a curiosity—an extravagant, overexcited piece of writing, terminating triumphantly and wholly implausibly with the announcement that the Greek name "Pythagoras" is identical with the Sanskrit "Bud'ha Gooroos," where the reference is to the spiritual teacher of Buddha. Sadly, the pages of the copy lodged in the Bodleian Library in Oxford are uncut. No one ever read it.

In 1825 Karl—or Carl , the name is spelled both ways—Otfried Müller had published his *Introduction to a Scientific Mythology*[26] (George Eliot refers to it in a review she wrote of R. W. Mackay). This work, as John Clark Pratt and Victor A. Neufeldt point out, decisively rejected the design of resolving the many into the one by means of etymological demonstration. [27] This line differentiates him from Max Müller, who was always haunted by the pursuit of the One. The scientifically respectable principle of Ockham's razor: the simplest or most economical explanation is to be preferred—and is potentially the most powerful—is itself dangerously close to a pre-rational dream of original oneness. The two are easily confounded, especially when myth is itself the subject matter. Max Müller, like Mr. Casaubon, stresses the notion of a *key*, which will unlock mysteries: "The key that is to open one must open all; otherwise it cannot be the right key."[28]

Much of the immediately relevant material is expertly set out in the Pratt and Neufeldt edition of the *Middlemarch* notebooks. They cite Müller's hieratic sentence on the key that will open all locks, and then the words of R. W. Mackay, written in a cooler time some twenty years after the period at which *Middlemarch* is set: "No writer on mythology is sceptical enough to assert its memorials to be without meaning, nor, on the other hand, so credulous as to claim to possess an infallible key for the solution of all puzzles."[29] John Mayor, however, sober lexicographer though he was, wrote with fervour about the duty of the modern grammarian to "pierce beneath the veil to the idea. . . .A key will be placed in their hands, which will open ways long barred up by hopeless difficulties and seeming contradictions . . . a master-key."[30] Pratt and Neufeldt observe that, while Mayor does no more than investigate some Roman proper names, this passage may indeed have given George Eliot the fundamental idea of a key.[31] They rightly contrast Charles François Dupuis's *Origine de tous les cultes* 1794) as an example of the kind of book Mr. Casaubon might have read with the far more important and fundamental *Symbolik und Mythologie der alten Völker besonder der Griechen* (1810–12) by Georg Friedrich Creuzer, from which he would have averted his gaze, but of course George Eliot was equal to Creuzer's German and did read him. We must be careful, however, not to forget that Dupuis is himself no "biblical centrist" as Mr. Casaubon was. His book bears on its title page the symbols of the Revolution, the year of publication is "l'an III de la République." Dupuis, in the eighteenth century, is clear that Christ is Apollo or the Sun in another form.[32] In contrast, the 154-volume *Allgemeine Encyklopëdie der Wissenschaften und Künste,* from which George Eliot transcribed notes on such things as euhemerism (the idea that ancient myths are modified accounts of real, historical persons who lived in the remote past), is exactly the sort of thing a bright young man like Will Ladislaw could swiftly consult — and extract in five minutes information that could overthrow at a stroke hundreds of pages (had they ever been written!) in Mr. Casaubon's "Key to All Mythologies."

Other grandly explanatory books were available to George Eliot and inaccessible to Mr. Casaubon, not because they were in German but because of chronology. They were written after 1832, the date at which *Middlemarch* is set. Henry James Sumner Maine's *Ancient Law: Its Connection with Early History of Society and Its Relation to Modern Ideas* (1861) is one. George Grote's eight-volume *History of Greece* (1849), with its strong emphasis on mythopoeia, is another. It is true that Pococke, the author of *India in Greece,* derided Grote's *History* because of its author's professed contentment with the surface sequence of events — " 'The curtain,' as Apelles said, 'does not conceal the work; it *is* the work' "; for Pococke latency is all — behind the curtain of Hellenic history lies the real picture, which is Indian.[33] For all that, Grote is an Explainer — but he comes too late. By contrast, Jacob Bryant, whose three-volume *New System, or, An Analysis of Ancient Mythology* appeared first in London in 1774–76, is immediately pertinent. Bryant was a sort of biblical euhemerist; he saw Greek legends as corrupt versions of the real historical events set out in *Genesis.* "The war of the Titans," he observes, "was no other than the war mentioned by Moses, which was carried on by the four families of Shem against the sons of Ham and Chus."[34] His work, like Mr. Casaubon's, is unenlightened by German philology. His eyes, like Mr. Casaubon's, were weak.[35] Ladislaw scornfully places Mr. Casaubon with Bryant when he describes him as "living in a lumber room and furbishing up broken-legged theories about Chus and Mizrain" (2.22:219). The physical event that heralds the final descent towards death of Mr. Casaubon, his sudden collapse on the library steps as he reached for a book (3.29:281) is curiously reminiscent, for those who relish extra-textual allusion, of Bryant's death. Pratt and Neufeldt point out that Eliot could have read in her own copy of Charles Knight's twenty-two-volume *English Cyclopaedia* (1854–70), under "Biography," how Bryant died as a result of a chair slipping from under him while he was reaching for a book.[36]

The narration of Mr. Casaubon's fall is not comic but seriously sympathetic, but for all that one senses that a kind of Sternean learned farce, a comedy of erudition and abstraction incompetently at war with the ordinary physical world, lies in the background. In E. M. Forster's *Howard's End*, Leonard Bast, the lower-class young man taken up by the well-read Schlegel sisters, is killed when a bookcase falls on him. Here too the writing is serious, but at the same time it is very nearly funny, partly because of the sudden crudeness of the symbolism: poor Leonard clobbered by learning. Mr. Casaubon belongs in many ways, like his unfashionable shoe-ties, to the eighteenth century. There is nothing bizarre about this. The eighteenth century is no more remote from the townsfolk of *Middlemarch* than the 1970s are from us. Mr. Casaubon would probably have despised William Hurd's *New Universal History of the Religious Rites, Ceremonies and Customs of the Whole World* (1788). Hurd's lavishly illustrated Cook's tour of the religious practices of the world, from China to Peru, is a highly entertaining work. He gives a fair account of the Ophite Gnostics, who thought that the serpent in Genesis was Christ, opposing the tyrant Jehovah. This indeed is one of the ways in which Gnostic William Blake could have learned about the Ophites (a copy of Hurd's work in the British Library bears annotations by W. B. Yeats, which show that Yeats had the same thought, when he was working on Blake). Of the antinomian Muggletonians (another pretty clear influence on Blake), he writes that they "are now a jolly set of fellows, who drink their pot and smoak their tobacco."[37] The *New Universal History* seems almost to be aimed at a mass market; it announces itself as "designed to form a complete family library" (one thinks of the sets of Wells or Dickens, "handsomely bound in Skivertex," "a must for every family," which were advertised for the readers of the great mass newspapers of the 1930s). The book is completely innocent of footnotes and learned references. Mr. Casaubon's own book, we may surmise, would, had it ever been completed, have been less genial. It would certainly have been encumbered with a vast apparatus of footnotes. Yet "The Key to All Mythologies" might well have ended by being closer to Hurd than, say, to Mosheim (J. L. Mosheim's fact-packed *Ecclesiastical History* appeared in English in 1758–68). The trumpeting ambition of both titles, Hurd's and Mr. Casaubon's, are in each case joined incongruously to a parochial narrowness of understanding. Although Robert Lowth's *Sacred Poetry of the Hebrews* belongs to the eighteenth century, it is slightly surprising to find that it is a favourite of Mr. Casaubon's (he asks Dorothea to read aloud from Lowth at 4.37:369). Mr. Casaubon appears momentarily to have deviated into good taste and judgement. Lowth was a profoundly original thinker whose views on poetry anticipate those of the Romantics.[38] He is remarkable perhaps more for his imagination than for his historical insight. But the effect of the introduction of his name is to reawaken our earlier anxiety. Mr. Casaubon's seems, obstinately, a great dream, too great for Mr. Casaubon.

I have suggested that the meta-narrative of myth-history can easily become itself another myth. To show in a given case that this has happened is usually to discredit this case in some degree according to the standards of "scientific" history. By the same token, however, the demonstration may magnify the same work, if it is seen as inadvertent mythic art. Freud, once the alarming, dubious scientist, is suddenly a *great* mythographer. So, to place Mr. Casaubon with the manifest myth-makers will operate, in an entirely smooth manner, to discredit him intellectually, but at the same time may operate in his favour, at the level of imagination. It is as if we have reached the point of saying, "Mr. Casaubon is not a judicious historian, but he is certainly creative." Creativity, surely, is the last characteristic Eliot wishes us to associate with this figure. Once more, however, the difficulty can be, at least in part, dispelled. Although Mr. Casaubon is writing heavily mythical history he is not creating his own myth; rather it is the old myth, inertly repeated.

Nevertheless Max Müller perhaps emerges as a little more like

Mr. Casaubon than Will Ladislaw would like us to think. Müller really does seem to have believed that the key to nearly all mythologies lay in philology. He traced "Apollo" and "Daphne" from Sanskrit words signifying the triumph of the sun over the dawn. The death of Heracles signified sunset.[39] Oscar Wilde's remark, "Religions die when they are proved to be true; science is the record of dead religions," looks like one of his damper squibs but becomes merely reasonable if one thinks of sun-worship.[40] The priests used to say that the Sun was Source of All Life, and now the scientists say exactly the same thing, but without the capital letters. George W. Cox's *Mythology of the Aryan Nations* (1870) came out too late to be drawn on in *Middlemarch* but exhibits the solar obsession that was by this time a sort of craze. A certain ingenious clergyman call R. F. Littledale waggishly argued that Max Müller was himself a solar myth.[41] But, if Max Müller's quest for a key links him to Mr. Casaubon, one has still to say that, despite the Frazerian promise of its title, Mr. Casaubon's "Key" does not come across as especially "solar." Why is that? The answer is that George Eliot is unwilling to give solar myth to Mr. Casaubon because she wants it for herself.

The novelist is not immune to the excitement in the air. She is herself caught up in the nineteenth-century dream of a new mythography. *Middlemarch* is itself a solar myth, transposed into the bourgeois detail of the contemporary novel. Mr. Casaubon's "Key" cannot be solar because he, within the myth of *Middlemarch*, is the dying winter, to be overcome in due course by the sun, Ladislaw. Felicia Bonaparte observes in her introduction to the World's Classics *Middlemarch* that the novel begins in the autumn and ends in spring.[42] When Mr. Casaubon is first attracted — in his own attenuated fashion — to Dorothea, his face, as we saw, is lit momentarily "by a smile like pale wintry sunshine" (1.3:25–26). His winter of frigidity is here touched by the sun's ray of a possible love, but only just. When Dorothea first visits Mr. Casaubon at Lowick it is a "grey but dry November morning." Bonaparte thinks that, since solar myth is allied to vegetation myth, so Ladislaw is as much a fertility god as he is the sun (hence the life-giving showers of rain that accompany several of his appearances in the book). Sunny he certainly is.

At first it is gently done. Celia walking round the village of Lowick glimpses a young man (who proves to be Ladislaw) "with light brown curls" (1.9:74). The phrase when the first-time reader meets it has no particular resonance, but as the book unfolds it assumes a greater force. The first syllable of "light-brown," "light," grows, so to speak, brighter and the curls become flames. Later we are told that Ladislaw's smile is like "the breaking of sunshine on the water" (5.47:464). In a curious play of independent mythopoeia Eliot has Will worry at one point that he will become "dimmed and for ever ray-shorn in her eyes" (4.37:364); the Sun God fears for the loss of his own powers as he encounters a possibly greater luminary. A more ordinary rationale, of course, operates simultaneously at the human level; Will is worried that Dorothea may think less of him. The odd thing is, however, that if one tries to read the passage simply, within the realistic mode, one is brought up short by the oddity of "ray-shorn." One would not expect a young man in the earlier nineteenth century to think of himself as emitting rays. The word marks the invasion of myth as distinct from the parallel evocation of myth. The realistic novel can easily, without violence to its own logic, suggest solar qualities in a figure by having him enter in sunlight. Initially the sunlight is simply sunlight, an ordinary part of the story; this was what the weather was like when the hero came in. But at the same time, by a separate logic, the mere mention of sunlight (especially if it is repeated elsewhere and so begins to compose a pattern) can begin to operate figuratively. The two worlds easily co-exist, do not collide, because one is literal, the other metaphorical. But in Ladislaw's words at this point there is a faint collision. A metaphor that begins to break into the literal mode must be more, we sense, than mere metaphor. When Mr. Casaubon and Ladislaw are together in the same room, Mr. Casaubon looks dim and faded, while Ladislaw projects "a sunny brightness," "His hair seemed to shake out light." Mr. Casaubon, we are told, meanwhile "stood rayless" (2.21: 206). What chance for poor Mr. Casaubon against this walking sunburst? Rays appear again when Ladislaw is pleading for an ethic of enjoyment against Dorothea's asceticism: "Enjoyment radiates" (2.22:217). Will's smile is "a gush of inward light illuminating the transparent skin as well as the eyes, and playing about every curve and line as if some Ariel were touching them with a new charm"

(2.21:203). This novel species of illumination seems electric rather than solar. Although one does not expect Shakespeare to have anything to say about electricity, the mention of Ariel may take us to just that. In *The Tempest* Ariel, the spirit of air and fire, tells how he "flamed amazement" on the ship's rigging (1.2:198). The passage is based on the account given, in a contemporary report of a shipwreck, of Saint Elmo's fire, an electrical phenomenon. When Will hears Dorothea's name announced, "he started up as from an electric shock, and felt a tingling at his finger-ends" (4.39:382). Later still, when Dorothea and Will are placed tensely together, though not touching, "It was as if the same electric shock had passed through her and Will" (6.54:537).

Later Frazer will have much to say in *The Golden Bough* about the Mithraic ritual of the sun's nativity and also about, for example, the importance attached by certain cultures to the requirement that the sun should not shine on girls at puberty.[43] In *Middlemarch* this feeling is reversed. Dorothea is a virtual or real virgin on whom it is urgently necessary that the sun should shine.

It is odd to find Eliot employing in the nineteenth century the same myth that her great namesake will draw on in the twentieth, yet it is so. It must be said that she does it less well than he. Ladislaw fizzes like a firecracker, but he does not engage the reader. The very negativity of Mr. Casaubon is somehow more vivid than the radiance of Ladislaw. Will is indeed like Shelley (with whom he is compared at 4.37:355)—as read by hostile readers: scintillating yet short on substance. It is as if George Eliot became aware of this difficulty and has sought to deal with it by an infusion of blood drawn from powerful ancient sources. The primal Mind of Europe must supply what is evidently not happening within the realist mode. But the old gods are not to be used in this implicitly cynical fashion. George Eliot is so deeply godless at the profoundest level, so lucidly rational, that the reader twigs at once that what might once have been a central source of energy is here a compensatory decoration. The imagination of T. S. Eliot, on the other hand—long before his intellect fell into line with it—is at the deepest level religious. So in *The Waste Land*, in what might have seemed a far less promising time—

a season, indeed, of dryness — the branch grew green again and the power returned.

Mr. Casaubon is not alone in having designs on a total understanding of things. Outside the book, as we have seen, in this period keys to all mythologies tumble from the presses. Inside the book others besides Mr. Casaubon are intent upon the same task of radical explanation. Mrs. Garth's eldest son, Christy, wishes to be "a Porson, and to study all literatures" (6.57:562). The passage is half-humorous, but the word "all" carries unmistakably the dark resonance of Mr. Casaubon's dream — of so many scholars' dreams — of a "key to *all* mythologies." Or take Lydgate, the doctor. The Renaissance adventure of gnosis split, as we saw, into scholarship on one hand and science on the other. Scholarship becomes asexual but science remains sexually charged. Therefore Lydgate, who, far more than Ladislaw, is the true gnostic anti-type of Mr. Casaubon, is sexy. Lydgate is a scientific knower. Dr. Faustus said dangerously, "A sound magician is a demi-god" (1604, 1.1.63). In her *Middlemarch* notebook George Eliot carefully wrote down a Greek phrase, *Iētros gar philosophos isotheos*, "The philosophic physician is equal to the gods."[44] When Faustus speaks his line he has just rejected medicine, but for all that, the steps from Faustian magic to science and thence to medicine are small ones. Lydgate like Faustus has sold his soul. Unlike Faustus, however, he has sold it not in order to gain knowledge (George Eliot would see no hint of wickedness in such motivation) but, more simply, for money — and for blonde, beautiful, evil Rosamond. She perhaps returns us to Dr. Faustus; she is very like that Helen who sucked out Faustus's soul (1604, 5.1.94).

In science as in scholarship it appears that the Germans are the formidable party. Lydgate is worried that "some plodding fellow of a German" will beat him to his great discovery (4.36:345). Mr. Casaubon, Eliot tells us, had "a theory of the elements which made the seed of all tradition (5.48:472), but then she at once differentiates this theory, in a passage that anticipates Karl Popper's demand for falsifiability in science, from the chemistry of an Antoine Lavoisier, by pointing to its "endlessly flexible" character, its avoidance of sharp collision. Yet when Lydgate speaks of his wish "to demonstrate the homogeneous origin of all tissues" (5.45:449) one senses that he and Mr. Casaubon, for all the fatal difference of method, may have *something* in common. The dark word, "all," has reappeared. Lydgate speaks elsewhere (2.15:147) of his impatience with Bichat's plurality of tissues and his own wish to find the "primitive tissue." When Lydgate talks about finding the "origin" of tissues he speaks modestly, but the word has within it a Darwinian grandeur. It is a "bigger word" than "key."

Dorothea, who had her own modest gnostic dream of assisting in a great enterprise of the mind, finds, instead, happiness with Ladislaw. Will becomes a member of parliament, working ardently for reform (Finale, 819). Stated in this way, the conclusion might appear triumphant. Karl Marx said that the important thing was not to interpret the world but to change it.[45] It might be thought that Ladislaw, alone of the persons of the novel, has made the critical transition from gnosis to praxis; instead of rewriting history, he is rewriting the world. In the words of Browning's grammarian, "Actual life comes next" (l. 57). But none of this will survive an attentive reading of the last pages of *Middlemarch*. Ladislaw's political life remains faint and inchoative, like Ladislaw himself. The author sadly promises that all his various small achievements in the way of reform will run away into the sand. Again we feel that the very negativity of Mr. Casaubon is more vivid, more substantial than the supposed positiveness of Ladislaw. His futile, enormous dream eclipses the ineffectual decency of Ladislaw. Dorothea, into whom George Eliot put so much of herself, the girl who dreamed of learning ancient languages (something George Eliot actually did), brings off no feat of intellection in the book. Her heart develops indeed, but she makes no striking journey in her mind. If this is a *Bildungsroman* the *Bildung* is weirdly negative, an undoing rather than a raising-up or completion. Dorothea's aspirations never flower as complex knowledge, scholarly or scientific. She learns negatively: that Mr. Casaubon is not really wise at all. Her religious ideals wither, no less surely than Mr. Casaubon's theories "withered like an elfin child" (5.48:472). She is fulfilled by wifehood and by motherhood. Her mind goes nowhere. She is "absorbed" (Eliot's word) into the life of her husband (Finale, 819). No Theresa she. One might say, "But Ladislaw would have been nothing, if the love of a good woman had not set him on the right track." The trouble is that Ladislaw, even when on the right track seems, though a pretty fellow, not to amount to very much after all.

It would be easy to conclude that the harsh anti-feminist thesis, "This is the story of a girl who thought she needed to employ her mind in a life of high ideals but all she really needed was some strong sex from a man, followed by motherhood" — that this thesis is simply confirmed by the Finale of *Middlemarch*. But this is a travesty of the book. Browning in the poem to which I have returned at intervals mocks his sickly, dead-from-the-waist-down grammarian but also makes felt a certain admiration for this strange being who would rather know than live (l. 139). Browning's grammarian is like Mr. Casaubon in many ways, but there is one great difference; *he* is a real scholar. In *Middlemarch* there are no successful positive models — not even Lydgate — for the life of the mind, but it would be crass indeed to conclude from that fact that the ideal is itself scorned and rejected. The intellectual incapacity of Mr. Casaubon, a thing quite separate from his sexual incapacity, is felt in the book as tragic, not funny. This immediately entails a high value placed implicitly on intellection.

It is often said that the story of Lydgate is a brilliant study in invisible tragedy, that is in tragedy muffled but not erased by the trivialising detail of bourgeois existence; that Lydgate is destroyed no less surely than Lear, yet the world sees only a rich doctor with a successful practice. Dorothea's story, conversely, is a comedy of love. It ends happily. Yet within that very happiness — and somehow the more poignantly because of the clear reality of that happiness — there is a latent tragedy of gnosis, more deeply invisible than that of Lydgate — almost, but surely not quite, invisible to George Eliot herself.

It may be said that the latent tragedy I am suggesting might have been credible if Eliot had given us a Dorothea with a genuine intellectual plan at the centre of her life (wishing to learn languages is not enough); then indeed her final absorption in Ladislaw and his less-than-successful efforts at reform might have been felt as terrible. In fact, when she explains her high hopes and talks of assisting a great husband she is if anything closer to the "child wife" Dora in *David Copperfield* (ch. 44) who wants to be allowed to hold the pens for her clever husband than to Theresa of Avila. Eliot in forming the character of her heroine withheld intellect. She allowed her moral ardour, but at the same time she, no less than the cold clerical husband within the fiction, denied her access to that life of the mind which has haunted the European imagination for centuries. This, the argument would run, must mean that the novelist backs the explicit happy ending against any implicit tragedy, that there is indeed no tragedy here. Dorothea really is a being who *properly* finds fulfilment in being a wife and mother, and in nothing else.

This argument has force, but it would be a mistake to suppose that it exorcises all demons, eliminates all regret. One is left suspecting that George Eliot intuits a kinship we might at first have thought absurd, a kinship between herself and Mr. Casaubon—a kinship in incapacity. In a letter she wrote, "I fear that the Casaubon tints are not quite foreign to my own complexion"[46] and, when challenged by a young friend as to the source of Mr. Casaubon, pointed to her own heart.[47] We, looking back at George Eliot, see a major literary artist. She saw someone who had never written, would never write a great work of philosophy or history. It is as if she projected her resentment at her own confinement to romantic fiction on to her heroine, and confined her to a conventional, romantically determined happiness. The strange disappointment at the end, in relation to Dorothea, is made greater by a sense that Dorothea no less than Mr. Casaubon was in any case never really made for intellectual achievement. The overarching contrast with Theresa of Avila remains, to disquiet the reader. The tragic fall of Dorothea is to be measured by the distance between her and the great saint with whom she is compared at the beginning of the book. Theresa founded a religious order and wrote books that are still read today; Dorothea does none of this. *Middlemarch* is sadder than most people think.

The slow accumulation of asphyxiating, counter-heroic ordinariness in nineteenth-century middle-class life has produced, very naturally, a nineteenth-century three-decker novel ending in marriage and a baby. But George Eliot began the novel as she did because she wanted the reader to be aware of another kind of book and another kind of life. The novelist herself meanwhile is enmeshed. Not only will she never be able to write like Hume or Gibbon, she will never be able to write like Sophocles or Shakespeare. The Other Story is as un-narratable for George Eliot as "The Key to All Mythologies" was unwritable for Mr. Casaubon.

2

Mark Pattison

Mr. Casaubon and Mr. Pattison

Mark Pattison, the rector of Lincoln College, Oxford, was born, six years before George Eliot, in 1813, and died, four years later than the novelist, in 1884. The idea that he was the model for Mr. Casaubon took root early. Mrs. Oliphant in a letter explains how she met Pattison — "a curious wizened little man" — in 1879, referring to him as the man "supposed to be the Casaubon of Middlemarch"; she then adds, "at least his wife considers herself the model of Dorothea."[1] The use of the word "supposed" clearly implies that others have been saying this. The latter part of Mrs. Oliphant's sentence, seemingly an afterthought, implies a certain reservation as to the identification of Pattison and Mr. Casaubon and shifts the centre of the story to Mrs. Pattison, who is roundly declared to have seen herself as Dorothea Brooke. Mrs. Pattison, née Emilia Francis Strong, was, like Dorothea, twenty-seven years younger than her husband. They were married in 1861 in the beautiful little Norman church at Iffley, just outside Oxford. Like Dorothea she settled to a life of study directed by her learned husband. Like Dorothea, she was attracted by mystical Christianity (Dorothea was a Puritan, Francis an Anglican, but this does not dissolve the similarity). Like Dorothea, she travelled with her husband, visited galleries and collections in Rome. Like Dorothea, she later found true love with a man much younger than Pattison, a radical politician. A year and a month after the death of Pattison, Francis married Sir Charles Dilke. The contrast must have been evident. Dilke was not only younger than Francis; he was a noted oarsman and fencer and a great collector of works of art. The second marriage seems indeed to have liberated the energies of Francis. She became a leading figure in the history of women's trades unions. George Eliot was on intimate terms with the Pattisons and visited them in Oxford. When Mrs. Oliphant says Mrs. Pattison believed she was the model for Dorothea, we have high authority for the identification as, at least, a thought that could be — was — thought, confirmation so to speak, from the horse's mouth. If this is accepted, the secondary identification of Pattison with Casaubon seems to follow inevitably from the first. Francis Pattison, we can be sure, felt that she resembled Dorothea partly because of her situation, because she was joined in marriage to a much older, scholarly man. This joins Pattison and Mr. Casaubon. Quite apart from these interior feelings of affinity there remains one oddly exterior link, in the name "Casaubon." Mark Pattison was deeply interested in Isaac Casaubon, the Renaissance scholar, and wrote what is still the standard work on him. All this is underlined when we find Sir Charles Dilke (another of the principals in the story) saying that "Dorothea's defence of her marriage to Casaubon, and Casaubon's account of his marriage to Dorothea" are "as a fact given by the novelist almost in Mark Pattison's words," and "the religious side of Dorothea Brooke was taken by George Eliot from the letters of Mrs. Pattison."[2] Dilke also wrote in his unpublished autobiography, *Memoir of Sir Charles Dilke*, that "Casaubon's letter to Dorothea at the beginning of the fifth chapter in Middlemarch, from what George Eliot herself told me in 1875, must have been very near the letter that Pattison actually wrote, and the reply very much the same."[3] Now we have it from the *author's* mouth.

There is however one small problem. The dates are slightly wrong. John Sparrow, although commonly seen as an uncritical advocate of the Pattison-Casaubon identification, himself points out that by 1870, the year in which she visited the Pattisons in Oxford, George Eliot had already begun work on *Middlemarch,* and of course *Middlemarch* itself begins with Dorothea Brooke and Mr. Casaubon. Francis's visits to Italian galleries and her marriage to Sir Charles Dilke happened after the publication of *Middlemarch* in 1871–72. Finally, with regard to the "external" link in the name of "Casaubon," Pattison's *Isaac Casaubon* was published after, not before *Middlemarch.*

Gordon S. Haight, the biographer of George Eliot, is unimpressed by the proposed identification. He urges instead the case of one Dr. Brabant. George Eliot would have remembered vividly how in 1843 she had responded eagerly to the interest taken in her by this learned gentleman and how it had terminated in embarrassment for all; Dr. Brabant's attention to young Marian Evans (George Eliot) became a little too keen, and Mrs. Brabant got her out of the house as swiftly as possible. Meanwhile there is no evidence that Mrs. Pattison actively encouraged George Eliot to turn Mr. Casaubon into a caricature of her husband. It is inherently improbable, Haight argues, that Eliot would have attacked a man who was her friend and, still more significantly, continued to be her friend after *Middlemarch* was published. Mark Pattison later sent George Eliot a copy of his book on Casaubon.[4] The matter is clinched for Haight by fundamental differences of character and physical appearance. Mr. Casaubon is a grey, sedentary figure. Mark Pattison was a great walker, rider, angler, whose hair retained its redness to the end. Most important of all, Mr. Casaubon is, intellectually, a hollow, futile creature while Mark Pattison was a truly formidable mind.

Is there then no link at all between these two men? Certainly Pattison speaks in his *Memoirs* (1885) of his devotion in his youth to fast riding and hunting.[5] V. H. H. Green in his book on Lincoln College in the nineteenth century says that Pattison was an excellent tennis player.[6] It is difficult to imagine Mr. Casaubon at any period of his life playing tennis at all, to say nothing of playing well. Sparrow himself, though Haight sees him as monolithic in his advocacy of the simple identification of the two, notes a major point of difference, in Pattison's uproarious social success with young women. Sparrow reports, with a degree of scepticism Walter Pater's description of the rector of Lincoln "romping with great girls among the gooseberry bushes."[7] Green goes further: "It is unquestionable that he had the power to the very end of his life to allure female admirers; they fluttered round his candle indifferent to the danger of being burned by his caustic utterances. It would seem that for all his lack of physical and social graces Pattison was in some way sexually attractive!"[8] This, perhaps, taken separately, is not completely persuasive. Clever women who like talking to an exceptionally clever man need not have been attracted *sexually*.

The huge difference remains the difference of intelligence. Once again Sparrow is clearly aware of the vast distance, in this regard, between Mr. Casaubon and Mark Pattison. It is his sense of this difference which leads him to suggest that Roger Wendover in Mrs. Humphry Ward's *Robert Elsmere* is the truer image of Pattison. No one doubts that Mr. Gray in *Robert Elsmere* is based on T. H. Green of Balliol College, the philosophically scrupulous liberal Christian who reasoned his way to a searching critical analysis of Hume in his introduction to a new edition of Hume's works in 1874–75, finding his way at last to a species of Kantian idealism. If Gray is Green, why should not the acidly sceptical Wendover be Pattison, who moved from the excited High Church Christianity of the Oxford Movement to find more congenial company in the eighteenth century? The physical resemblance is close and this time the I.Q. is right. Henry Nettleship, who collected and edited Mark Pattison's essays after his death, observed in the obituary he wrote for his friend that "some have fancied" that Mr. Casaubon was based on Pattison (again we become aware that this suggestion, however well- or ill-founded, is *being made* by people); but then he goes on to say sternly that there was "nothing in common between the serious scholar at Lincoln and the mere pedant frittering away his life in useless trivialities."[9] Mrs. Humphry Ward made the same point: "the dreary and foolish pedant" could not be Mark Pattison.[10] Even Sir

Charles Dilke, despite his tantalising observation that Pattison's very words were echoed in *Middlemarch,* joins the chorus of the sceptics at this point, affirming that only the simple-minded will be happy to identify "a mere pedant" with "a great scholar."[11]

Haight's counter-case is strong, but he is perhaps too absolute on his dismissal. Something must have prompted all that talk, started not by John Sparrow but by contemporaries of Mr. and Mrs. Pattison. Nor does the gossip come from the frivolous-minded only. Sidney Lee in his article on Lady Dilke in *The Dictionary of National Biography* says roundly, "There is no doubt that Mrs. Mark Pattison suggested to George Eliot the character of Dorothea in her work 'Middlemarch' . . . and that the novelist's conception of Casaubon was based on Mark Pattison." Haight seems scarcely to know what to do with Dilke's remark that Pattison's own words were echoed in the novel. Haight says that no such letter has been found. This, in the face of a plain assertion from a contemporary of George Eliot, is obviously weak. Richard Ellmann, supporting Haight, cites a letter of George Eliot written in 1846, making up the terms of a pedantic marriage proposal, a quarter of a century before she met Pattison, and knowingly observes that second husbands like to disparage first husbands.[12] One senses that Haight and Ellmann are desperately trying to explain away an unwanted piece of testimony. Sir Charles Dilke's words are perfectly clear. The burden of disproof is on Haight and his allies, and they have not disproved. Haight slightly overplays his hand when he contrasts the sporting, sandy-haired Pattison with the grey Mr. Casaubon. The horse-riding and the angling belong to Pattison's youth. It is as if it is now the professional biographer, of all people, who has become hazy about dates. We are looking at a later time in Pattison's life when many were struck by the difference between the dried-up don and the young, beautiful wife. Even Green, with his belief in the strange sexual power of Pattison, concedes in the very same sentence a lack of physical and social graces. Pattison seems indeed to have been a deathly figure in his later years. Sparrow cites A. C. Swinburne, who linked Pattison's name with "the Dead Sea," and Stephen Gwynne, who admittedly was describing Pattison at a still later stage (around 1882 or 1884), as saying that he was more like a corpse than a living thing.[13] But in any case, by 1870 there was an evident contrast between the "withered" Pattison and Francis. Lord Rosebery described him as looking "wizened and wintry by the side of his blooming wife."[14] This is precisely the imagery of "death and winter" that is systematically applied to Mr. Casaubon in *Middlemarch*.

Most vivid of all is Mrs. Ward's picture of Mark Pattison at the time of George Eliot's visit in 1870 (George Eliot is here referred to as "Mrs. Lewes"):

> As we turned into the quadrangle of Lincoln—suddenly, at one of the upper windows of the Rector's lodgings, which occupied the far right corner of the quad, there appeared the head and shoulders of Mrs. Pattison, as she looked out and beckoned smiling to Mr. Lewes. It was a brilliant apparition, as though a French portrait by Greuze or Perronneau had suddenly stepped into a vacant space in the old college wall. The pale, pretty head, *blond-cendrée,* the delicate smiling features and white throat; a touch of black, a touch of blue; a white dress; a general eighteenth-century impression as though of powder and patches:—Mrs. Lewes perceived it in a flash, and I saw her run eagerly to Mr. Lewes and draw his attention to the window and its occupant. . . . If she had lived longer, some day, and somewhere in her books, that vision at the window, and that flower-laden garden would have reappeared, I seemed to see her consciously and deliberately committing them both to memory.[15]

This indeed makes no mention of Pattison, but it requires no great exercise of the imagination to guess that beside this, he stands "rayless" as Mr. Casaubon did in the twenty-first chapter of *Middlemarch*. The contrast of husband and wife is replicated in the setting. If Mrs. Pattison is like the flowers, Pattison must be like the grey, flaking "old college wall."

The whole passage deserves to be placed beside George Eliot's picture of Dorothea with the sleeping Ariadne in the Vatican Gallery (2.19:186). We saw there how *ecphrasis,* the literary description of a work of art, was doubled as Eliot arrested her live heroine, momentarily, as if *she* were the work of art. A similar doubling happens here. Mrs. Pattison is like a Greuze portrait and is, at the same time, herself framed, like a picture, by the window. The entire sequence in *Middlemarch* is concerned with sexuality, acknowledged and un-acknowledged. Dorothea, who was disconcerted by the "Corregios-ities" of Italian art (1.9:72) is herself "voluptuous," like the sleeping Ariadne (2.19:186). In the passage by Mrs. Ward we again have an example of a woman describing a female sex object. The effect is far more muted than in *Middlemarch*. Jean-Baptiste Greuze was seen as a "moralist-painter" in nineteenth-century France, but for all that his work is full of rosy bosoms and delicious young women. If one has been looking, just before, at paintings by François Boucher or Jean-Honoré Fragonard, his work may appear chaste (though never en-tirely so). To easily shocked English eyes the lubricious effect is inescapable. I suggested earlier that George Eliot *wanted* her hero, Ladislaw, to see Dorothea as a sex object at this point. In Mrs. Ward's account "Mrs. Lewes" (George Eliot) eagerly draws George Henry Lewes into the experience. Of course in *Middlemarch* Eliot, Pandarus-like, is bringing two young people together, fomenting a match. In the real-life situation she would presumably not have wished to match Lewes with Francis. But she does want him to see the beauty of Mrs. Pattison. One thinks of the paintings Queen Vic-toria bought for Prince Albert. . . .

We are left with the curious, obstinate fact that Francis said she was the model for Dorothea. This, as we saw, was where the dates suddenly became awkward. *Middlemarch* was not published until after the Oxford visit but work on it was well advanced. Other parts of the intricate analogy, the art galleries, the later marriage to a young ardent politician — haunting as they are — all follow the publication. Yet Mrs. Pattison said it.

Everything would be different if she had not used the word "model," if she had said simply, "I am like Dorothea." It is entirely possible that, if George Eliot was not describing Francis in the novel, Francis afterwards modelled herself upon the heroine. We know that she was intensely interested in George Eliot and her work. It is not just possible but probable that in her visits to galleries in Rome later she identified imaginatively with Dorothea Brooke. That nature im-itates art is both an old joke and an occasional truth. Sadly, one cannot extend the idea to account for her second marriage (as if she fixed on Dilke only because she had to find a Ladislaw). But, once again, it is not just possible but probable that a consciousness of the analogy, in Francis's mind, was a contributing factor. And now, one can easily add, in this new relaxed atmosphere, something of the Pattison marriage as perceived from outside, could after all have fed into Eliot's picture of Mr. and Mrs. Casaubon, as composition proceeded (together of course with innumerable other influences).

We have now loosened the tyranny of the chronological sequence imposed by the conventional notion of a real-life model for a literary character. We know that Mrs. Pattison felt that there was a likeness between herself and Dorothea. What then of Mark Pattison? John Sparrow who is often represented as holding that Pattison was the model, actually says that he does not believe that the idea of Mr. Casaubon was first presented to George Eliot by Mark Pattison.[16] He argues only for a qualified resemblance. Both Sparrow and Haight in fact agree (with the support of various well-informed nineteenth-century persons) that he is simply much too formidable, intellectually. But if Francis thought she was like Dorothea, could Mark have thought himself like Mr. Casaubon? Haight is right when he says that the evidence is actually against any such direct identification on Pattison's part. The continuation of friendly relations between George Eliot and both Pattisons after the publication of *Middlemarch* must mean, at the very least, that no such resemblance was explicitly acknowledged, within the group. But if we ask, more loosely, is there any sign that Pattison thought of himself not as a great scholar but as a futile failure, the answer is, "Yes, a great deal."

Haight says, as if it settled the matter, that Mr. Casaubon's absurd "Key to all Mythologies" is quite unlike Mark Pattison's *Isaac Casaubon*.[17] Pattison's book on the Renaissance Casaubon is a work of careful, scrupulous — limited — scope: a scholar writing about another scholar. "A Key to All Mythologies" by contrast was, in design, a work of comprehensive explanatory power. Pattison was never fool enough to think that he could explain the mind of Europe, but he certainly did long incubate a work of comprehensive history that he was never able to complete. His life's work, a history of scholarship built around the figure of Joseph Scaliger,[18] was never written, and Pattison was keenly aware of the failure. Certain sentences in his account of his own life are marked by a desolate *diminuendo*: "One's ambition is always in the inverse proportion of one's knowledge. I soon discovered how much I had miscalculated my powers. I contracted my views to a history of one only of the schools of philology. It should be the French school, beginning with Budaeus, and coming down at least [*sic*], to Huet and the Delphin editions. It was not long before I found that even on this reduced scale, I could not hope to execute a thorough piece of work . . . of the ambitions I had first conceived I have only executed fragments."[19] Suddenly one sees that Haight's comparison of *Isaac Casaubon* with the "Key to All Mythologies" is misconceived. The "key" as it figures in *Middlemarch* is, so to speak, *essentially* an unwritten work. Clearly the analogue in Pattison's life, if any is to be found, will not be an achieved publication but something that eludes him, as the "key" eluded Mr. Casaubon. It is odd how often what looks to the outside world like resounding public success can feel, from the inside, like failure. I have already suggested that George Eliot, who wrote so much, may have felt that she had never achieved a real work of intellect. So with Mark Pattison, the world sees a distinguished intellectual of the nineteenth century, the head of an Oxford college in a time of reform. To Pattison it all tasted like dust.

Of course, although our figures have moved closer together, differences persist. Pattison, unlike Mr. Casaubon, knows, clearly and grimly, what he cannot do and faces the fact — one cannot say without flinching, because Pattison was no Stoic, but bravely. When Pattison speaks with reference to an early phase of his life of "the fatuity of my arrangements" and "snail-like progress" (*Memoirs*, 149), we may feel that it is as if George Eliot in *Middlemarch* took Pattison at his own self-lacerating word and formed the character from that, but of course the *Memoirs* came after *Middlemarch*. It remains clear that there is a string of likenesses between the way he sees himself and the way George Eliot sees Mr. Casaubon. "No progress" is a leitmotiv of the *Memoirs*. Eliot despises Mr. Casaubon, but she pities him too. Pattison despises Pattison — but he is also very sorry for himself. I have said that he is no Stoic. In fact the style of the *Memoirs* is stoical, but the inner emotional charge is at odds with the cold cadence of the sentences; the stench of self-pity is everywhere.

Against Haight's picture of the vigorous, successful Pattison, Pattison saw social failure. He explains in the *Memoirs* how he longed for intellectual companionship but then found that he could not warm to his fellow undergraduates. Interestingly he makes it clear that it was not that they were cold to him; he did not like *them* — but this too is very characteristic. He was, he says, repelled by the "rampant and imperious" character of the "bodily appetites" of the young who surrounded him (*Memoirs*, 46). "I had no taste for drinking," he adds gloomily. How different from Dickens, of whom it has been said that the very record of his conviviality is exhausting! Pattison finishes the picture with the terrible words, "I . . . dared not raise a glass to my lips for fear it should be seen how my hand trembled" (*Memoirs*, 50). The taste of failure is most bitter in the account Pattison gives of his non-election to the rectorship of Lincoln College in 1851 (some time later he was successful). He saw this, with no trace of irony, in terms of the hellish torments visited on Sisyphus: "My new-cut ambition was dashed to the ground. . . . The stone I had rolled to the top of the hill with so much pains had rolled back upon me in a moment." He continues, "A blank, dumb despair filled me, a chronic heartache took possession of me, perceptible even through sleep" (*Memoirs*, 289–90). The last four words are especially frightening. Pattison's despair, surely pathological in its peculiar intensity, continued throughout the succeeding year. At perhaps the lowest point, on 13 November 1852, his diary passes from English into Latin (the language of the book Pattison loved best, the *Ephemerides* or "Journal" of Isaac Casaubon): *Hunc diem satis misere, ut semper, transegi,* "This day I passed wretchedly enough, as always."

The failure here is not the failure to write a great book but a practical, political failure, the defeat of his ambitions in relation to his college and the university. This at once separates him from Mr. Casaubon, who has no political life at all. Pattison insists that his personal disappointment over the rectorship was a minor element, that he had invested all his hopes and energies, his whole "heart and pride" in the success of the college, in other words, that he really did care more about the college than about himself (*Memoirs*, 289). This we can believe. But although his aims were unselfish and he really was badly used, there is a streak of megalomania in his reaction, which once more echoes the weirdly grandiose dream of Mr.

Casaubon, labouring among the ruins of the past to build his labyrinth. Pattison says of J. L. R. Kettlewell, who let him down in the
voting for the rectorship, "The proverb says, 'One fool can destroy
in an hour what ten wise men cannot build up in a generation.' To
gratify his designs he had burned down the Temple of Ephesus"
(*Memoirs*, 289). Pattison's resentment escapes his control and transforms his scheme for the college into the mightiest temple of antiquity. The whole passage trembles on the edge of an inadvertent absurdity. This too is reminiscent of Mr. Casaubon. Just as we noted
earlier that imagery of death and winter is attached to both Pattison
and Mr. Casaubon, so here the architectural allusion appears in the
novel. At the beginning Mr. Brooke engages Mr. Casaubon in talk
about "the ruins of Rhamnus" (1.3:25). Much later he is associated
with Dagon, the god of the Philistines whose temple Samson destroyed (5.49:477).

Empiricists used to argue that the so-called creative imagination
never really creates, but merely rearranges percepts. The unicorn
may appear to be a pure innovation, but in fact the unicorn is made
by joining a horn to a horse. Both horses and horns were previously
available in experience. There is some truth in the general contention, but we need to allow that, quite literally, thousands of percepts
and memories went into the formation of Dorothea Brooke and Mr.
Casaubon and no doubt continued to feed in, after the first conception of the characters, as the writing proceeded. This means that it
is entirely on the cards that something of Mr. and Mrs. Pattison may
have modified the fictions in *Middlemarch*, as they gradually reached
their final form. In the earlier part of 1973 a series of issues of the
Times Literary Supplement printed letters from various parties on Sparrow's suggestion that Mr. Casaubon and Pattison are linked. One
luminary after another weighs in on the side of Haight. Yet Sparrow's modest assertion of an evident similarity — no more than that —
remains luminously credible. To show that A differs from B in the
respect of x in no way disproves the simultaneous contention that A
resembles B in the respect y. The fact that Pattison was clever does
not obliterate the fact that he was a dry, erudite figure married to a
blooming young wife. Already the similarity is palpably greater than
any we find in the case of Haight's chosen candidate, Brabant. Bra-

bant never married George Eliot, was married already, was sexually susceptible. When contemporaries looked at Mr. and Mrs. Pattison, they said, "This is Mr. and Mrs. Casaubon." They did not say these things unprompted by any data, wilfully, in a fictive vacuum. Mrs. Pattison herself agreed with them. It is hard to account for the strength of the hostility to John Sparrow. It is perhaps a compound of resentment and misplaced chivalry; resentment of Sparrow's upper-class, Establishment style and chivalry to the dead Mark Pattison, whom they deem unjustly insulted by the comparison. But no one — certainly not Sparrow — is saying that Pattison is really level with Mr. Casaubon in all respects. One last detail remains to nag at the back of the mind. The eerie link to the name "Casaubon," formed by the fact that Pattison's best book had this for its title, is deemed to have been blown out of the water by the further fact that *Isaac Casaubon* came out after *Middlemarch*. This, however, turns out not to be the knock-down argument it seemed to be. As John Sparrow gently pointed out, Pattison had been working on and obsessed by Isaac Casaubon for years before he met George Eliot and had indeed already published an article on him in the *Quarterly Review* in 1853).[20] As soon as George Eliot asked, "What are you working on?" Pattison would have answered, "Casaubon," and away he would go.

For Mrs. Pattison, evidently the current flowed *from* the book *into* her own life; it is likely that in some degree she formed herself upon the pattern of Dorothea. With Mark Pattison we can be much less sure. It would however be strange if this scholar, who clearly perceived himself as a failure, could have read all the way through *Middlemarch* without any uncomfortable twinges from the parts dealing with Mr. Casaubon. Nevertheless, when all this is said, the empiricist reduction of imagination to (reshuffled) percepts will not finally hold. The act of synthesis is neither trivial nor random. It is an active, complex feat. The resultant fiction is much more than the sum of the pre-existing, non-fictional parts. Mr. Casaubon, though he never existed, is so to speak a person in his own right.

Mark Pattison's Oxford

And so of course was Mark Pattison. To adapt the words of Bishop Butler, "Everyone is himself or herself, and not another person." Is there a "key" to Pattison—a governing humour, a ruling passion, around which the other elements of the personality fall into place? Very near the end of his life he said that since 1851, when his political hopes were dashed, he had lived only for study.[21] A more generalised love of learning and of the world of learning had been present in him from a much earlier time. Pattison's father, the rector of Haux-well in Yorkshire, had been a commoner at Brasenose College, Oxford, at the beginning of the nineteenth century. He loved to talk about his days at the university, to tell stories of the strutting, larger-than-life figures of the day—of his tutor, Frodsham Hodson, who drove into Oxford with post-horses, in order "that it should not be said that the first tutor of the first college of the first university of the world entered it with a pair" (*Memoirs*, 3). Mark Pattison was clearly hooked from the beginning by a successfully transmitted vision, a picture of the shining city of learning, but he is oddly unloving, oddly critical towards the transmitter of the picture. He gives a cold beta minus both to his father's intellectual aspirations and, still more cruelly perhaps, to his social aspirations. Hardy's stonemason, Jude, excluded from the university by his low social status, knows clearly that those within the institution are separate from him; what he never suspects is that *within* the university there were further, painful divisions, those who were in and those who were out. Pattison Senior was, the son bleakly observes, excluded from the highest set by his want of money and from the intellectual set by his "lack of literary cultivation" (*Memoirs*, 5): "My father never professed any understanding of Aristotle, and had a very faint idea of Logic, as I discovered when he tried to read Aldrich with me" (*Memoirs*, 6–7).

"Oxford," we must notice, carries a double charge: on one hand, intellectual distinction and on the other, more troublingly, social elevation. It is a very English mix. In Scotland, seemingly, things were different. The boatman, Cameron, in J. M. Barrie's *Mary Rose* is quite unlike the cheerfully servile Oxford boatman, genially overcharging "the gentlemen," whom we shall meet later in this chapter. Cameron, a softly spoken Highlander, is a ghillie and, simultaneously, a student at Aberdeen University. He carries a pocket Euripides (in Greek). His father, a crofter, is also a student at Aberdeen University; when he has finished his course he will go back to being a crofter. Cameron carefully explains to the English party who are employing him for the day that he is formally their servant but humanly their equal. He confesses, however, that he would love to acquire the easy manners of Simon Blake, a young upper-class Englishman who is one of the group. Cameron is very clear that it is Simon's "deportment" rather than his education that he finds enviable: "He has not much learning, but I haf always understood that the English manage without it."[22] *Mary Rose* came out in 1920, but the scene with Cameron the boatman is set in the nineteenth century.

Mark Pattison is unloveably quick to disparage both the scholarly and the social pretensions of Pattison Senior. Yet the father's vivid anecdotes remained in the mind of the son and kindled in him a love of the imagined academy, a love that would assume an increasingly austere character as time passed but would never be extinguished. One sympathises with the older Pattison under the searching gaze of his hyper-intelligent offspring. Once, during the time I spent at the University of Sussex, an old Oxford friend was coming to dinner. Our small children set the table, laying at each place a small grubby piece of paper, headed "Topics of Conversation." Chief among these, to my amazement, was "Stories of Oxford Days." Here, note, I have begun to identify myself with Pattison Senior as Mrs. Pattison identified with Dorothea Brooke. Art seeps into life and, now, personal reminiscence spills incongruously into a supposedly neutral work of literary history. Obviously I used to tell picturesque stories. Equally obviously my children actually enjoyed these — at least for a time. So with the Pattisons. Pattison Senior is the source of another story, recounted by the son in his *Memoirs*. Hodson, the tutor, found his pupil one night climbing on the statue of Cain and Abel, which stood then in the principal quadrangle of Brasenose. Asked what he was doing Pattison Senior replied, "Aerobatō kai periphronō ton helion." Mark Pattison explains that his father's favourite reading was Aristophanes, the comic poet, but does not deign to translate the Greek. Pattison Senior — then very young of course — is quoting from Aristophanes *Clouds* 225. There Socrates, the intellectual, is discovered hanging in a basket inside his *phrontistērion*, or "thinking shop" (94). When asked what he is doing by Strepsiades, he answers in the words borrowed by the delinquent undergraduate, "I walk upon air and consider the sun." Mark Pattison supposes himself to be telling his reader about a half-educated specimen of the old, bad time, before Oxford was reformed. We meanwhile in the first years of the twenty-first century, often assume that the standards of our own time are higher than ever before. Yet how many students today could come up with so clinchingly apposite a reply, when blind drunk, *in Greek?* Suddenly Mark Pattison's unhesitating scorn seems eloquent of a cracklingly high standard. If the half-educated man was like this, what must the educated man have been like?

It is odd that our account of Mark Pattison, the Oxford don, should begin with the citing of a phrase from the great Greek comedy written, as Shakespeare's *Love's Labour's Lost* was written, against the Academy. So far the terms which have engaged us have been: "scholar," "scientist," "philosopher," "historian." We must now add a Greek term, "sophist." This was the word applied to the professional lecturers and teachers who became the object of an intense mistrust in the fifth century B.C. Plato laboured to distinguish his teacher, Socrates, from the sophists, always insisting for example that he had never taken money for his teaching. Aristophanes simply sees Socrates as the star sophist. Here, in the play, he is intent upon astronomy. This too may seem to conflict with the essentially ethical and metaphysical thinker we meet in the pages of Plato, but then one remembers that in the *Phaedo* Socrates — Plato's Socrates — actually says that in his youth he was interested in scientific explanations of things (97D–98D). The Sophist, note, is more dangerous than contemptible, closer to Faustus than to Browning's grammarian, though here he is clearly funny. These sophists are the people who by argument can make the worse appear the better cause. Like the subtle serpent in Genesis they can destroy the innocence of those they teach, afterwards perhaps destroying the pupils themselves. Pattison Senior, clinging drunkenly to the statue, unthinkingly sets in motion a wheel that has rolled on from Aristophanes through the centuries, through Shakespeare and Burton to Browning: the knower feared, hated, derided, despised.

As Pattison tells it, the story is wholly happy. "It's only Aristophanic Pattison!" cries Hodson in the darkened quadrangle, the tone seemingly friendly. Mark Pattison says the effect of his father's stories was to make him "familiar with college life from as early a time as I can remember" (*Memoirs*, 7).

A. E. Housman in his childhood, we are told, never actually knew that Shropshire which forms the golden landscape of his poems, but it was in fact visible to him as distant hills in the west, where the sun went down. The world of *A Shropshire Lad* is not as we might have thought, wholly mythical, having no connection with experience. The experience of things half-seen, distant, inaccessible can have its own special intensity. It is not indeed "a given" of experience, but rather a "half-given." Hardy's Jude as a child saw the lights of Christminster (Oxford) from a hill. For young Pattison, better placed to be sure than Jude, the lights of a remembered Oxford shone in the genial tales of his father, long before he made the journey south from Yorkshire. The sweetness of the moment when the letter inviting him to go to Oxford arrived comes through the more powerfully, because of the Pattisonian aridity of the surrounding prose. This is the crux of the whole story, the beginning of Pattison's long love affair with learning. *Incipit vita nova*, "The new life begins."[23] Very occasionally the reader of the *Memoirs* is given a concrete glimpse of a particular moment, in a particular place. It happens here: "I remember that I was in a remote corner of the garden, where I cultivated a special plot called my garden. It was dusk. My father appeared, agitated with delight, holding up the letter with the Oxford postmark, before he opened it" (*Memoirs*, 40).

It is a haunting picture. The sense of a *hortus conclusus*, a garden enclosed but now invaded by a quickening influence, is made still stronger by reduplication. Mark is standing in a garden (his own) within the larger garden. This much is touched by the old myth of Eden and the sin of knowledge. But the father's face, dimly seen in the fading light, has extraordinary actuality. Pattison does not tell us what his father said, but the reader seems to hear his voice in the cold evening air. Darkness is falling on this March evening in a northern county, but spring is near.

Father and son set out together by coach on Monday morning and arrived at The Angel in Oxford High Street (where the Examination Schools now stand) at four o'clock in the morning on Wednesday. Pattison writes of the excitement that mounted in him over the last ten miles, followed at last by "exultation" (*Memoirs*, 41) as they reached the lights of Saint Giles, the road into Oxford from the north. There was no "North Oxford then, no suburban city." This was in 1832. But it was not Pattison's first visit. In 1830 he and his father had travelled to Oxford to select a college. Pattison writes,

> It was May and Oxford, not then overbuilt and slummy, looked — as Oxford can still look in May — charming. I was intoxicated with delight, and my father was as pleased as a child. His constant recurrence to his reminiscences of this place had so riveted it in my mind that I had, by aid of an old guidebook I found at Hauxwell, mastered the topography by anticipation, and was proud as we walked about the streets to show that I knew where to find the colleges. In all other respects I was an ignorant country bumpkin, and incapable of learning from what I now saw for the first time. My father, of course, took me "on the water" — his own favourite amusement. We were sculled down to Iffley, and he enjoyed paying the overcharge, "eighteen pence each gentleman as went in the boat, and two shillings the man." [*Memoirs*, 14]

I hinted that Pattison left a Yorkshire Eden to eat the fruit of the Tree of Knowledge, but in this passage Oxford is itself another, brighter garden. It is seen here of course through reminiscent eyes. Instead of inducing a sudden maturity it makes even the elder Pattison into a child again. The usual Pattisonian tic of censure is nevertheless active. He notes his own inability to learn from what was before him, but, for all that, everything is bathed in a forgiving radiance. His ignorance is rural, pastoral — he is a "bumpkin." We smile both at him and with him, as we smile both at and with Mr. Verdant Green on his first encounter with Oxford, in Cuthbert Bede's immortal work. Beauty and happiness easily predominate. The Oxford of 1830 was still the perfect city we see in Rudolph Ackermann's aquatints, as yet unviolated, aesthetically, by the Victorian revival, virtually without suburbs. But it continued — continues — to be very beautiful. This, however, is not obvious to Pattison. He has to remind himself that the Oxford he can gaze at now, in his latter years, can look in May as it looked in 1830.

Pattison also describes his love of the northern landscape at this period of his life, so that when, afterwards, he read William Words-worth's *Prelude*, it was as if he was reading his own history. Suddenly and characteristically, however, he stamps on any incipient intuition of a special felicity: "I hasten to say that in these first years of the 1830s there was nothing in me that could be called intelligence, nor any manifestation of sensibility of feeling" (*Memoirs*, 35–36). The reader experiences this as pure contradiction, the ostensibly rational self-contempt as conceivably irrational, at base. The radiance of that beginning is unsubduable and is indeed essential to the subsequent tragedy.

Those days when father and son together walked the streets of Oxford in sunlight were not to last. While for his father the idea of Oxford as a kind of Arcadia covered the entire period of his time there as an undergraduate, for the son, things changed at once, from undifferentiated exultation to a harsh, almost ascetic sense of an op-pressive destiny: he was there, not to live, but to read. Pattison tells how his father was fond of repeating a certain sentence in the Eton Latin grammar: *Concessi Contabrigiam ad capiendum ingenii cultum*, "To Cambridge I went, to acquire cultivation of mind." The younger Pattison writes, "This was the proverb which presided over my whole college life" (*Memoirs*, 22). The presumption must be that what had formed a part of Oxford life for the rector of Hauxwell has become everything for the son.

It may seem that Pattison Senior differed from his son as one with a natural talent for happiness differs from one constitutionally liable to depression. But clouds gathered in the older man's mind. When Mark Pattison was drawn into the Tractarian movement in the early 1840s, Mr. Pattison, who had written regularly and very affectionately to his son, broke off all correspondence. John Sparrow says that it appears that he never wrote another letter to his son.[24] Earlier, in 1834, Mr. Pattison had to be taken for a brief period away from his rectory and placed in a private lunatic asylum at Acomb, near York. After his release his behaviour was intermittently violent. Indeed for the last thirty years of his life he was a tyrant to his family. Sometimes he merely locked himself in his room. At the same time, however, he implacably opposed the marriage of his daughter and made a will in which his children were disinherited. Mark Pattison was strange, but he was never as mad as this. In 1835 he had to return to Hauxwell for a considerable period because of his father's uncontrollable behaviour. Ten years later we find Mark Pattison visiting one John Mavor, who was incarcerated, in a crazed condition, in Oxford prison. Mavor believed that the whole world was against him: "All the world he looks on as in conspiracy against him" (*Memoirs*, 192). Later Pattison himself fell into excesses of self-pity—and we feel, when we come to this stage in his story, that he is beginning to turn into Mavor, the man he had tried to help.[25] More faintly but still discernibly he is also turning into his own father, the man who sent him south to a world of learning, the man who in the end was to be heard ranting from his pulpit against the iniquities of his family. But the process of mental disintegration was never completed in the son.

What kind of academic community did young Pattison enter? It is difficult now to disentangle myth from fact—especially difficult, because Oxford generates mythical feelings and memories not just in those who misunderstand, from a distance but in—especially in—those who were actually there. These heightened responses then have a material effect on the real lives of those concerned. Over and over again, as generation succeeds generation, one finds writers saying, with strong emotion, "I saw the last of the old Oxford." The writer of this book, who should be defended by a clear, cool awareness of the presence here of a repetitive myth, certainly feels, vividly and intuitively, that he did. Evelyn Waugh's lost innocent Academe "irrecoverable as Lyonnesse" (*Brideshead Revisited*, book 1, ch. 1) is perennial, as real and as unreal as a rainbow. Usually the old Oxford is a "soft-primitivist" Arcadia (soft-primitivist pastoral commends the life of the shepherd, lolling at ease in the shade of the beech, while "hard-primitivist" Georgic poetry commends back-breaking toil, ploughing the stubborn earth, because it forms a hardy race).[26] A similar myth attaches itself to Cambridge, but with less intensity and less frequent recurrence. "Old Damoetas" in the nostalgic part of Milton's "Lycidas"—the rubicund figure who seems to have stepped from a painting by Nicolas Poussin—old Damoetas was a Cambridge, not an Oxford don. The sense is that once there was a time when leisure was endless, as was the wine and the good fellowship: Oxford was an Eden as yet unvisited by the curse of toil.

The university in the early years of the nineteenth century was very small. Even by the late 1840s there were only fourteen hundred undergraduates.[27] More importantly, perhaps, the university was all male. While we cannot doubt that the young men of the time found ways of dealing with their sexual needs, this all-male existence, lived to the sound of church bells, with stern physical exercise on the river and long, long country walks, certainly produced a sense of innocence, especially when remembered later. Remember how in the second chapter of Thomas Hughes's *Tom Brown at Oxford* the hero sets out joyously on a fine February morning for his first trial run on the river, remember the lines in Matthew Arnold's "Scholar Gipsy" about walking home through flooded fields or seeing on a winter night the "line of festal light in Christ-Church hall" from the top of Hinksey Hill (ll. 122, 129). The supposed leisure on the other hand, the other component of the pastoral picture, is a little more problematic. In the undergraduate community there were those who had no intention of taking a classified degree. These really did lead lives of sporting conviviality. Most fellows of colleges did no teaching. Sparrow says with reference to the late 1840s that of the five hundred or more fellows, only two-thirds were resident in Oxford.[28] M. C. Curthoys points out that James Heywood's 1842 survey shows that at that point only a minority, 196 out of 550, lived in the city.[29] Clearly those who were absent, whether working or not, make no impact on the Oxford scene as such. But the fact that so many of those who did live in college had nothing to do but eat, drink, and talk while they waited for livings as parsons, means that there is, once more, a verifiable area of real leisure or idleness. What is surprising, after all this rosy slackness, is the life led meanwhile, by those in college who did work.

In 1832 the "Schools," or final examination, consisted of "the rudiments of religion (the Gospels in Greek, Old and New Testament History, the thirty-nine Articles and Paley's *Evidences*)," Literae Humaniores (the Greek and Latin languages, ancient history, rhetoric, poetry, and moral and political philosophy, as taught by classical writers), and the elements of mathematics and physics. Literae Humaniores on one hand and mathematics with physics on the other were regarded as separate Schools. An "honours" candidate was required to do both (hence the possibility of achieving "a double First").[30] Oxford had its professors of law, medicine, Anglo-Saxon, and so forth, but, notoriously, their lectures were thinly attended, simply because they lay outside the curriculum. The curriculum itself, absurd as it may look to us, may well have been very demanding.

Sparrow says that, in 1822 and after, the "examinations were entirely oral."[31] This, it seems, is not quite correct. Curthoys observes that written work had been set in the B.A. examinations since 1807; however it played a minor part only. But he then adds that, within twenty years, the role of written exercises had grown; in 1827 William Jacobson worked on written answers for three days, before being examined viva voce. In 1830 we have the first printed papers (brief, craggy, dauntingly precise factual questions, to be answered at high speed—oddly like the kind of examination that could be dealt with by a computer). The candidates suffered. Curthoys quotes C. K. Sharpe's description of the viva voce (oral) examinations as they were in 1801, including his own terror on the day before (he was unable to eat, sleep, *or even talk*). George Moberley, later headmaster of Winchester, fainted before his examination in 1825, and Francis Jenne had a breakdown during his, in 1827.[32] Those fellows who were given tutorships (two or occasionally three persons in a given college) were in general expected to cover the whole range of subjects, though occasionally a division of labour was arrived at.[33] Since tutors were not chosen on the basis of academic expertise, it is likely that the standard of teaching was low. It does not follow that the life of a tutor was easy. Today an ordinary working fellow of an Oxford college is expected to do twelve hours of tutorial teaching a week and sixteen hours of lectures or classes in the course of a year. Outside Oxford the requirement is commonly lower than this. At this point it should be explained to readers not familiar with university work that "contact hours" are a small proportion of the total input of work. Quite recently I remember reflecting with relief that I could *just* keep Christmas Day completely clear. Of course in making the comparison with the present day, we must add the burden of graduate supervision, something that simply did not exist in nineteenth-century Oxford. Frederick Temple, who became mathematics lecturer at Balliol in 1843, had to do fifteen hours of lecturing a week.[34] Mark Pattison describes how he gave four lectures, end to end, "every day" (this probably means six days a week) and how, in addition, he would turn out after dinner to see his pupils individually between 8 and 10 P.M. He lightly adds that he took a reading party to Bowness *for a month* (*Memoirs*, 261, 262). Your twenty-first-century don might countenance a week but would blench at the thought of a whole month out of the vacation, out of research time.

In seeing his pupils separately Pattison is helping to invent what is known today as "the tutorial system." The phrase "tutorial system," readers should be warned, was in frequent use in the nineteenth century but had a completely different meaning. It referred to the classes laid on by the college, on the principle of "one man teaching everything."[35] It may be thought that this surge of industry is peculiar to the 1840s, with their atmosphere of intense reform, but D. K. Sandford, who graduated from Christ Church in 1820, reckoned that Oxford tutors were teaching for about seven or eight hours a day (this may include private teaching taken on as an extra).[36] Again we have Mark Pattison telling us how abysmal, intellectually, these occasions were: "the class construing, in turns, some twenty lines of a classical text to the tutor, who corrected you when you were wrong" (*Memoirs*, 64). In other words it was, in our terms, much more like school teaching than university teaching. But, when all this is admitted, seven or eight hours a day of "contact hours" can hardly be described as an Arcadian existence.

Nor is it always understood that the shift away from oral examination was not, at the time, perceived as a move from idyllic amateurism to strenuous professionalism but rather as a means of reducing a workload that had become intolerable. In 1822 it took the examiners twelve solid weeks to work through the two hundred candidates, one by one.[37] By the 1830s it was taking half the year to process the list, which had now grown to four hundred candidates. These oral examinations were quite unlike modern "vivas"; the examiners were able to do at most six in one day. In *Tom Brown at*

Oxford, which appeared in 1861 but is set in the 1840s, Thomas Hughes describes the examiners as dealing with four candidates a day and then laying on a further oral examination for those seeking honours.[38] The examination Hughes describes still took place in the Bodleian quadrangle; the Examination Schools were as yet unbuilt. The setting for Hughes carries with it an atmosphere of extreme dread. The wonderful painting by S. P. Hall of a viva, *We Pause for a Reply*, which now hangs in Pembroke College, Oxford, despite the fact that it was exhibited at the Royal Academy in 1895, is discernibly set in the Bodleian quadrangle. When the printed examination papers came in the 1830s it was expressly stated that this was in order "to try several persons at the same time."[39] The atmosphere, as recalled by Thomas Hughes was indeed the reverse of carefree. There is, we must grant, an element of hyperbolical Victorian facetiousness in the style, but it is fundamentally a grim picture. He writes, "I suppose that a man being tried for his life must be even more uncomfortable than an undergraduate being examined for his degree, and that to be hung — perhaps even to be pilloried — must be worse than to be plucked."[40] As one reads on, Hughes's metaphor of *peine forte et dure* feels less and less wild: "Through the long day till four o'clock, or later, the torture lasts. Then the last victim is dismissed; the men who are 'sitting for the schools' fly all ways to their colleges, silently, in search of relief to their over-wrought feelings, probably also of beer, the undergraduates universal specific."[41] Hughes then reminds us that we are looking at a time when, while fellows of the colleges were required to be celibate, undergraduates could be married men. He urges the married candidate never to send his son to hear the result: "Oxford has never seen the sight over which she would more willingly draw the veil with averted face than that of the youth rushing wildly, dissolved in tears, from the schools quadrangle, and shouting 'Mamma! Papa's plucked! Papa's pluck'd!' "[42]

As the examiners toiled, so did many of the candidates. They frequently paid for private coaching, on a one-to-one basis. This was wholly unofficial and happened alongside the classes provided by the colleges. This private tuition is the source of the Oxford "tutorial system" as it is understood today. But whereas the modern undergraduate has about two tutorials a week (sometimes only one), it was then common to be coached for an hour every other day.[43] Mark Pattison says that it was the coaches and not the elementary college lectures that worked a man up for a first (*Memoirs*, 26). He himself went six times a week to C. P. Eden, "for a fee of £17.10s., nearly as much as the college tuition fee, £21, which I was also paying and getting nothing in return" (*Memoirs*, 140). In *Tom Brown at Oxford* the character Hardy, whose social origins and finances are straitened, gets a first without coaching, and this is expressly commented on by his college tutor. "He called attention, in more than one common room, to the fact that Hardy had never had any private tuition, but had attained his intellectual development solely in the *curriculum* provided by St Andrew's College for the training of the youth entrusted to her."[44]

One must imagine a society more sharply divided than anything we see today. It was divided not so much along lines of class as between workers and idlers. Most fellows did little, but some did a great deal. The same was true of the undergraduates. The various vivid contrasts within the undergraduate body, "aesthetes" versus "hearties," "reading men" versus the rest, still very evident in the 1950s and traceable even today, were in the earlier nineteenth century strongly rooted in economic fact and practice.

Pattison came south, from the beautiful remote northern village of Hauxwell (where the near perfect, small medieval church still stands unspoiled, though the rectory has gone) to an equally, or still more beautiful Oxford, just before the spate of nineteenth-century building. He was, he says, socially inept, and this might lead us to suppose that fear or some sort of anxiety was his ruling passion, but that was not the case. The readiest impulse in him was contempt, liberally applied both to himself and to others. Looking back on his first term at Oxford he despises his own performance and castigates himself for not using compendia and summaries of information in his undergraduate years: "I dawdled from a mixture of mental infirmity, bad habit, and the necessity of thoroughness" (*Memoirs*, 151). This self-contempt is however laced with feeling of another kind. Part of Pattison actually approves of his youthful refusal to trust "epitomes," and dawdling because of "*the necessity of thoroughness*," so far from being a matter of real, keen shame, is almost something of which a scholar might be proud.

But his immediate contempt for the college teaching is unequivocal, as is his later contempt for the scholarship of Benjamin Jowett[45] and John Conington. Pattison's style is so powerful that we believe him—perhaps too readily. His cold, measured, analytic judgements are uttered with an eerie confidence. He writes as the ultimate External Examiner, separate from the fray. Jowett in fact began as a brilliant youth, and this brilliance included striking ability as a Latinist. Dr. John Sleath, high master of St. Paul's school, said Jowett was "the best Latin scholar whom he had ever sent to college."[46] In 1835 he gained an open scholarship to Balliol and in 1837 won the Hertford (University) Scholarship for Latin. Then, in 1838, he was elected to a fellowship while still an undergraduate. In 1841 he won the chancellor's prize for a Latin essay. Thereafter he may be seen as moving away from strict scholarship into the world of ideas. The political and moral conflicts aroused by the Oxford Movement absorbed a good deal of Jowett's energy. He was one of the first people in Oxford to take an intelligent interest in the writings of G. W. F. Hegel. In 1855 he brought out his edition of Saint Paul (Thessalonians, Galatians, and Romans) and was soon attacked by the stricter philologists, such as the formidable Joseph Lightfoot, bishop of Durham, for supposing that he could glean the meaning of Saint Paul better from the context (as apprehended by him, Jowett) than from a careful scrutiny of the Greek text.[47] This was followed in 1871 by his translation of all the dialogues of Plato (his hopes of completing a commentary on Plato having faded). The translation remains a superb piece of work, linguistically scrupulous, philosophically intelligent.

So was Pattison right? By some very severe standard, perhaps he was. Did Pattison do more, as a scholar, than Jowett? Surely not. With Conington the case was similar. His main work was his edition of Virgil. Although critics said he took too little account of developments in European scholarship, it is a work alight with intelligence. Anyone who can notice, for example, as Conington did, that those lines in the *Eclogues* which describe the Golden Age (3.89, 4.30, 5.60) are oddly like other passages in which we are shown a world gone crazy (1.59, 8.53) deserves the gratitude of posterity.[48] The whole notion of the *adynata*, the "fishes-in-the-trees" topos which proved so fertile for twentieth-century literary criticism, is there, in germ. Of Conington, Pattison writes, "he abandoned himself to the laziest of all occupations with the classics that namely of translating them into English" (*Memoirs*, 25). Pattison says nothing about Conington's editions, causing an embarrassed nineteenth-century editor to add the note, "He also edited, with notes, Virgil and Persius." Pattison's sentence may not be absolutely unjust in itself, but one can nevertheless feel that the real Conington has not been adequately conveyed to the reader. There is one point in the *Memoirs* (146) where Pattison records, with a certain surprise, an occasion when he felt genuine pleasure in the success of a friend, thus inverting the duc de La Rochefoucald's grim maxim, "Dans l'adversité des nos meilleurs amis, nous trouvons toujours quelque chose qui ne nous déplaît pas," "In the misfortune of our best friends we always find something not displeasing to us."[49]

The Man Out of His Time

This instinctive failure of warmth to all around him arises, in part, from a simple but very mysterious fact. Mark Pattison, 1813–84, had an eighteenth-century mind. Revealingly, he wrote of England's greatest eighteenth-century poet, "Pope has so much the modern air that we are apt to forget that his poetry is now a century and a half old."[50] One struggles to make sense of this by conjecturing that there may have been, after the Tractarians, a reaction in favour of cool epigram, but nothing will make the sentence plausible. The truth is that Pattison was writing well on in a century that had by this time grown heavy with the cadences of Tennyson. No one with an ear for what was in the air in the 1870s could have supposed for one second that Pope belonged to the later nineteenth century. The idea is forced upon us that Pope felt contemporary to Pattison because he is indeed *spiritually* contemporary with Pattison — or rather Pattison was contemporary with *him*. Pattison's coevals, meanwhile, were always in a manner strangers to him. Pope, Johnson, and Gibbon were, immediately, his friends. When he writes about the period 1835–36 he describes his slow savouring of Johnson's *Lives of the*

Poets, knowing from the first that these would be "congenial." Here, he concludes, "I would set up my habitation" (*Memoirs,* 153). Similarly his instantaneous dislike of Victorian Gothic architecture, which he disparages as merely imitative, is revealing of the man.[51]

Yet Pattison was for a certain period a Tractarian. In the fateful summer term of 1833 he moved into "better and more expensive rooms" on the same staircase as John Henry Newman (*Memoirs,* 117). Looking back, Pattison is clear that the entire episode was a bizarre disaster both for Oxford and for himself. Where many see the 1830s and early 1840s as the high point in the fortunes of Oriel College (the time of John Newman and Edward Pusey) Pattison gravely points to 1831 as the moment at which Oriel began to slip, and Balliol to shoot up. His personal experience he likens to being "drawn into a whirlpool" (*Memoirs,* 171). He sums up this time in his life with these words: "It was soon after 1830 that the 'Tracts' desolated Oxford life, and suspended, for an indefinite period, all science, humane letters, and the first strivings of intellectual freedom which had moved in the bosom of Oriel" (*Memoirs,* 100–101). Pattison himself was soon to be found, toiling away at the very centre of all this repression of intellect, translating Thomas Aquinas for Newman. Indeed he was, as he confesses, an extremist among extremists. At first the Tractarians argued for the Church of England as an acceptable *via media,* or middle way, between Roman Catholicism and Protestantism, but the inner tendency of the movement was not to adhere to this middle course but rather to edge, consistently, nearer and nearer to Rome, further and further from Protestant principles. *Tendimus in Latium,* "Our path lies towards Rome," became a catchphrase. Jokes, always a good indicator of growing trends, are, again and again, jokes at the expense of the Anglican Church (*Memoirs,* 185). It seems clear that when the "crash" came and Newman went over to Rome in 1845, Pattison very nearly followed him.

All of this seems quintessentially nineteenth century and so to overthrow our basic premise, which is that Pattison belonged mentally to the eighteenth century. But, while his sincerity is not in question, we may still wonder about the precise nature of his temporary allegiance. One suspects that Pattison may have resembled those in our own time who are drawn briefly into cults. He was lonely and ill at ease and must have been hungry to belong to *something*. Pattison's narrative of the Tractarian episode in his life presents it as a temporary darkening of the intellect, a brief extinction of reason. Yet he also makes it clear that what really energised him in the actual work he undertook for Newman was not a surge of passionate piety but a gritty taste for getting things right. The text he took on was Aquinas's *Catena Aurea,* on the Gospels. Pattison at first hoped to translate the parts dealing with Matthew's Gospel and Mark's but, as things turned out, never got as far as Mark. He soon hit the difficulty of Aquinas's quotations; Aquinas does not give references when quoting from Church Fathers. Pattison writes, "I hunted up the whereabouts of all the quotations in each case in the best edition of the Fathers; I spent hours and days over the work in the Bodleian, and would not be beat" (*Memoirs,* 181). The last four words are eloquent of a strange happiness that Pattison has found in the midst of so much half-distasteful *piétisme*. While the spiritual young man is all at sea, the scholar in him finds work to do and functions.

Pattison says that after 1845, just *before* the strange suspension induced by the secession of Newman, he plunged into the secular literary history of the eighteenth century, reading Thomas Gray, James Prior's *Life of Goldsmith,* and Hume's *Life and Correspondence* (*Memoirs,* 187). Even earlier there are signs that the germ of his interest in the Fathers lay not in Tractarianism but in Gibbon's great, unbelieving History (*Memoirs,* 173). V. H. H. Green completely misses this aspect of Pattison's motivation in the account he gives of the episode.[52] Pattison gives extended passages from his diary written in the Tractarian years in order to show how completely his mind had been submerged. Yet within these pious pages there are odd twitches. In the middle of an apparently admiring account of the great ascetics of the early church, he writes, "The Cistercians never had their minds in vigour; could hardly even be said to be thoroughly awake" (*Memoirs,* 206). This is from 1843. He is clearly on the Cistercians' side, but a Gibbonian humour is, so to speak, within call. After all it was in 1833 that Gibbon's *Autobiography* made a strong impact on him. In the *Memoirs* he falls at once into Gibbon's manner when he describes Newman and his associates.

Gibbon tells us how he conceived the idea of his history on an autumn day in the ruins of Rome; he watched the barefoot friars on their way to sing Vespers in what had once been the Temple of Jupiter Capitoline and resolved there and then to tell the long story of the decline and fall of the Roman Empire, which was also, as he would later put it, the story of the triumph "of barbarism and religion."[53] For Gibbon, the felicity of the Antonine age gave way to priestcraft and superstition; the strong were defeated by the weak. Here indeed lay the special challenge, to the explanatory historian. Pattison writes of Newman, "Athanasius was his hero; he was inspired by the triumph of the Church organization over the wisdom and philosophy of the Hellenic world; that triumph which, to the Humanist, is the saddest moment in history—the ruin of the painfully constructed fabric of civilisation to the profit of the Church" (*Memoirs*, 96). A little later he adds, with reference this time not to Newman but to clerical Oxford in general, "Of the world of wisdom and sentiment—of poetry and philosophy, of social and political experience, contained in the Latin and Greek classics, and of the true relation of the degenerate and semi-barbarous Christian writers of the fourth century to that world—Oxford, in 1830, had never dreamt" (*Memoirs*, 97).

Pattison is clear that the natural bent of his mind is "nominalist," as distinct from "realist." These are the notoriously misleading terms of late medieval philosophy. One has to explain that "realist," in this usage, has a meaning almost directly opposite to that which we expect: a realist is a person who believes that universals ("abstractions") such as "humanity" or "beauty" refer to real, immaterial entities, whereas nominalists hold, conversely, that universals are *flatus vocis*, mere breath, and that concrete particulars (setting aside God for the moment) alone exist. There is no such thing as "humanity"; there are only human beings. Pattison, not unreasonably, sees realism as conducive to the hegemony of the church and nominalism as inherently resistant to any such dominance (*Memoirs*, 165–67). He swiftly identifies realism in this technical sense with apriorism, the idea that there are important truths which *precede* experience, instead of being drawn from experience. He can then effortlessly slot the rising interest in Immanuel Kant and German idealism into the Enemy Doctrine. He is delighted by the effect of J. S. Mill, who "repudiated at once sacerdotal principles and Kantian logic" (*Memoirs*, 166). He is puzzled, however, that it should have been the staunchly liberal T. H. Green, who brought idealism into Oxford.

Pattison was always more willing to essay crisply censorious general descriptions of intellectual positions than to enter into exacting philosophical argument. It is likely that the scrupulous objections to Humean scepticism which Green set out in his majestic introduction to the *Works* (1874–75) simply passed Pattison by. In Mrs. Humphry Ward's *Robert Elsmere* the problem is, after a fashion, resolved. There Green, as we saw, became the character Gray who, liberal as he is, emerges as the true friend of Christianity. Pattison on the other hand, as John Sparrow loved to maintain, perhaps appears in the book as the frightening sceptic Roger Wendover.[54] It is a curious case. One can almost argue that here fiction is truer than fact. Pattison perhaps never knew, clearly and explicitly, that he was opposed to Christianity itself. If he were asked (and, after all he should know!), he would say he was a Christian and he would not be lying. But the deepest impulses of his mind are all anti-religious. Just as a caricature of Tony Blair can be more like Blair than Blair is, so Wendover is more Pattisonian than Pattison.

In the essay "Tendencies of Religious Thought in England, 1688–1750," which he wrote for *Essays and Reviews* (1860), Pattison actually says that it is a mistake to think of the eighteenth century as Godless or anti-theological; rather it is anticlerical.[55] He could easily have been brought to admit that he likewise was against the clerics. He likens the open contempt visited on the clergy in the eighteenth century to that visited on monks and priests by Wycliffites in an earlier age. Pattison is conscious that he likes the Deists, those critical spirits who sought to replace the fierce specificity of Christianity with a religion-of-all-sensible-persons, as evident to the civilised Chinaman as to the London merchant. He knows very well, however, that almost no one in his own century likes the Deists. One can detect a certain relief as well as joy when he discovers that Professor Fraser has called the eighteenth century "the golden age of English theology."[56] Pattison shrewdly singles out John Locke's *Reasonableness of Christianity* (1695) as an important opening move in the game. Although Locke differs from the Deists in the weight he places on the revealed text of Scripture and in the space he reserved for faith, this little book can indeed be seen as the beginning of that movement of rationalism which was ended by *Tracts for the Times*.[57] In the period up to 1750 "the main endeavour was to show that there was nothing in the contents of revelation which was not agreeable to reason."[58] This for Pattison was the essence of the matter. Reason is here, implicitly, made prior to revelation. Although Locke, unlike John Toland, held that certain truths were above reason, it was for reason to decide which those truths were.[59] As Deism developed the effects of this revised priority became slowly more evident. Religion becomes natural. It is judged according to the standards of reason, not vice versa.

At the same time, however, Pattison affirms the idea that reason is itself implanted in us by God. Jonathan Swift once wrote (not for publication), "I am not answerable to God for the doubts that arise in my own breast, since they are the consequence of that reason which he hath planted in me, if I take care to conceal those doubts from others, if I use my best endeavours to subdue them, and if they have no influence on the conduct of my life."[60] There is an ethical dividedness — a sheer weirdness — about this which is characteristically Swiftian: doubts are nothing to be ashamed of because they are the natural result of a divine gift; doubts must be hidden from others, crushed, never permitted to influence behaviour! The Deists hoped of course that reason would provide not doubt but certainty.

Once more it remains, at least, an open question whether in the mind of rational Pattison doubt or certainty had the upper hand. When he refers to this essay later, in the *Memoirs*, he says his aim was to account for the demise of Deism, but he never allowed that it died because it was refuted. It was never refuted. A little later he expresses, as his own opinion, a general view of theology that is itself thoroughly Deist: "If God interferes at all to procure the happiness of mankind it must be on a far more comprehensive scale than by providing for them a church of which far the majority will never hear" (*Memoirs*, 313, 327). This is essentially the argument later set out as fundamental to Deism by Leslie Stephen, with the memorable phrase, "The scenery had become too wide for the drama."[61] It makes sense to judge everyone by his or her response if the crucifixion takes place, so to speak, on a stage twenty yards wide. When, however, it takes place on a stage many miles across, out of sight and hearing of most of the people on that stage (so that they neither react nor, meaningfully, "fail to react"), such a judgement becomes obviously unfair. The early Deists were strongly affected in particular by merchants' reports on the Chinese, who behaved in so many ways like decent businessmen and not like devils at all.

Pattison published his essay on eighteenth-century religious thought some sixteen years before Stephen brought out his massive study. In general Pattison stands up well in a comparison with his indefatigable successor. Pattison knows about Toland, Henry St. John, Viscount Bolingbroke, and William Warburton (all of whom figure prominently in Stephen's book) and finds his way to more obscure persons such as Humphrey Prideaux, dean of Norwich.[62] When he comes to tell how Deism died in its tracks with the writings of Lord Bolingbroke, one becomes aware of a profound difference between Pattison and Stephen. Pattison notes how unfashionable, how boringly obsolete Deism seemed by the 1750s. The works of Bolingbroke were brought out in 1754, three years after his death, by his Scottish executor, David Mallet. Pattison, doubtless writing from memory since his quotation is inexact, cites Johnson's comment as given by James Boswell: "It was a rusty blunderbuss, which he need not have been afraid to have discharged himself, instead of leaving half a crown to a Scotchman to let it off after his death."[63] To be sure, Pattison has more in the way of explanation: the very intellectual fairness of Deism, when set beside the punitive terrors of traditional Christianity, made it, relatively speaking, a weak inducement to moral behaviour. Stephen, however, has an altogether deeper strategy. He too refers his readers to a Scotsman, but to one greater than Mallet. Sceptical Stephen knew that he could afford, in the earlier part of his *History*, to disparage the hasty, shoddy little books of the early Deists because he had up his sleeve the greatest sceptic of all, David Hume. In due course Hume would produce a wholly unanswerable case against Christianity. When Hume discharged *his* gun, the explosion was simply too great to be immediately apprehended. Deism and scepticism vanished not because they had become boring and weak but because they had become too strong. They were now intractable.

Pattison is fascinating, however, on the freethinker Anthony Collins. He seems for a moment to concede that on the occasion of the famous clash between Collins and Richard Bentley, Bentley won. Of Bentley's onslaught (*Remarks of Phileleutherus Lipsiensis*) on Collins's *Discourse of Freethinking,* Pattison writes, "perhaps the best of all his works."[64] But then he adds, almost lightly, that Bentley did not actually reply to Collins's *argument*. Suddenly the coin flips over, and Bentley becomes the more dubious character of the two: "Collins was not a sharper, and would have disdained practices to which Bentley stooped."[65] Bentley went to work, solely, on narrow points of scholarship in Collins. The whole story is curiously reminiscent of the account Pattison gives in his *Isaac Casaubon*[66] of Philippe Duplessis-Mornay, who wrote a reasoned criticism of Roman Catholicism and was afterwards fiercely attacked by the Roman Catholic establishment, but solely on the accuracy of his citations. Pattison is willing to concede that his favourite century, the eighteenth, is not strong on history as distinct from rational theology. He allows Gibbon as the one, huge exception.[67] He also allows that the "Lectures at Cambridge" of Herbert Marsh (who was born in 1757 and died in 1839, thus overlapping substantially with Pattison himself) did institute a real enquiry into the origins of canonical writings: "That investigation, introduced by a bishop and professor of divinity, has scarcely yet a footing in the English Church." As with Collins, so with the historical criticism of Marsh: "It is excluded, not from a conviction of its barrenness, but from a fear that it might prove too fertile in results."[68]

In general Pattison tends to assume that you explain a thing by eliciting its history, rather than by exposing its metaphysical presuppositions. Pattison was not incompetent in philosophy; George Eliot was impressed[69] by an article he wrote on the present state of Oxford philosophy in the first issue of the journal *Mind* (January 1878), but it is history that engages his intelligence. His love of the period led him to edit Alexander Pope's *Essay on Man,* but his philosophical understanding of this work is less than sure. He denies that the poem is Deist[70] (though he sees that it is "Théodicée"—G. W. Leibniz's term for a "justification of God") on the ground that Deism is essentially the exclusion of revelation, the setting aside of Scriptures given to some but not to all. He fails to see that Pope begins his poem by echoing Milton, "Vindicate the ways of God to Man" (1.16) but then, instead of recounting the story given in Genesis, seeks to justify the Creator through synchronic philosophical argument. The fundamental design of the poem is Deist in exactly the sense laid down by Pattison. Yet when he says he found in Butler a "solid structure of logical argument in which it surpasses any other book that I know in the English language," and adds that nevertheless Dugald Stewart (most of whose work belongs, once more, to the eighteenth century) led him to resist Joseph Butler's account of conscience (*Memoirs*, 149, 140), one can feel that real philosophical argument is under way. But it is neither vigorous nor sustained. The passion lies elsewhere. Hume's *Treatise of Human Nature*, the greatest philosophical achievement of the eighteenth century, the book that so absorbed the energies of T. H. Green, seems to have had virtually no impact on Pattison.

Wordsworth's poem "There Was a Boy," about the child who lay buried in a Lakeland churchyard, is, pretty plainly, a poem about himself. The biographers who labour to identify "the Hawkshead schoolfellow" are on a wild-goose chase. The earliest manuscript drafts of this poem actually employ the first-person singular. Wordsworth is mourning the visionary child he once was and is no longer. Pattison ends his account of his immersion in the Tractarian movement by telling the story of "a female cousin." This lady possessed extraordinary intellectual powers. She had an unmatched command of ancient and modern history, taught herself Latin, Greek, Italian, German, and mathematics. Like Pattison she was carried away by the tide of Puseyism and became an extreme, anti-Anglican Tractarian. In the end, like Newman, she went over to Rome. When Pattison joined the Tractarians his father, as we saw, broke off all communication by letter with his son. This moment of rupture finds a kind of echo in words Pattison applies to his cousin: "All intellectual intercourse between myself and my cousin was at an end. . . . Can such a wreck of a noble intellect by religious fanaticism be paralleled?" (*Memoirs*, 228). The cousin, unlike the boy in Wordsworth's poem, is unequivocally real, but for all that Pattison in writing about his cousin is writing about himself. However, this is an elegy, not for one's own best self, now irretrievably lost, but for a death of mind that might have been his own but then, magically, was borne by another party, a sacrificial figure. There, but for the grace of scepticism, go I.

Cold, scholarly, self-castigating Pattison is really one of the most egotistical writers we possess. Everywhere we trace, in the stories he tells, his own ravaged lineaments. The episode of his cousin is one example. His account of the conversion of Conington ("From this time forward Professor Conington never roused himself to any intellectual exertion worthy of him"; *Memoirs*, 250–51) is another. Once more it is the story of something that might have happened to Pattison himself. His writings are an echo chamber.

At one point in his essay on "Tendencies of Religious Thought in England, 1688–1750," Pattison quotes at length from Bishop Berkeley's *Alciphron*, a passage on the new kind of smooth *un*-learned philosopher: "You may now commonly see a young lady, or a *petit-maître*, non-plus a divine or an old-fashioned gentleman who hath read many a Greek and Latin author, and spent much time in hard methodical study."[71] The whole passage can be read as an inadvertent anticipatory sketch of the implicit alliance of Dorothea and Will Ladislaw against Mr. Casaubon in *Middlemarch*. Berkeley's sympathies are entirely with the older party, but here Pattison has a grain of sympathy with the *petit-maître*, the Ladislaw of the scene presented. He pulls back from giving full assent to Berkeley: "Among a host of mischiefs thus arising, one positive good may be signalized. If there must be debate there ought to be fair play." Pattison knew that Berkeley was the hammer of the Deists, while he, Pattison, was their (late-born) friend. His opposition to the Oxford Movement is in fact a curious mixture of the kind of scepticism we associate with youth and an old-fashioned (eighteenth-century) worldview, which refuses to entertain new notions. Certainly young Ladislaw is no Tractarian and is, on this particular issue, just a little closer to the views of Pattison than Mr. Casaubon would be. The entire picture is both tantalising and tricky.

Proponents of a simple identification of Pattison with Mr. Casaubon will always run into such difficulties. Take for example the emphasis placed by George Eliot on the painfully slow progress of Mr. Casaubon. Pattison, in what might appear to be a precisely parallel manner, refers in his *Memoirs* to his own "snail-like progress" (149). One thinks for a moment, "George Eliot has simply taken Pattison at his own, self-lacerating word; she has formed her picture of an intellectual failure from the pathologically depressed self-image of one who was really very clever indeed." But this will not do. Once more, the dates are wrong. The words in the *Memoirs* are later than *Middlemarch*.

Milton: The Face in the Glass

Mr. Casaubon in *Middlemarch* looked, it will be remembered, very like the poet John Milton. When Mark Pattison came to write his book on Milton the faculty of self-projection, of discovering his own features in those of his subject, is powerfully evident. The book is not especially good. If we compare it with David Masson's massive biography of Milton, the first volume of which was published in 1859, it is clear at once that Masson is the true scholar, in command of his thesis, while Pattison is the gifted amateur, getting some things right, some wrong. For example there is the vexed question of Milton's heretical views on the Trinity in *De Doctrina Christiana* (if this is indeed the work of the poet). Was Milton an Arian? The Arians denied the divinity of Christ. Pattison speaks hesitantly of a "semi-Arian" scheme — that is, a scheme which, admitting the co-essentiality, denies the eternal generation of Christ. The Arians did indeed deny the "co-essentiality" of Christ with the other persons of the Trinity at the time of the Council of Nicaea (A.D. 325). But Milton in fact does not allow co-essentiality, any more than the original Arians had. The whole matter has been cleared up by Michael Bauman in his *Milton and Arianism*.[72] Milton indeed allowed that the Father and the Son were of the same "stuff" or "substance" (*substantia* in Milton's Latin); indeed for Milton all created beings are of this "substance," but meanwhile Milton's word for "essence" (*ousia* in the Nicene deliberations) is *essentia*, and this is *not* shared. Therefore the author of *De Doctrina Christiana* is an out-and-out Arian. This Masson clearly saw.[73] We cannot fault Pattison for failing to check Masson's views, because the volume in which Masson dealt with *De Doctrina Christiana* came out after Pattison's book on Milton. Nevertheless, we can fairly say that Pattison fumbles where Masson will go straight to the point.

Meanwhile Pattison's self-projection shows first, in minor details, small egocentricities. He lightly observes that Milton's *Tractate of Education to Master Samuel Hartlib* is probably known even to those who have never looked at anything else of Milton in prose.[74] Of course Pattison's eye would be caught by this work because he was professionally interested in schemes of education. But why should he suppose that everyone else sees as he does? Then, as now, Milton's *Areopagitica* was, surely, far better known (Pattison later in the book pays high honour to *Areopagitica; Milton*, 80–81).

All his life Pattison was fascinated by the notion of a programme or record of reading. In his *Memoirs* he writes, "In July 1833 I began a student's diary on the same plan as I have kept up, with intervals, to the present date (December, 1883). This diary only exceptionally mentions what I do, or see, or hear, it deals with what I read or write. It is strictly the student's journal, being, in this respect, the exact counterpart of Casaubon's *Ephemerides*, of which I had not then heard" (119–20). There is a streak of bizarre fascination here with the subordination of what is called "actual life" in Browning's "Grammarian's Funeral"—"what I do, or see, or hear"—to reading. The closest analogy is, as he says, to the Latin journal of Isaac Casaubon, but in Milton he found his way to a similar cast of mind, to similar behaviour. Milton himself believed that the prime cause of the loss of his eyesight was reading: "prima oculorum pernicies fuit."[75] Weak eyes, as Browning knew, are conventionally part of the literary topos, "scholar." Milton's life, by a kind of heroic exaggeration, carries the process further, to the point of absolute blindness.

Pattison seizes at once on the programme of reading followed by Milton at Horton, in his youth. Characteristically Pattison displays an itch to diminish his subject even as he discovers this congenial appetite for reading. He observes that although Milton was a scholar he was not a truly learned man—less learned than his antagonist Salmasius (that is Claudius Salmasius, the French royalist who wrote "A defense of the King against the people of England"). Milton's reading, Pattison tells us, was "industrious," but it was also "select" (*Milton*, 210); Johnson was careless in his *Life* of Milton when he said Milton read all the Greek and Latin authors at Horton; Milton's own words in the *Defensio Secunda* are that he "enjoyed a complete holiday in turning over Latin and Greek authors." In fact Milton's "own words" were Latin, not English. The key word is *evolvendis*,[76] which may seem to support Pattison. But the English "turning over," which can easily suggest desultory browsing, differs importantly from the Latin *evolvere*. Although the root meaning is certainly "turn" or "unroll," as with a scroll, the sense here is "read through" (see *The Oxford Latin Dictionary, evolvo*, 6c). When Cicero tells a person to *evolve* a certain book of Plato's (*De Finibus Bonorum et Malorum* 1.72), he clearly means, "Read it from end to end." Pattison, in a manner that could itself be stigmatised as showing slovenly Latin scholarship, here indulges in tendentious redescription and is quite unjust to Johnson. Of course Milton's claim to have read through the Greek and Latin authors may still be false, but that is another matter. Even here, however, we must, in our turn, tread carefully. There is no definite article in Latin, no "the." In English "I have read the Latin authors" makes a larger claim than "I have read Latin authors." Some may decide that the exhaustive reading cannot have happened because it is simply impossible. Anthony Grafton is willing to believe that Joseph Scaliger, Pattison's hero, read through the entire corpus of Greek literature "within two or three years."[77]

Could it be that in Milton, Pattison had met learning beyond his own? He says tetchily that the Miltonic poem-title "Il Penseroso" is bad Italian, presuming that good Italian would require "Pensieroso" (*Milton*, 23). In 1889 W. H. David pointed out that Milton's spelling can be justified by reference to a French-Italian dictionary published by Chouet in Geneva in 1644.[78] Sometimes Pattison is forced slowly to withdraw the disparagement that has become almost instinctive to him. He begins to be scornful when he finds Milton telling a friend how he had been long entangled in the obscurities of early medieval Italian history, observing that it is obvious from the commonplace book that Milton had merely been reading one volume of Carolus Sigonius's *Historia Regni Italici*. But then the tone changes: he concedes that Milton was genuinely fluent in Italian and discusses the poet's plan to read separately about the different Italian states (*Milton*, 20).

He succeeds better in his attack on the un-learned, empirical side of Milton's writings. Pattison here produces a passage of virtuoso writing, exposing the inaccuracy of the poet's epithets and general imprecision in describing plants and flowers, laying bare not want of reading, this time, but a "real defect of natural knowledge." Pattison draws the usual conclusion that Milton sees nature through the spectacles of books, but then has the grace to add (despite all his reservations) that, nevertheless, "he still sees it" (*Milton*, 25, 26).

There are many moments of insight. Predictably, Pattison gives a sharp, intelligent account of Milton's Italian journey: the academies were still bearers of culture, keeping alive "the traditions of a more masculine Medicean age," though the descent had just begun; Milton was rashly forthright in Roman Catholic Italy about his Protestantism but did not get into any serious trouble, perhaps because the Italians were embarrassed by the Galileo case, an episode which they knew had done them little good in the eyes of the world; the scholars told Milton that they were oppressed by the church and that England was the home of freedom (*Milton*, 24, 35–36).

Moreover, Pattison is capable of seeing that Milton's Latin verses are real poetry, by a real poet. They are "distinguished from most Neo-latin [sic] verse by being a vehicle of real emotion" (*Milton*, 41). He is thinking here of the *Epitaphium Damonis*, which Milton wrote for his friend Charles Diodati. Readers who expect frigidity from Latin compositions have again and again been surprised by this poem. Dr. Johnson famously complained of the unreal pastoral apparatus in "Lycidas," Milton's English elegy for a dead friend, and affirmed that the poem lacked real personal grief.[79] Meanwhile, no doubt, "Lycidas" does other things. But the *Epitaphium Damonis* really seems to be the poem Johnson was looking for. For Pattison, as for Johnson, the whole business of pastoral remains a tissue of artifice, needing to be defeated or transubstantiated by vivid feeling. This, however, is exactly what he thinks happens in the *Epitaphium Damonis*. Suddenly we find him writing with startling power: "This factitious bucolicism is pervaded by a pathos which, like volcanic heat, has fused into a new compound the dilapidate débris of the theocritean [*sic*] world" (*Milton*, 41).

Pattison gives an excellent account, given the time at which he was writing, of Milton on sexual relations. He observes that "the Puritan had thrown off chivalry as being parcel of Catholicism, and had replaced it by the Hebrew ideal of subjection and seclusion of woman," but then adds, a page later, that Milton is simultaneously strongly drawn to the idea of companionate marriage. Pattison writes with feeling about Milton's picture of husband and wife reading together, calling it "matrimony as earthly paradise" (*Milton*, 54, 56). The word "paradise" may make us think of Adam's conversation with Eve in *Paradise Lost* and of William and Catherine Blake sitting naked together in their arbour at Hercules Buildings. They too were reading—what? *Paradise Lost*.[80] Next, we may think of Dorothea Brooke and Mr. Casaubon. Dorothea dreamed of a matrimonial paradise of learning in which she was prepared to play a subordinate role, but even this Mr. Casaubon was not prepared to allow. Here the path twists back, away from the Miltonic vision of marriage, to the sad Miltonic fact. The account, as Pattison gives it, of Milton's marriage to Mary Powell reads like a harsh parody of Mr. Casaubon's marriage to Dorothea, seen through the eyes of a censorious scholar: "He found that he had mated himself to a clod of earth, who not only was not now, but had not the capacity of becoming, a helpmeet to him" (*Milton*, 54). Last of all we may think, as Pattison is clearly thinking, of Mrs. Pattison. Dorothea was no clod of earth and certainly Mrs. Pattison was a woman of quite remarkable ability, but all these marriages are stories of the paradisal ideal—the meeting of minds, the reading together—going tragically wrong.

Pattison explains that Milton came to marry Mary Powell, the daughter of a raffish, debt-ridden Cavalier family, because he was more susceptible than most men to female attraction (like Adam, "fondly overcome by female charm"—*Paradise Lost*, 9.999—where "fondly" means "foolishly") (*Milton*, 53). Earlier he noted Milton's responsiveness to good-looking Italian ladies (*Milton*, 37–38). Now the self-projection of the writer begins to grow stronger. As long as Milton is seen as a fellow scholar, he is the object of nervous criticism from Pattison. When he is seen as suffering sexually, the two become one. Considering Milton's divorce pamphlets Pattison writes, "The suggestion . . . is that Milton's young wife refused him the consummation of the marriage. . . . if Milton was brooding over this seething agony of passion all through July, with the young bride to whom he had been barely wedded a month . . . then the pamphlet, however imprudent, becomes pardonable" (*Milton*, 58). This is disquietingly direct. The sheer pain of frustration is as clear in these few lines as it is in the extended treatment it was to receive from Hardy in *Jude the Obscure* (1894–95) — Hardy's book about Oxford, scholarship, and the life of the mind. The fact that, after her reconciliation with Milton, Mary Powell bore three daughters and died giving birth to a fourth at the age of twenty-six simply fades from Pattison's mind, abstracted, one guesses, by his own resentful recollections. The sympathy with Milton is suddenly complete and heartfelt. That something was wrong between Mr. and Mrs. Pattison is clear. Lord Roseberry wrote, "The secret of his character cannot well be published, for I presume that in his case his relations to Mrs. Pattison gave the key? . . . I remember him about 1866 looking wizened and wintry beside his blooming wife."[81] Pattison warms to Milton at this point, one surmises, because he has suffered in the same way. That he is thinking — and thinking very realistically — about the nineteenth century as well as the seventeenth is suggested by his adding that Milton "refused to console himself as other men would have consoled themselves" (*Milton*, 58). The reference must surely be to the employment of prostitutes.

Pattison says that it is only because Milton's political hopes were wrecked, causing him to withdraw from the world, that we have *Paradise Lost* at all: "But for the Restoration and the overthrow of the Puritans, we should never have had the great Puritan epic" (*Milton*, 65). Again there is a curious parallel with Pattison's own experience. In his *Memoirs* he finally decides that the great catastrophe of 1851 in which all his political, educational, reformist hopes were dashed, was a blessing in disguise: "I might have wasted years in the idle and thankless pursuit which they call doing university business" (*Memoirs*, 331). But no visible monument, no great Pattisonian work resulted, which we could begin to think of setting beside Milton's. Pattison was freed for an enterprise that remained heavily introverted. "I am fairly entitled to say," he writes with strange complacency, "that, I have lived entirely for study" (*Memoirs*, 331).

Earlier I argued that the workhorses of the nineteenth-century college system did not lead a life of Arcadian ease but, on the contrary, toiled long and hard. Here I pointed to the strenuous work put in by Pattison at this stage in his career. But at the same time I allowed the existence of other strata, undergraduates not seeking honours, fellows without duties, who did indeed lead such a life. As Pattison describes his life after 1851, we find just such an existence, consisting wholly of leisured, scholarly activity. Though still a fellow of the college he no longer has to give classes or lectures. He is sent exceptionally able pupils by Jowett and others, but he is able to do all his private tuition in the Lent and Michaelmas terms, taking off for a prolonged fishing trip in April, staying from April to July at a country inn and then going off to ramble over vast distances in Germany (*Memoirs*, 300). It may be well that both Milton and Pattison felt, at one level, that the kingdom of which they dreamed was not of this world. Pattison had begun by despairing of the amateurism of the port-sodden teachers of his youth; he ended by hating the fiercely competitive examination system brought in by the reformers (*Memoirs*, 303). It is as if, in our time a literary academic were to begin by attacking "foundationlessness" in fashionable deconstructive literary theory and were then to find that he was, curiously, less grateful than he ought to be when the gritty scrutiny of factual evidence came back into fashion under the flag of New Historicism.

We may seem to have reached a point at which the division between the scholar and the man of action has become strangely absolute — more plainly so, even, than in Browning's poem. From this seemingly perfect separation there will derive, in due course, a new species of paradox: the scholar who is simultaneously — and therefore weirdly — a figure of action. In George MacDonald Fraser's *Flash for Freedom!* (1971) and *Flashman and the Redskins* (1982), John Charity Spring, the former fellow of Oriel turned slave trader in the American Wild West of the mid-nineteenth century, whose conversation is as copiously larded with Latin tags as his behaviour is violent, is a case in point. Still better is Arthur Ransome's Missee Lee, in the novel of that name written for children. Arthur Ransome, the son of a professor of history, became a journalist. In 1913 he travelled to Russia, intending to learn the language, and found himself covering the Russian Revolution. The succession of children's books came much later, in the 1930s and 1940s. *Missee Lee* opens with a group of English children, becalmed in the China seas. They are on a protracted sailing holiday, in the care of one James Turner, uncle to two of the children. Gibber, their pet monkey, snatches a lit cigar and drops it in the fuel tank of the emergency engine. The ship is burned to the waterline and all on board take to the two lifeboats. In the night that follows, the boats become separated. One finds landfall on a small deserted island. There they discover a temple and, in the temple, a Virgil and a Latin dictionary, in which someone has written, in Chinese and English. The Latin dictionary also has, in the flyleaf, some lines of doggerel Latin:

> *Hic liber est meus*
> *Testis est deus*
> *Si quis furetur*
> *Per collum pendetur.*

("This book is mine, God is my witness. If anyone should steal it, he hangs by the neck.")

Roger, the youngest and the least well behaved of the group, writes in the book, below the Latin words, "Like this poor cretur," and draws a crude picture of a man hanging from a gallows. Meanwhile those in the other boat are picked up at sea by Chinese pirates. These pirates later catch the children who entered the temple, and so they find themselves all together again but in a terrifying situation. If the pirates cannot obtain satisfactory compensation, the captives will be killed. The entire racket, "protection," piracy, and the rest, is run from the "Three Islands" by three taicoons, Chang, Wu and Missee Lee, the most important of the three. The men who find the children work for Chang. But the book in the temple belongs to Missee Lee, who has, so to speak, a non-criminal past. Years before, she was educated at Girton College, Cambridge. Hence the facetious Latin inscription in her book. When her eye falls on Roger's scribble, she perceives that he has understood the Latin, memories flood back, and she is seized by the glorious thought of having regular Latin classes—like old times. So she purchases the children—and later Uncle Jim—from Chang. Roger's delinquency saves them all. Missee Lee reveres her pirate father, from whom she inherited her present job, but her allegiance to Cambridge is complete: "At Oxford the scholarship is poor, but the marmalade is velly good."[82] Where the terrifying agency of Doctor Faustus was fused with his intellectual power, in the new order the scholar who is also frightening is a kind of walking zeugma.

Pattison, his riding days now past, is no zeugma, but has made himself into a peculiarly unalloyed intellectual, isolated not only from physical action but also from political participation, turned in upon himself so utterly that even the act of writing now seems coarsely public, a tainting of the mental life. The change indeed is great. In November 1850 Pattison (then in his thirties) gave in his reply to the printed questions circulated by the Royal Commission on Oxford, a shining vision of what a college—a community, not an individual—could be. The time had been, he pointed out, when all were students alike, differing only in being at different stages of their progress. Hence their life was truly a life in common. Then was obtained that which, then as now, constitutes the "truly invaluable element of the College system—the close action of the teacher on the pupil . . . not indeed without a very beneficial reaction of the young on the aging man." In 1850, Pattison observed, all this lay in ruins: "College life has ceased to be the life in common. The relation between the student and the College official is, in general, as distant and technical as that between the officer and the private in our army."[83] But this wrong could, he then believed, be set right. The chances of the older Pattison reacting fruitfully in his turn to the mind of a pupil would appear to be zero. He insulates himself from all communication whether by teaching or writing; he continues to read and to think.

But to describe Pattison's love of learning as introverted may be misleading, for all that it never issued in a published, written monument. There is perhaps a danger of mistaking a disinterested love of truth-for-its-own-sake for an inwardly turned preoccupation with

115

self. There are certainly moments in Pattison's book on Milton when he seems to relish the idea of non-participation in life (reminding the reader of Browning's grammarian): "No good man can with impunity addict himself to party. . . . But when one with the sensibility of a poet throws himself into the excitements of a struggle, he is certain to lose his balance. The endowment of feeling and imagination which qualifies him to be the interpreter of life, *unfits him for participation in that life*" (*Milton*, 66, my italics). Notice, however, that in this passage the presumption persists that such a mind, before it recoils into privacy, still strives to interpret the world. Earlier in the book he takes a different line. He observes with obvious approval that Milton did not go in for knowledge and learning for their own sake, but in order to form the poet's mind (*Milton*, 15).[1] Bishop Butler liked to argue that disinterested actions were not necessarily virtuous and that, conversely, interested actions were not necessarily wicked; an action is interested if its *telos*, or end, lies outside the agent. Thus Iago in Shakespeare's *Othello* may delight in cruelty even when, as we say, there is nothing in it for him. The pain of the other person is valued in itself. Iago is therefore disinterestedly malicious. Meanwhile the person who is actuated by motives of self-improvement may behave in a genuinely virtuous manner.[84]

By this analysis it begins to look as if my word, "introverted," was after all entirely in order. In this earlier passage Pattison carefully distinguishes an objective, disinterested regard for truth from developing the mind of the subject, and prefers the latter. It is a revealing passage. There are points in the *Memoirs* when he can pause in his track of habitual self-contempt and turn, for the moment, oddly cheerful. These moments occur, not when he considers a reform successfully achieved or a book completed, but when he notes that his own mind was growing.[85] Very near the end he says how foolish he was in his youth to think publication important. The mere *living* at the higher level is enough. But by the end of his study of Milton, the towering example set by the poet, with his evident, public achievement, moves him to revise the picture, to direct us back to extra-personal realities, in a reconciling sentence: "He cultivated not letters but himself, and sought to enter into possession of his own mental kingdom, not that he might reign there, but that he might royally use its resources in building up a work, which should bring honour to his country and his native tongue" (*Milton*, 211). In both places Pattison is writing simultaneously about Milton (openly) and himself (covertly), but there is a difference. In the first Pattison subsumes Milton; in the second Milton is taking over. The very cadence of the later sentence is Miltonic. We think of the famous words in *The Reason of Church Government* where the poet speaks of the great Italian academies and then of the inward prompting to undertake a great work, that "I might perhaps leave something so written to aftertimes, as they should not willingly let it die" — all this seen as tending to the "honour" of his country.[86]

Pattison is pretty consistently clear that settling "*Hoti's* business" and "properly basing *Oun*," the gritty linguistic detail which for many constitutes the heart of disinterested learning, properly understood, is no fit object of admiration. We saw earlier how he mildly disparaged Milton's learning, remarking that his reading, though extensive and industrious, was "select" (*Milton*, 210), and affirmed that Milton's antagonist, Salmasius, was meanwhile truly learned (it is incidentally true that Salmasius, or Claude de Saumaise, discovered and did crucial work on the Palatine Anthology). But then Pattison writes, "If anyone thinks classical studies of themselves cultivate the taste and the sentiments, let him look at Salmasius's *Responsio*" and backs his point with an appalling passage in which Salmasius makes fun of Milton's blindness (*Milton*, 108). We may remember now that in the world of university politics Pattison was a surprisingly "enlightened" figure, anxious to promote the study of science in Oxford even at the expense of classics: he writes, "Even more astonishing . . . was the blindness in which we still lived as to the claims of science in the world of knowledge, and our naïve assumption that classical learning was a complete equipment for a great university" (*Memoirs*, 306).

Thus it should be no surprise that Pattison should cast the admired Milton in the role of Ladislaw, not Mr. Casaubon. He recounts Milton's engagement, in *The Reason of Church Government*, with James Ussher, archbishop of Armagh, as the story of an encounter in which aged learning was easily overthrown by youthful smartness (*Milton*, 76). When he describes his own early relationship with Newman,

Pattison writes, "I had too little knowledge to see how limited his philosophical acquirements were. . . . A. P. Stanley once said to me "How different the fortunes of the Church of England might have been if Newman had been able to read German. . . . All the grand development of human reason, from Aristotle down, was a closed book to him" (*Memoirs*, 210). It is as if Pattison missed his moment to be Ladislaw, to explain the living intellectual imperative of the times, manifest to the alertly discerning, invisible to the hidebound: "Read the Germans!"

German learning, German historiography were in the air. It was a mark of cultural awareness to refer to them. One remembers how, in the heyday of logical positivism in the first half of the twentieth century, the question to ask, in a suitably challenging manner, was "Have you read Carnap?" V. H. H. Green quotes from an essay by Pusey the words "A thoughtful German mentions among the causes of the destruction of belief in Germany, the misapplication of the principles of Heyne on Greek mythology to Holy Scripture."[87] This comes from a central pillar of the Oxford Movement! German incredulity is indeed censured, but, notice, it takes a German to demonstrate the fact. Pattison publishes his essay "The Present State of Theology in Germany" in the *Westminster Review* in 1857. In this piece he is, perhaps surprisingly, contemptuous of Voltaire's wittily sceptical "Dictionary."[88] One suspects a cluster of reasons for this. Voltaire is too openly derisive of established religion to be safely used in the 1850s. More importantly, perhaps, he is French, and flippant. The Germans are the serious ones.

Later we are told about Mosheim's "colossal capacity for details."[89] Johann Mosheim, author of the gigantic *Ecclesiastical History* still useful for its sheer range of information, is, notice, an essentially narrative work, telling the story of Christianity, not examining its philosophic credentials. Pattison's natural temper shows itself from time to time. When he considers the Christology presented in German "Meditation Theology" he finds it vacuously metaphysical, at this point swiftly anticipating, seemingly without effort, most of the objections to metaphysics that were to make the name of A. J. Ayer when he presented them in the twentieth century.[90] Pattison says of the German Pietists who attacked Friedrich Schleiermacher,

"It is ideology; a theology of rhetoric, not of facts."[91] It is interesting to see Pattison using Napoleon's half-contemptuous word "ideology" as early as 1857. Karl Marx and Friedrich Engels had already written *The German Ideology* in 1845–46, but it was not to be published until 1932.

Richard Rothe's *Theologische Ethik* (1845) is gently handled by Pattison. Rothe's notion of redemption working within human beings, enabling man through "a unity of self-consciousness and self-activity" and through loss and suffering, to attain full moral development, thus undoing the sin of Adam — this notion is ripe for sceptical demolition. One thinks of what F. H. Bradley did to Matthew Arnold's not dissimilar doctrine of "the enduring power, not ourselves that makes for righteousness."[92] But Rothe was influenced, Pattison says, by Schleiermacher,[93] and Schleiermacher as have already seen, was attacked by the Pietists; anyone detested by the Pietists cannot be all bad. Pattison also shrewdly notes the influence of Hegel. Indeed the bizarre notion of a supra-personal process of learning is immediately reminiscent of Hegel's idea of the Absolute thinking itself in history, memorably caricatured by Bertrand Russell as the Universe gradually learning Hegel's philosophy.[94] But Pattison holds back. When he comes to comment on Rothe he avoids fundamental philosophical analysis and confines himself to a sharp, schoolmasterish distillation of the general character of Rothe's mind: "Seemingly intent on its own work, it is unconsciously labouring to comprehend as much of existing opinion as it can. With all its appearance of vigorous logic, it has a side-eye for the received dogmatic forms. Conscious of not having the right to compel assent, it would insinuate itself."[95] Nevertheless there may be a latent sting, a fully philosophical argument lurking in Pattison's words. In this brief sketch the Absolute, slowly comprehending itself, or God, undoing the fallen nature of man, together shrink to an ordinary, historically located human mind, eagerly assimilating the vacuous requirements of pious fashion.

Pattison's talent — he must have known this — is for the succinct, damaging comment, written as it might be at the end of a student's essay, in the days before there was any pressure on teachers to make such comments "upbeat." Fundamental conceptual analysis is something he instinctively avoids. When he notes that his hero, Joseph

Scaliger, was less interested in Plato and Aristotle than Scaliger Senior had been, he seems implicitly to be smiling approval at the defection.[96] In the essay on Montaigne he wrote for the *Quarterly Review* in 1858 he states firmly, "We shall confine our remarks to Montaigne's life. We are not going to re-dissect the *Essais*."[97] Things are to be understood by being placed in time, by being narrated. Thus, in the long run, history not philosophy will prove to be the more powerful agent of criticism.

To encapsulate the idea, Pattison speaks of the "historico-critical school."[98] Here he gives a high place to Ferdinand Christian Baur, author of *Symbolik und Mythologie* (1824). This book is far better, Pattison tells us, than the more famous (later) *Leben Jesu* of David Friedrich Strauss (1835–36). Yet if Baur has a fault in Pattison's eyes it is precisely that he, within his history, gives undue importance to the part played by thought in the development of doctrine: "the law of development of thought has become in his hands the master-key of the history of doctrine."[99] Note here the appearance of the word "key," which will be so important in *Middlemarch* ("The Key to All Mythologies"). The sentence in isolation could be taken for praise. In context it is clear that Pattison thinks he is pointing to a weakness. Once more, by this minor assertion of scepticism he falls on Ladislaw's side. To question the idea of a Key to All is to be against Mr. Casaubon rather than to be implicitly identical with him.

But the dried-up life and the great work unwritten continue to unite them. The completed *Isaac Casaubon* can never have been in Pattison's mind an adequate substitute for the *Joseph Scaliger* he was never to carry through. In effect he was scooped by Jacob Bernays. Bernays's work turned Pattison from the man who would write the great book on Scaliger into the man who reviewed Bernays. His critical notice in the *Quarterly Review* for July 1860, is indeed a long, admirable essay, full of a life and acuity of its own. [100] Henry Nettleship printed surviving fragments from Pattison's own projected book in the *Essays*.[101] It is clear that Pattison continued to preserve his dream after Bernays's book had appeared. But one senses that, really, it is all over. Pattison's only course would have been to challenge Bernays in some fundamental way. As it is, the two references to Bernays are both deferential. [102]

Pattison delights[103] in Scaliger's free, vigorous Latinity, which can look sloppy to linguistic purists, rejoices in the great scholar's openness to the unclassical, whether in the form of monkish Latin or border ballads, here anticipating classical Joseph Addison, who surprised everyone in the early eighteenth century by praising Chevy Chase, "the favourite ballad of the common people of England," at the expense of the polished Augustanism of the Town.[104] Pattison is also attracted by Scaliger's largeness of mind and at the same time, as we should by this time be able to predict, by his commitment to undogmatic, historical understanding: "It was a cherished principle of Protestant exegesis not to bring any secular knowledge to the interpretation of Holy Scripture. Scaliger was the first to perceive that the history of the ancient world, so far as it could be known at all, could only be known as a whole."[105] Pattison, who is ready to scorn the notion of a "key" to understanding, unhesitatingly admires the drive to attain exhaustive knowledge. Like Browning's grammarian, he would "know all" (l. 61) — or, at least, praise those who came nearest to doing so.

The modern reader may feel that there is something crazy in Scaliger's plan to restore the original Greek of Eusebius of Caesarea (Eusebius survived only in Jerome's Latin; Scaliger thought he could arrive at the Greek by deleting the places where Jerome was likely to have introduced changes). Anthony Grafton points out that Scaliger's fascination with the idea of reconstructing lost literary works began early.[106] My friend Stephen Medcalf used to dream that all English literature was lost and that he, Medcalf, was entrusted with the task of reconstructing the entire corpus, using the quotations in *The Oxford English Dictionary*, plus his own memory. Of course Scaliger later found, in Paris, a manuscript containing Syncellus's transcription of Eusebius's Greek, and shortly after that the entire Eusebian chronicle turned up in an Armenian version. These discoveries showed that Scaliger had been absolutely right in his daring hypothesis that there had been, originally, two books and that Jerome had translated the second only.[107] What appears at first to be a wholly unrealistic scheme to restore a text on an insufficient evidentiary basis proved in the event to have provided a stiff, salutary training in scholarship. Pattison, the former adherent of Newman, rejoices to see Scaliger welcomed and respected in Protestant Holland and to see him confounding the Jesuit interpretation of history.[108] For once, Pattison's writing is artlessly dazed. Hero worship has taken over. The final sentence reads, "The most richly stored intellect which ever spent itself in acquiring knowledge was in the presence of the omniscient." He means, "Scaliger was dead." This pious grandiosity is not what the moment required. Pattison should have known better.

3

Isaac Casaubon

The Real Thing

An Almost Silent Life

So Pattison wrote, instead, about Casaubon. The reader should not jump to the conclusion that Pattison found after all, *per accidens*, the proper subject for the planned great work. In the event he did not do for Casaubon what Jacob Bernays had done for Scaliger. *Isaac Casaubon* is not a monument of exhaustive historical scholarship.[1] But it is, for all that, a very fine book, with a lot of hard reading behind it, written, as everything by Pattison is written, with that special sombre elegance of which he was master. Even today there is no better single study of Casaubon available. We at the beginning of the twenty-first century must still see Isaac Casaubon through the eyes of the rector of Lincoln. If Ovid is the poets' poet, Casaubon is the scholars' scholar. Those in the trade know how good he is. Today most informed persons asked to name the greatest scholar of the early modern period would say, "Scaliger." Joseph Scaliger himself thought otherwise. After genially condemning Casaubon's vile Greek script, he suddenly offers a judgement: Casaubon is "le plus grand homme que nous ayons en Grec. Je luy cède; est doctissimus omnium qui nunc vivunt."[2] Scaliger's French is strongly worded but still guarded: "Casaubon is the greatest man we have in the field of Greek; I yield to him," but then as he passes into Latin the praise is absolute: "He [is the] most learned man alive today."

Casaubon's interior life was a vast, labyrinthine journey, through a world of books. The word "labyrinth" is important in *Middlemarch*. But while Mr. Casaubon was lost and wretched in his labyrinth, Isaac Casaubon was happy in his. The external life, by contrast, is fairly simple and can be given in a short space. Casaubon was born in 1559 of Huguenot stock. His father, Arnaud Casaubon, was at one time forced to flee from his native Gascony because he was in danger of being burned as a heretic. In 1572 the news of the Saint Bartholomew Massacre drove the family to hide in the hills, where they sheltered in a cave; and the father and son soldiered on with their Greek reading. Isaac Casaubon grew up in the Dauphiné. His father was his sole teacher until he was nineteen. This may remind us of Mark Pattison, whose father "read Aldrich" with him. For Pattison the memory provided ammunition for a cold disparagement of the intellect of the father who had tried to teach him. There is no such retrospective coldness in Isaac Casaubon. In 1578 he was sent as a student to Geneva, where he became professor in 1582. In 1583 he married Marie Prolyot, a surgeon's daughter, who died two years after her marriage, having borne him a daughter. In 1586 Casaubon's father died. Famously he breaks off in the middle of a note on Strabo, leaving the scholarly difficulty unresolved: "I have neither time nor spirit for the discussion of such things. My mind, overwhelmed by the intelligence it has just received, has no more taste for these classical studies." Strangely, all this survives in the printed commentary on Strabo.[3] Learned Latin works of the early modern period present a general appearance of frosty inhumanity. But, in fact, just as Milton could provide the sincere grief Johnson complained was missing from *Lycidas* in his Latin *Epitaphium Damonis*, so the Latin of Casaubon turns out to be a startlingly human, subtle, immediately responsive medium. There is a foretaste here of the extraordinarily immediate expression of emotion we shall find later in the *Ephemerides*, the Latin diary Casaubon began in 1597 and kept up to within two weeks of his death. Two months after his father died, Casaubon married his second wife, Florence Estienne, the daughter of Henri Estienne (that is, Stephanus, the editor of the great Thesaurus). Pattison suggests (*IC*, 29) that Casaubon fell in love with the father's manuscript collection before he paid court to the daughter. Whether this is so or not, it soon appeared that Casaubon could expect nothing from his new father-in-law. He was denied access to Estienne's library. Estienne was in financial difficulties, so there was no dowry (the young couple began their married life on a minute income), and relations grew still worse when Casaubon had the temerity to provide notes for an edition of Theocritus that had appeared in competition with Estienne's edition. But the marriage itself was profoundly happy.

In 1598 Casaubon moved from Geneva to Montpellier. Two years later he made his first visit to Paris and discovered the extent of the historian Jacques-Auguste de Thou's library. At first his heart sank — there they were too many books to read — but at the same time it was a thrilling sight. In 1599 he was invited by the king, Henri IV, to assist in the work of restoring the University of Paris, in a state of near ruin at this date because of the religious wars. Casaubon, who was sad at leaving Montpellier, and was perhaps half-aware that in moving within the direct sphere of the king he was in danger of compromising his own Protestantism, nevertheless accepted the invitation. It looks as if the sight of all those books was enough to hook the fish. The passage from Montpellier to Paris took a full year, as it turned out, partly because Casaubon turned aside to oversee the printing of his *Animadversiones* ("Comments") on Athenaeus, partly perhaps for more shadowy reasons: there may have been attempts to persuade Casaubon during this time to go over to Rome and there is some reason to suppose that he may actually have wavered for a while. When he finally reached Paris, the religious difficulty became evident.

Philippe de Mornay, seigneur du Plessis-Marly, the friend of Sir Philip Sidney, was in some ways the ideal nobleman, a statesman and a scholar with, in addition, charm — or perhaps one should say, more directly, lovableness, which one can still sense in him, across the intervening centuries. Duplessis-Mornay had been unswervingly loyal to his king, yet he had at the same time become a Protestant and had written a book, *De l'Eucharistie* (La Rochelle, 1598), which was critical of the Roman Catholic tradition. Henri IV himself had been a Protestant until 1593, when political pressure virtually forced him to abjure. It appears that Duplessis-Mornay continued to hope that the king would work within the system to safeguard Protestants. Indeed it might be said that Henri's Edict of Nantes in due course did exactly this, to a strictly limited extent. But on this occasion the effect of the royal intervention (whatever the intention) was to exacerbate religious differences. A tumultuous dispute followed Duplessis-Mornay's publication of his book, which finally gathered to a head. The king insisted upon a formal debate, to be held at Fontainebleau. Six commissaries, four Roman Catholic, two Protestant, were to adjudicate. Casaubon was called upon to serve as one of the Protestant adjudicators (the other, Canaye de Fresne, was a cipher — known to be seeking in any case a reason for converting to Rome). The terms of the debate were carefully restricted by the Catholic party to the accuracy or otherwise of Duplessis-Mornay's citations. The actual argument of the book was set aside. Today this looks like a confession of defeat before the argument begins, but this seems not to have been generally noticed at the time. Jacques Davy Du Perron, bishop of Evreux, Duplessis-Mornay's principal opponent, simply wished to win, and believed he could win on this point. In the end, the debate turned on only nineteen erroneous passages out of the five hundred Du Perron said he had discovered, and these, since in some cases Duplessis-Mornay had paraphrased his sources, were ambiguous. But the adjudication went against Duplessis-Mornay. Casaubon voted with the Catholics.

Doubtless he would have been vividly aware of his obligation to his new employers, but there is no need to suppose that he compromised on a matter of scholarly judgement. It may well be that he would have sympathised with Duplessis-Mornay's argument, but on that he was never asked to pronounce. With regard to the citations, if Casaubon applied to Duplessis-Mornay the rigour he applied to his own work, he would indeed discover error and imprecision. One can see why he voted — why in a way, by his own lights, he had to vote — as he did. But of course he knew that this small-scale truthfulness enforced a much larger lie. He, the most trusted intelligence in France, had told the world that Duplessis-Mornay had written a bad book. In his *Ephemerides* he begins to tell the story of the conference and then breaks off, as if flinching from the very thought.[4] Scaliger, aghast, would say nothing until he had heard Casaubon's own account. On 16 September 1600 Casaubon sent him a stilted, minimal narrative. Thereafter, while this great friendship of scholars continues, Scaliger says nothing at all to Casaubon about Fontainebleau. Once he was drawn in, whatever Casaubon did would have been ferociously criticised. One can easily see why he agreed to serve. His new boss, de Thou, urged him to do so. He was professionally well fitted for the task. But, as Scaliger observed afterwards, he should have stayed out.[5]

There were more difficulties. Casaubon could not become professor because he was not a Roman Catholic. Instead the post went to a notably unlearned twenty-two-year-old, one Jerome Goulu, a protégé of Du Perron, now a cardinal. Casaubon bore the title "lecteur du roi," "the king's reader," a designation that simultaneously marks his exclusion from the professorship which was his by right and yet includes him, still, within the king's party. In 1604 he was appointed sub-librarian, under de Thou (whose Latin name is Thuanus). De Thou is remarkable — one cannot say is remembered — chiefly for his astounding work, the *History of His Own Time*. The old joke about the schoolboy who wrote in a review, "This book tells me more than I wish to know about this subject," here finds its proper application. We are supposed to be grateful when historians tell us more rather than less about a given matter, but this, in the words of Groucho Marx, is ridiculous. The work's virtue is its vice. The history covers sixty-four years. Pattison writes, "It has been calculated that de Thou's folios would require twelve months at four hours a day for their perusal" (*IC*, 66). Those who know Bernard Wilson's English translation of de Thou (London: Samuel Buckley, 1733) may be surprised by this, since the English fills only two (very large) folio volumes. But Wilson was in fact defeated by the extent of the work before him, as Napoleon and Hitler were defeated by the sheer extent of Russia. Wilson got as far as the end of de Thou's twenty-sixth book. That leaves a hundred and twelve still to be translated. Clio, the Muse of History, indeed delights in irony. The world has forgotten de Thou because it cannot face the labour of reading him. De Thou himself contrariwise supposed that his work might be too exciting. In his preface addressed to Henri IV he says he was not unaware that his history would expose him to attack, and he displays an epigraph from Lucian, which says that history must be fearless and call a spade a spade (literally "call a tub a tub"). In fact, de Thou's preface was less foolish than it now appears; there were some attacks, such as Io. Bapt. Gallus's *Vanissima Historia Thuani* ("Vacuous History of Thuanus"), which the reader can find set out in the seventh volume. Statesmen all over Europe consulted it, before oblivion engulfed it. In 1600 de Thou had plenty of clout.

Once inside de Thou's library, Casaubon did what Pattison said no librarian should do: he began to read the books. The ambiguity of his position and its attendant anxieties were at once eclipsed by the joy of reading. J. E. Sandys describes his time in Paris as "the happiest period of his life."[6] In 1610 Henri IV was assassinated, and the Ultramontane party became powerful. Ultramontanists believed that power should be centralised, in Rome, as distinct from Gallicans (such as Casaubon's friend Pierre Pithou, who argued for a degree of independence to be enjoyed by the kings and bishops of France). Once more Casaubon was pressed to become a Roman Catholic. It seems that his mind was not the sort which stiffens under an attempt at persuasion. On the contrary, he saw great force in some arguments and none in others. But—and this is itself clear evidence that if he was "timid and wavering,"[7] he was always, still more, principled—he did not "convert." Instead, to his troubled intelligence, the *via media* of Anglicanism began to look more and more attractive. Therefore, when Archbishop Richard Bancroft invited him to England, Casaubon went. He was welcomed by James I, given a prebendal stall at Canterbury and a pension of three hundred pounds a year. Once in England Casaubon became friends with Lancelot Andrewes and was frequently called upon for conversations with the king, who liked bookish talk. There is no doubt that these conversations became burdensome, as Casaubon was dragged out every

Sunday to one hunting seat after another, but they were burdensome only because they interrupted his scholarly labours. Everything — even the society of well-loved friends — which kept Casaubon from his study exasperated him. The conversations in themselves he obviously greatly enjoyed. The king, who lives in our imagination today (principally because of the "Secret History" of Walter Scott) as a grotesque figure, uncouth of speech, unclean of person, and sexually bizarre, was a genuinely deeply read man, quite unlike the smiling upper-class barbarian who had ruled France. Casaubon wrote to de Thou, soon after his arrival in England, "The Sun sees nothing more cultivated [*humanius* in Casaubon's Latin], nothing kindlier, nothing which has a greater love of scholarship [*literarum*] and all virtue than this Prince."[8] There is no reason to doubt the sincerity of this, written as it is not to procure favour but simply to describe his situation, to an uninvolved friend. Some three years later his opinion had not changed. He writes that the king is much better educated than people suppose. "His love of learning is beyond belief; he makes judgements on works both old and more recent, more in the manner of a supremely learned scholar than of a most powerful prince."[9]

We may catch here a note of surprise, even after years spent in the king's company. We should not suppose that Casaubon's talk with James was mere literary chit-chat. Before he left France it was already evident that Casaubon was uncomfortable with the intolerant views of his more extreme co-religionists. Strong Calvinists were happy to describe the pope as "Antichrist," believed that human nature was "totally depraved," that is that we can do nothing of ourselves but sin, and that all human beings are predestined from before birth either to salvation or damnation. That such doctrines preserve the majesty of God at the cost of his goodness is fairly obvious, but this was a thought which, at the end of the sixteenth century and at the beginning of the seventeenth, one hardly dared to articulate, even in the privacy of one's own mind. One must remember that those in whom such notions might have begun to rise were not atheists. They thought that the predestinarian God was actually *there*, and had access to their thoughts. But the Arminian idea that human beings might be free to do either good or evil, the idea that restores a vivid moral life to God's creatures, was a little easier to entertain. In

James, Casaubon found a friend who was like-minded, both theologically and politically. It appears that, before the French scholar reached England the king had been reading his *De libertate ecclesiastica*. This elegant, tolerant little book appeared on 1607. It is a highly Casaubonian mixture of shyness and courage. The work is anonymous; no publisher's name is given, no place of publication (the Bodleian Library catalogue conjectures, "Paris?" the British Library, "Venice?"). The table of contents printed at the beginning promises a tenth chapter on the errors of Baronius's polemically Roman Catholic *Annales* — a work to which we shall come in due course — but we never reach the tenth chapter. The book breaks off in midstream. On the last page in the Bodleian copy a handwritten note reads, "Hoc opus inceptum iussu quorundam Principum Virorum imperfectum mansit iussu Henrici IV," "This work, begun on the orders of certain high-ranking persons, remained uncompleted, by order of Henri IV." The sentence nervously refers to powerful friends before acknowledging the greater power of the king of France. But the text as we have it nevertheless contains telling criticisms of Baronius (12, 256 f.). James rightly thought that he for his part had found in Casaubon a powerful ally in the great enterprise of healing the divisions that rent Christian Europe. Certainly James embroiled Casaubon in controversy. One senses that he really knew how to use the great engine of Casaubon's learning — something the French had never mastered. When Fronton du Duc ("Fronto Ducaeus") wrote a defence of the Jesuits and desired his old friend Casaubon to show it to James, the king's reaction turned out to be far from eirenic. He was incensed at the degree of temporal power given by Fronton to the pope and at once persuaded Casaubon to write a reply.[10] Casaubon, at bottom, agreed with James and disagreed with his old friend. He writes, therefore, gently and courteously but uncompromisingly. Casaubon also published, while he was in England, a reply to Cardinal Du Perron. Du Perron had argued that the distinctiveness of the Roman Catholic Church consisted in the mere fact of the communion of the members, within that church. For James, communion was itself, precisely, the problem. Du Perron's stance was in the circumstances absurdly pre-emptive: "It is because it is." Casaubon's reply to Du Perron, which was swiftly translated from Latin into

English,[11] was entirely in the spirit of James. The overarching motive, in both Casaubon and the king, was ecumenical. Casaubon expected this northern king to be a figure of benighted ignorance, just as we expect (from our own strongly conditioned perspective) the great European scholar to be contemptuous of the Scottish eccentric. But that is not what happened. Pattison, as we shall see, labours to assimilate Casaubon to his own personality, which means that he plays up the depressive elements and plays down the capacity for enjoyment.[12]

In fact Casaubon was not surprised by the king only; he was also agreeably surprised by England. He wrote in 1612 to his friend Claude de Saumaise, "The people are anything but barbarous"[12] and earlier to Daniel Heinsius, a pupil of the great Scaliger, that England was *makarōn nēson*, "the island of the blessed."[14] Casaubon was entertained in Cambridge and Oxford. These visits clearly delighted him. But while he was in England the task of rebutting the *Annals* of Baronius, a massive exercise in Orthodox Catholic historiography, fell to Casaubon. So his life in England, like his life before, was filled with unremitting toil. It is not unlikely that the unfinished labour of refutation killed him. Casaubon, notice (1559–1614), is an almost exact contemporary of Shakespeare (1564–1616). I do not know if they ever met, but it is most unlikely. There is no sign in the *Ephemerides* that Casaubon ever went to see a play in England. He arrived in 1610 when Shakespeare was withdrawing from active participation. Thus, he could have seen the greatest drama of post-classical times in its first, fresh presentation. Presumably it never occurred to him to go to so low, so godless an entertainment. Also, ironically, Casaubon, the profound reader of Aeschylus, was simply not equipped linguistically for Shakespeare; he could not have followed the dialogue.

Casaubon, a small, physically weak man, was afflicted in his time in England, by a hacking cough (*"tussis* attacked him," as it attacked Browning's Grammarian). At the same time, *calculus* racked him — or, at least, he exhibited symptoms normally associated with the stone, and remedies then thought applicable to renal disorders was applied. He experienced panic attacks. He wrote in his *Ephemerides* that he felt an onset of anxiety in St. Paul's Cathedral during a sudden thunderstorm.[15] Oddly, Lancelot Andrewes had told Casaubon of an occasion in Wells Cathedral about fifteen years earlier when various persons found crosses marked on their bodies, after a storm. Andrewes was told the story by the bishop of Bath and Wells. It is all strangely vivid even at this distance in time: the bishop's wife, first, tells her husband and is met with a sceptical laugh from her husband; he then finds the marks on his own body and discovers that others have been similarly affected.[16] Perhaps it stuck in Casaubon's imagination, for all the rational scepticism he expressed on hearing the story.

"Then mark what ills the scholar's life assail," wrote Johnson in *The Vanity of Human Wishes* (l. 159), and we sense at once that the writer, even as he pities the scholar, is beginning to enjoy himself, if only because he has struck a rich literary vein. *"Grammaticus non est foelix,* 'The grammarian is not a happy man,' " writes Burton, perhaps lifting the phrase from Haedus.[17] Burton, still more than Johnson, delights in listing the ills, in building a Rabelaisian inventory of the woes of *grammatici,* getting especially rich results when he comes to the medical details. We have good information about Casaubon's bodily condition at the last and it is certainly grotesque. Indeed it is so grotesque that it can be easily figure as comic writing, centuries later. For example, in our own time Nicholson Baker, in the middle of a hilarious account of his dream of becoming an authority on the comma (Browning's Grammarian, it will be recalled, had "settled *Hoti*'s business and properly based *Oun,*" was an authority, that is to say, on particles and similar linguistic minutiae), Baker suddenly conjures from the past the figure of the terminally ill Casaubon:

In 1614, even as he was dying of the strain of years of "unintermitted study" and of complications of a congenitally formed dual bladder, which, like a bag pipe, boasted (so the post mortem revealed) a secondary storage area in which painful calculi formed amidst a general purulence, in part caused by his chronic "inattention to the calls of nature, while the mind of the student was engaged in study and contemplation" (as Mark Pattison, his nineteenth century biographer, tactfully has it) and which calculi became when I read about them the emblems of learnedness without sufficient issue, knowledge that wasn't whizzed out but retained to the point of internal damage within the knower—this man, even as his bladder's expanding side-car was killing him, worked harder than ever on his ambitious (so I'd heard) refutation of the *Annales Ecclesiastici* of Baronius.[18]

One curiosity of Nicholas Baker's version is his observation that Casaubon, amazingly, "had found time to raise, or at least father a child."[19] It looks as if the myth of the anti-sexual scholar, "dead from the waist down," has invaded. Casaubon had nineteen children (poor Mme Casaubon actually endured twenty-two confinements). Not all of these of course survived. Meric Casaubon, the good son (unlike his faithless brother John, who greatly distressed his father by first stealing from him and then going over to the church of Rome), describes how, at the last, Isaac Casaubon gave his blessing to each of his children in turn. Pattison's death, amid the improved medicine of the nineteenth century, was, as it turned out, far worse. He died, screaming in agony, from cancer of the stomach.[20]

Pattison tells the story of Casaubon's last days at a slower, non-comic tempo. He explains how Casaubon's friends, alarmed by his deterioration, tried to persuade him to take a break. As last he agreed to a coach trip. In the event, the jolting he experienced on this journey (though he felt oddly well for a brief space, before the final phase began) seems to have precipitated a renal attack. Casaubon passed the night after the trip to Greenwich "voiding blood, calculi and purulent urine" (*IC*, 468). Even today medical textbooks coolly describe the agony of kidney stones as "the worst pain known to man." Casaubon, like Shakespeare's Mercutio, could manage a joke, in the intervals of his distress: "I am, like Theophrastus, dying of a holiday. When Theophrastus had passed his hundredth year he went to his nephew's wedding, and gave up a day's study to do it. But he never studied more, he died of it."[21] There is a streak of very likeable self-parody in this. Casaubon must have been conscious of the obsession with time, with the avoidance of any interruption of his studies, which runs through his diaries from the beginning to the end. Here, as it kills him, he sees the funny side. After his death they opened him up and found "a monstrous malformation of the vesica. The bladder itself was of natural size and healthy. But an opening in its left side admitted into a second, or supplementary bladder. This sack was at least six times as large as the natural bladder, and was full of mucous calculous matter" (*IC,* 469).

We may ask of Casaubon the question we asked of Browning's Grammarian: What did he do? In 1583 he published notes on Diogenes Laertius, the highly entertaining, gossipy biographer of philosophers, eccentrics, and bad poets; then in 1584 Casaubon contributed notes to an edition of a great poet, Theocritus. In 1587 he produced his commentary on the ancient geographer Strabo, who lived from 64 or 63 B.C. to A.D. 21, or later. In the same year he published work on the New Testament. The year 1588 saw his "Animadversiones" on Dionysius of Halicarnassus, the ancient literary critic who lived and taught at Rome about the time of the birth of Christ. In 1589 he produced his important *editio princeps* of Polyaenus, the Macedonian rhetorician of the second century a.d. who compiled the work known as "Stratagems," a collection of supposedly instructive more or less historical examples, indiscriminately gathered. In 1590 he published an edition of the whole of Aristotle with an accompanying Latin translation (this sounds impressive, but here the editorial input was in fact minimal). In 1591 we have nothing from him except a few corrections and explanations contributed to a reprint of Henri Estienne's edition of Pliny. Then, in 1592, Casaubon published his brilliant commentary on the *Characters* of Theophrastus. This ground-breaking work established that, among other things, the number of "characters" treated should be raised from twenty-three to twenty-eight (Casaubon had found five more in the library at Heidelberg). The following three years saw further contributions on Diogenes Laertius (who wrote the lives of the twelve caesars), and Theocritus. This may look like a thin output for three years, but it should be noted that Casaubon's comments on Suetonius were in fact continuously reprinted, so solidly useful were they, until 1736. In 1597 he published his text of Athenaeus's *Deipnosophists.*

Athenaeus lived in Egypt in the second or third century A.D.. The *Deipnosophists* is a cross between a treatise on cookery and a literary symposium. Its author cites about 1,250 authors, supplies titles of more than a thousand plays and more than ten thousand lines of verse. This may give an impression of glittering richness — an ancient equivalent of Thomas Love Peacock and Izaak Walton rolled into one. The snag is that Athenaeus is destitute of intelligence. This, nevertheless, was to be Casaubon's major scholarly undertaking (a commentary followed the text, in 1600). Though it may seem preposterous that a mind as good as Casaubon's should be applied for so long to a mind as bad as that of Athenaeus, it remains true that the manic allusiveness of the ancient proved an admirable instrument for provoking an explosion of general linguistic and cultural research among the commentators. Like Mark Pattison so many years later, Casaubon "would not be beat." In 1603 he published a collection of biographies of Roman emperors to which he gave the title *Historia Augusta*, "The Augustan History," a designation that has held ever since, though the precise nature of the contents has become a matter of fierce scholarly dispute. In 1604 and 1605 he was thrown into working on Christian materials; he contributes a "diatriba" of about a hundred pages to an edition of Chrysostom and supplies information on Gregorius Thaumaturgus, "Gregory the Wonder-worker," the panegyrist of Origen, for an edition of Origen. Meanwhile he kept his hand in by simultaneously publishing scholarly work on Persius the Roman satirist and on Greek and Roman satire more generally. His edition of the History of Polybius (second century B.C.) followed in 1609. His last years, as we have seen, were taken up with his controversy with the Roman Catholic historian Baronius (Cesare Baronio). A single volume of Casaubon's reply was published in 1614, the year of his death. This was the work in which, *en passant*, Casaubon demonstrated the late date of the *Hermetica*.

Thus summarised, it may well be that "what Casaubon did" may instantly evaporate in the modern reader's mind. Setting aside for a moment the redating of . . . the *Hermetica*, there is no world-transforming "thesis" or line of argument to fasten on. What is there is a cumulative, complex simultaneous assault on a vast range of problems (linguistic, historical), each, taken separately, minute, yet as a whole — because of the quality of the work of the explainer — of incalculable historical and cultural importance. If "truth" is construed not as some underlying Platonic formula but as indefinitely, incorrigibly plural, the real merit of Casaubon is suddenly apparent. He appears, in this century torn by grand theological disputes, by myth-making and myth-breaking, as the quiet truth-teller among the clamorous liars.

Pattison sees and responds to this. His description of the encounter, in Oxford, of Sir Henry Savile, the warden of Merton College, with the French scholar has become famous: "Casaubon, insignificant in presence, the most humble of men, but intensely real, knowing what he knew with fatal accuracy, and keeping his utterance below his knowledge. Sir Henry, the munificent patron of learning, and devoting his fortune to its promotion, with a fine presence, polished manners and courtly speech" (*IC,* 399). The phrase "fatal accuracy" suggests an unregenerate interest, on Pattison's side, in adversarial prowess — one may compare Boswell's interest in the gladiatorial side of Johnson — an interest Casaubon himself would not have immediately understood, but the linguistically curious use of "real" (anticipating the American idiom, "real" for "realistic," but not identical therewith) marks Pattison's recognition of the fact that truth lies at the centre of Casaubon's personality. The picture is very sharp and is likely to be accurate. At the same time it is coloured, perhaps, by Pattison's memory of interesting moments of awkwardness in his own life, encounters between the austere, unloved, genuine intellectual on one side and the smooth, grand figure on the other. Pattison conceived himself to be unattractive (there is real modesty here), but Pattison's self-identification with Casaubon is not based solely on the presumption of a shared social insignificance; there is a simultaneous presumption of a shared quality of mind, and this, if it is not simple wish-fulfilment — dreaming — implies a substratum of sheer pride in Pattison. Pattison is interested, first and foremost, in the idea of a life devoted to study, but he is also keenly interested in the social context of this life, in the way the life must have felt — tasted — then. This combination of perspectives makes his book a more vivid experience for the reader than one might have expected.

The attention to social detail shows early in the book. Pattison explains how, when Casaubon became professor of Greek at Geneva, the institution he joined was tiny. At the same time, however, the atmosphere there was intense. The academy at Geneva comprised a grammar school and the university. Calvin had been a founding spirit and had taught there; although both Papists and Lutherans were admitted as students after 1576, no dissident, not even a Lutheran, could actually teach at Geneva. This held until 1796. The number of students in the university, a hundred and sixty or even fewer (*IC*, 9, 13, 14), stands in vivid contrast with the University of Paris, which was enormous, quite as large as a large university today, having, until it was depleted by the religious wars and the founding of rival educational institutions in other parts of the country, about eleven thousand students.[22] The pay for professors at Geneva was very low (*IC*, 17–18). In summer work began at six o'clock, in winter at seven. The boys (boys, indeed, rather than men) brought their breakfasts in with them. The windows were unglazed in 1564. In November of that year, however, a master in the grammar school asked for the windows to be glazed and the authorities said, in reply, that the boys could be allowed to paste paper over the windows next to their seats. A charcoal brazier, in each classroom, allowed hands to be warmed (so that they could write! *IC*, 14). With such detail the supposedly deathly Pattison brings the world of Casaubon to life. It is not difficult to imagine the large, dark room on a winter morning, at least for those of us whose memories include crowding round the coke stove at school before being dispersed to our several places by the master. Meanwhile, the teaching, by Pattison's exacting standard, was of high quality, although there was no system of examination or set curriculum and attendance at lectures was not compulsory — lecturers had to *attract* an audience. Pattison writes, "We find a width of reading possessed by the teacher, and a level of philological inquiry pre-supposed in the learner, which it would not be easy to find surpassed in the most celebrated lecturerooms of our own time" (*IC*, 49).

Pattison's contrasting picture of a vast decay of the University of Paris is similarly powerful. Marlowe, in his play about the wars of religion, *The Massacre at Paris*, gives a hyperbolical account of what was in truth a vast institution: "Paris hath full five hundred colleges" (1.1.137). Paris never really had five hundred colleges, but it did have forty. Now, after the wars of religion, some of these stood empty, some were in ruins. In the Middle Ages it had all been very different. M. T. Clanchy observes that, by the end of the thirteenth century, Paris, Bologna, and Oxford had achieved an astonishing level of organisation, "with campus police, endowments, vacations, examinations, teaching assistants, copy shops and libraries."[23] By Casaubon's time Spanish and Neapolitan soldiers had used the furniture for firewood and stalled their horses in the chapels; peasant families were squatting in some buildings; others were overgrown with thistles and brambles. The whole account reads like a cross between the opening of *Brideshead Revisited* (the soldiers, the beautiful house) and *Blade Runner*.

It is a little surprising, given Pattison's profound respect for German scholarship in its later phase that his picture of German mores in the Time of Casaubon should be one of almost brutal grossness. "Refinement is perhaps a term hardly applicable to any German court of the period. Hunting and hawking, heavy feasts prolonged to swinish intoxication, were the serious occupation of the princes and the nobles" (*IC*, 279–80). One remembers Pattison's account in his *Memoirs* of the way the conviviality of his hard-drinking fellow undergraduates actually repelled him. Here, as he looks back at the Germany of the late sixteenth century, the picture is basically the same, but suddenly exaggerated in its physicality. A similar sense of German grossness pervades his account of the *intellectual* operations of the German Jesuits. John Sparrow in his book on Pattison does not explain how Pattison's interest in Scaliger, the friend of Casaubon, was quickened by a belief, planted in his mind by a conversation he had with Chevalier Bunsen at Charlottenburg in 1856, to the effect that the Papists and especially the Jesuits had systematically blackened the character of Protestant Scaliger. As Sparrow omits the context, with reference to Pattison, so Bernays, in his great work on Scaliger, the book that scooped Pattison, had taken too little account of the circumambient Jesuit malice. On the Jesuit pamphlets themselves Pattison observes that they are violent "compounds of the beer house, the cloister and the brothel" (*IC*, 244). The general level of the debate can be illustrated by a story that Heinsius, the friend of Scaliger, tells of Gaspar Scioppius, one of the Jesuit controversialists. Scioppius accused Scaliger of liking pornography. But meanwhile, Heinsius gleefully pointed out, Scioppius had expressed his envy of the sexual potency of sparrows: "While I lived at Ingoldstadt, I saw opposite to my study a sparrow repeating the act of love twenty times, and afterwards so faint and weary that he fell to the ground when he attempted to fly away. Unequal fortune! Why is this given to sparrows and in denied to men?"[24] Those readers who remember Luther's preoccupation with his own excretion may question whether the crudity discerned by Pattison was confined to German Papists.

Pattison can also convey the curious manner in which low financial rewards went with exalted status and high ceremony. He gives a wonderful account of Casaubon's entry to the University of Montpellier after he left Geneva. On 31 December 1596 Casaubon was met, one mile beyond the gates of the city, by "a cortège composed of his own friends, of the regents of the faculties, and, at their head, more than one of the consuls of the year" (*IC*, 92). This of course was a great occasion, and one is not surprised to find it carefully recorded. But Pattison can also supply telling detail where it is less expected. For example he finds, and tells the reader, that when Casaubon had his long conversations with James I, they spoke neither in English nor in Latin (which Casaubon employed when speaking to the English bishops) but in French. Once more the scene springs to life.

Inside the Labyrinth

But what really fascinates Pattison is Casaubon himself, as a curiously pure specimen of a life devoted to personal learning. Wordsworth famously wrote of Newton, "Voyaging through strange seas of thought, alone" (*The Prelude*, 1850, 3.63). Casaubon, less spectacularly but nevertheless movingly, is voyaging through seas of *intricate fact* alone—alone, because he knows so much more than his contemporaries. Pattison remarks (*IC*, 268) that when Scaliger died in 1609 Casaubon lost his only competent reader. Even here, however, there is a certain picturesqueness, an eccentricity, which Pattison can relish. Casaubon's continual complaints about being overwhelmed with administration and business ("Negotiis obruor") are partly absurd: Pattison says anyone might think that he was running a bank or a vast industrial enterprise (*IC*, 474). But then he adds, a page later, in generous deference, that no amount of leisure would ever have been enough for Casaubon's intellectual need. Casaubon was almost comically unskilful in financial affairs, giving wildly inappropriate tips when in England (he was never clear in his mind about the value of English coins) and frequently losing large sums. He bore these losses philosophically, so philosophically as momentarily to exasperate Pattison, who acidly observes that real philosophy teaches the importance of money. It looks as if Casaubon's fault was inattention rather than irresponsibility; he was desperately worried when Sir Henry Wotton, who had a real aristocratic contempt for money which Casaubon himself could never feel, ran up huge debts with Casaubon standing as surety (*IC*, 46). All this suggests a loveable unworldliness. But Casaubon had the scholar's vices. He failed to return borrowed books. Here one may think of the nineteenth-century Shakespearean scholar J. O. Halliwell (later, Halliwell-Phillips), who actually stole books in great numbers and remarked, complacently, late in life, that he was the worthier possessor because better able to look after the material he lifted.[25] It appears that Casaubon, like Halliwell-Phillips, was conscious that he would at least use what others would merely neglect. He wrote to Hieronymus Commelin in 1596 asking him to get hold of a certain book, "at any price," in order that it should not fall into "hands that would do nothing with it" (*IC*, 39).

Those in our century who write contemptuously of the scholarship of earlier periods would do well to reflect on the degree to which our path is smoothed by adequate works of reference, by good dictionaries. To put it simply, Casaubon had no Liddell and Scott, no Paully-Wissowa. Instead he is himself an important part of the reason why we now have these things. "We are still living," wrote Ulrich von Wilamowitz, "on the capital accumulated by the industry of Casaubon."[26] He gets what books he can, when he can. One thing that still exists today, the Frankfurt Book Fair, existed then, and was of crucial importance to Casaubon. But he also bought dodgy (inaccurate) manuscript transcripts of classical texts by Damarius, one of the last of the "calligraphers," "a race which long survived the invention of printing" (*IC*, 38). "Incessant reading, seconded by capacious memory" (*IC*, 206), remains the essence, for Pattison. Scaliger said of the Dutch scholar Marcilius that he had "read himself, into ignorance" (*IC,* 189). Hobbes would later say that if he had read as much as other men he would have known no more than they,[27] and Pope wrote of "the bookful blockhead, ignorantly read, / With loads of learned lumber in his head" (*An Essay on Criticism* 612–13). Behind the topos of the scholar unfitted for life or sex by erudition lies a more paradoxical topos: that of the person unfitted for *intellection* by study. But with Casaubon it was otherwise. His understanding grew with his reading.

Pattison sees the scholarly drive as being in natural antagonism with the religious impulse: "the theologian and the scholar were in tension" (*IC,* 56). He has to concede that Casaubon's piety, though unostentatious, was intense and that he was utterly unaware of any collision between it and his classical work. Indeed, so far from the Christianity impeding the scholarship, it looks as if Casaubon himself felt that the impediment operated in a contrary direction. While he was working on Polybius he actually wished that he was working on the Greek Church Fathers. He was not permitted to do this, because he was a Protestant (*IC,* 215). The *Ephemerides,* Casaubon's Latin diary, recording his reading from day to day, is the peculiar delight of Pattison. As we saw, he was excited to find out similar it was to his own record of reading. It is necessary to add, however, that, although the similarity is there, Pattison (true to his usual practice of reading himself into the great French scholar) exaggerates it. Pattison's journal is much less expansive and humane than Casaubon's. Whole years go by — 1854, 1855 — in which we have nothing but the authors and titles of works read, jotted down day by day. Admittedly the diary of the younger Pattison is a little more like the *Ephemerides.* The diary for 1839 records his joy when "Mozley came up to tell me I was elected at Lincoln" (8 November). This was the point at which Pattison became a fellow of an Oxford college. The intensity of the experience, interestingly, causes him to break into (very pious) Latin, as he prays that all will turn out to work for the glory of God and the Church. In the 1839 diary he berates himself for idleness, and tells us a little about what he does, as distinct from what he reads. The entry for 1 March reads, "Took a skiff and pulled [i.e., rowed] to Sandford." He often notes how he "walked alone" to this place or that. The word "alone" carries a charge of pathos wholly foreign to the *Ephemerides*.

The first thing to meet the eye when one opens the *Ephemerides* is its author's preoccupation with time and the lack of it. The very first words, before the entries proper begin, read, "Cum sit *pantōn polutelestaton analōma to tou khronou*, Vereque dixerit Stoicus Latinus unius rei honestam avaritiam esse, temporis," "Since *the worst extravagance is the squandering of time*, the Latin Stoic will have spoken truly when he says that avarice is virtuous in one case only, when it is greed for time." We then have, in the first entry (volume 1, page 2), a series of quotations from Seneca, all about the shortness of time available. He is berating himself for rising as late as five o'clock — "A quinta (heu quam sero) surreximus," "Got up at five (gosh, how late!)." I have translated this into colloquial modern idiom in order to reflect the extraordinarily easy, free immediacy of Casaubon's Latin. He writes of books as though they were friends or acquaintances. This may momentarily confuse the unprepared reader. Casaubon keeps referring to time given to "Basilius." At last one realises that Basilius is a long-dead author (he is reading Hieronymus Froben's 1598 edition — 698 close-packed folio pages). One sentence sticks in the memory: "Dein pro more pexo capillo museum ingressi," "Then I combed my hair in the usual way and went into my study." Why does Casaubon, the least narcissistic of men, record in his diary that he combed his hair? One wonders for a moment if there is a strain of ritual in this careful preparation of his person before engaging in the wholly private activity of study. Machiavelli famously tells posterity that he put on his court robes before passing into the world of the ancients and reading for four hours, alone.[28] Keats told his brother George on 17 September 1819 in a letter how he would brush his hair, put on a clean shirt, and "in fact adonize as I were going out" before sitting down to write poetry.[29]

There are, however, for Pattison, three factors that have lowered the popularity of the *Ephemerides:* it is in Latin; it does not deal with public events; "it is surcharged with the language of devotion" (*IC*, 100). Geneva, for Pattison, is a puzzling cultural phenomenon. It produced Bibles and works of Calvinist theology, which is bad enough, but at the same time it produced something worse — surreptitious editions of Jesuit publications. Lyons, meanwhile, presents a mirror image, on the Papist side, producing missals and books of hours together with Calvinist hymnbooks to satisfy the Protestant market. Pattison affirms that the University of Paris, which had been "a supreme centre of intellectual life and freedom," was, near the end of the sixteenth century, ruined by "religious fanaticism." One senses that Pattison's thought is partly clouded for a moment by the charge of hostility ever-present, for him, in the word "religious," as if "religion," rather than dissension, were the cause of the decline. After all, before the wars of religion, the University of Paris was a thoroughly Christian institution.

Pattison tells the story of how the Papist "convertisseurs" attempted to persuade Casaubon's daughter, Philippa, to go over to Rome. Casaubon told her that it was greatly in her interest to convert, because in this way she could marry well, something he wanted for her, wholeheartedly; meanwhile he could do nothing for her financially if she chose to resist the blandishments. To his great joy she spurned the worldly inducements and remained true to her Protestant upbringing. The story is a real-life equivalent of those "I did this but to try thee" episodes in early modern drama (say, Malcolm trying the virtue of Macduff by pretending to be vicious, *Macbeth* 4.3), which can make uncomfortable reading for modern sensibilities. Alternatively it may be that Casaubon was not erecting an artificial hurdle for her to surmount but was stating as honestly and fairly as he could the case for making the move — following the scholar's instinct to state the contrary position as strongly as possible. Pattison tells how Philippa said that God would provide for her, and adds, "God did provide for her; she was removed from this world at the age of nineteen" (*IC*, 241). I imagine that most of Pattison's readers in the nineteenth century would take this sentence to be wholly unironic. Certainly Casaubon himself would take it so, if *per impossibile* he were able to read it. But in fact Pattison's comment is trembling on the edge of a bitterly ironic scepticism.

One senses, again, that Pattison is obscurely annoyed by the fact that his hero takes little notice of Greek poetry but is endlessly moved by the Hebrew psalter (*IC*, 495–96). Milton's notorious lines about the "Songs of Sion, to all true tastes excelling" the poetry of Greece (*Paradise Regained* 4.347) have of course attracted similar mild hostility. C. S. Lewis observed with some force, "The rest of us, whose Greek is amateurish and who have no Hebrew, must leave Milton to discuss the question with his peers."[30]

For George Eliot and for Mark Pattison there is an inescapable conflict between the essence of intellection and the essence of religion. For both, also, there is a similar conflict between religion and sexuality and possibly (but much less clearly) between intellection and sex. Once again Casaubon, the real intellectual, fails to evince the proper marks of agonised conflict. His long second marriage was as we have seen a love match. "Dolor ex uxoris absentia studia mea impediverunt," "I am missing my wife so much that I can't work" (June 1599), is a characteristic entry in the *Ephemerides*. In another place he writes, "O quando ego te, coniux charissima . . . videbo?" "Dearest wife, when shall I see you? When will we be together?" Here he goes on, in the privacy of his journal, to call her his heart, his dove (*columba*), and says that he will live and die with her.

Florence Casaubon, after twenty-two confinements, might reasonably have had cause to look upon her husband with something less than enthusiasm. Scholars were not always, it seems, dead from the waist down. The sixteenth-century scholar Tiraquellus (Andrée Tiraqueau) was said to have fathered forty-five children. Pierre Bayle, who reports the claim, is admittedly sceptical. After citing Thuanus's observation that Tiraquellus produced one book and one child every year, Bayle says that in his opinion the true number may have been a mere thirty or so. He wonders whether the fact that Tiraquellus drank no wine — he was a Total Abstainer (apart from sex) — may have contributed to his longevity.[31] With the stories of Tiraquellus one senses that one is in the world of hilarious gossip. With Casaubon we have, as always, the real thing: the sober evidence of the diary. In fact after her husband's death Mme Casaubon exhibits all the signs of a devoted widow, treating his literary remains including the commentary on Polybius as sacred, pressing indefatigably for publication. She is therefore the exact opposite of Dorothea in *Middlemarch*, for whom the idea of carrying on her husband's work after his death was simultaneously repugnant and desolating. Florence appears just once in her own right, so to speak, in the *Ephemerides*. Suddenly the Latin of the husband is cut across by the vernacular of the wife. "Ce jourduit Monsieur Casaubon a este absent, que Dieu veulle garder et moi et les nostres avec lui," "Today M. Casaubon is away; whom God protect—and me and all of us with him."[32] She is writing on a day when the fanatical Papists were roaming the streets, looking for Protestants to beat up. Her sentence is devout, frightened, and wholly loving.

A year before he died we find Casaubon in England, fretting desperately at the absence of Florence, who is away in France. The anxiety builds gradually: "De uxore nihildum," "No news yet of my wife," he writes.[33] Then on 31 August he sends his son's tutor to meet her at Dover (Florence had never learned to speak English). The tutor missed her at the port. Casaubon, as usual, was trying to work. Suddenly he interrupts himself, as long before he had interrupted his commentary on Strabo to give vent to grief at the news of his father's death. This time it is not grief but joy that breaks over him: "O laetum diem! Circa decimam horam matutinam serio aliquid meditanti uxor adstitit in museo et me suo conspectu beavit," "Happy day! About ten o'clock this morning while I was working on something or other abstruse my wife was there, standing, and blessed me with the sight of her."[34] Pattison, commenting on this entry, calls Florence "the guardian angel of the house." It is hard to know if he is consciously alluding to Coventry Patmore's sequence, about his wife, Emily, "The Angel in the House," which appeared in 1854–63. Certainly if he did he would have been wholly unaware of course of the way in which feminist criticism has undermined such modes of praise. In Pattison the phrase is touched by a certain wistfulness. For no two things could be more different than this sixteenth-century Protestant marriage and his. In a precisely parallel manner the contrast with *Middlemarch* is equally strong.

Yet, despite the evident contrast, Pattison himself is clearly energised by a sense of affinity with Isaac Casaubon. Contemporaries thought he was George Eliot's Casaubon; he thought he was Isaac Casaubon. Or rather, since he was simultaneously aware of the plain fact that he was outclassed, as a scholar, by the early modern figure, he chose to draw Casaubon into the circle of his own personality.

Hugh Lloyd-Jones rightly observes that Pattison's *Isaac Casaubon* is "a concealed autobiography."[35] He goes on to notice how Pattison, when writing on an earlier epoch, describes the escape of the scholar from the doubts and perplexities engendered by religion into the heaven of the life of learning. This again leads us, naturally, back into the experience of Pattison himself. We saw earlier how the rank misery recounted in Pattison's memoir of his own life gave place, unexpectedly, to a strangely happy ending. The very last page, indeed, breathes pure contentment. But, for all that, Lloyd-Jones paints too rosy a picture. Pattison's dyspeptic intelligence was always ready to discover causes for grief, even within the world of books. Describing not the religious but the scholarly character of the age, he writes,

> We are now in the age of erudition . . . the Renaissance, the spring tide of modern life, with its genial freshness, is far behind us. The creative period is past, the accumulative is set in. Genius can now do nothing, the day is to dull industry. The prophet is departed and in his place we have the priest of the book. Casaubon knows so much of ancient lore, that not only his faculties, but his spirits are oppressed by the knowledge. He can neither create nor enjoy; he groans under his load. The scholar of 1500 gambols in the free air of classical poetry, as in an atmosphere of joy. The scholar of 1600 has a century of compilation behind him, and "drags at each remove a lengthening chain." [*IC*, 122–23]

As always, Pattison has the writerly knack of enjoying his misery. Notice how the myth of the sexless scholar that is so strong in Browning's poem and pervades George Eliot's novel is breaking in, behind the phrase "neither create nor enjoy." At the same time, to be sure, there is intelligent cognitive reference to the real object. Pattison is half-remembering, as he evokes from Oliver Goldsmith's "Traveller" the image of the chained man, Casaubon's description of his toil over Athenaeus as "catenati in ergastulo labores," "labours of one chained in a stalag" (*IC, 123*). Undeniably there are wholly objective points of coincidence between the two. Casaubon described himself as *opsimathēs*, "a late learner,"[36] and Pattison in his *Memoirs* speaks of his own slow reading and a snail-like progress (123, 149).

In like manner Pattison seizes eagerly on those hints in the *Ephemerides* that Casaubon was briefly tempted to go over to Rome. This of course mirrors his own wilder oscillation in 1847. For Casaubon, though not of course for Pattison, conversion to Rome would have been, materially, in his interest. Resisting Rome in sixteenth-century France is very different from resisting Rome in England, whether in the nineteenth or in the sixteenth century. Notoriously Casaubon's younger contemporary, John Donne, born into a fiercely Roman Catholic family, seceded from Catholicism to Protestantism and did very nicely out of the move. Donne's relations used to talk together about the chance of being martyred. Donne's queasy witticism — "For some, not to be martyrs, is a martyrdom" ("The Litany" ll. 89–90) sounds merely shifty beside Casaubon's clearly heartfelt declaration that the memory of the time when his family were driven into the hills because of their faith was sweeter to him than honey or sugar (*IC*, 7).

Casaubon's Protestantism was neither monolithic nor insulated from counter-argument. Though Du Perron could not persuade him, the ethical appeal of Arminianism, which unlike strict Calvinism finds room for free will and thus for real moral agency, clearly moved him and played a part in his decision to go to England. Casaubon was attracted for a while in Paris by the Arminian preaching of John Uytenbogaert. Pattison cites a minute of a conversation between Casaubon and Uytenbogaert in which it is observed that if one accepts predestination it is very difficult to avoid the conclusion that God is the author of evil.[37] In the event, Casaubon was to find that Arminianism was heterodox even in England. It is interesting to discover that when James I wanted someone to rebut Arminianism it was felt that Casaubon could not be used. When one Richard Thomson was accused in Cambridge of drinking and Arminianism, he turned for help to Casaubon. Similarly, when Casaubon read the Catholic Robert Bellarmine he was in general unpersuaded. But when he came to Bellarmine's account of the sacraments he felt there was force in the Catholic argument. This scrupulous fair-mindedness made him very vulnerable in a time of violent political and religious factionalism, as he was squeezed on both sides, by Protestants of divided opinion and by Catholics eager to secure a prize convert. One detects, once more, the accent of personal experience when Pattison considers the truth of the claim that Casaubon was killed by overwork, occasioned by the obligation to refute Baronius. Work alone, he decides, could not have this effect. He goes on, "What depresses the powers of life is prolonged labour when combined with anxiety" (*IC*, 473). The bleak observation hangs in the air. It is as much about Pattison as it is about Casaubon. We find the same grim confidence of assertion, the same unacknowledged yet clear reference to himself when he explains that Casaubon's criticism of Baronius was in fact a fragment of what he had hoped to accomplish on the archaeology of the Church (*IC*, 383). Here we encounter once more the topos of the Great Unwritten Work, which permeates *Middlemarch*. Pattison writes, "Writers are apt to flatter themselves that they are not, like the men of action, the slaves of circumstance. They think they can write what and when they choose. But it is not so. Whatever we may think and scheme, as soon as we seek to produce our thoughts and schemes to our fellow men, we are involved in the same necessities of compromise, the same grooves of motion, the same liabilities to failure or half measures, as we are in life and action" (*IC*, 383). The shift of pronouns betrays all. Pattison begins with the distant neutrality of the third person: "Writers are . . . ," "They think. . . ." But then, as he turns from the illusion to the converse reality of the situation, he begins to use the first person plural: "whatever we may think. . . ." By the end of the last sentence the reader is keenly aware that "we" includes — is the thinnest of disguises for — "I."

Although, however, Pattison is able to discover in his hero Casaubon his own failures and incapacity, it remains true that the whole is generalised. All writers, he, you, we, I, are thus. Casaubon is both an anti-hero and a hero. He lacks the dynastic glamour of his friend Scaliger, who believed himself (wrongly, as it happens) to belong to the great della Scala family. Nor had he the social grace of Henry Savile. In person he was unimpressive. Within the intellectual sphere, he is not *immediately* dazzling. Casaubon never shows off. But then we become aware of the real cumulative impressiveness of his achievement, his status as unequivocally, unironically embodying a certain intellectual ideal.

The basic term is *knowledge:* "The one only motive which can support the daily energy called for in the solitary students live, is the desire to know" (*IC*, 491). "Objectivity" almost became a term of abuse among theoreticians in the last decades of the twentieth century. But it is clear that objectivity figures crucially in this picture. It is because Pattison reverences objectivity that he can rejoice in the very absence of personal colour from Casaubon's writings: "He has the enviable gift of presenting the object as it is (*Veranschaulichung*). This was due not to the possession of a poetic imagination, but to its absence. He likes the object with no subjective radiance, and decorated with no ornaments. He had the inestimable advantage, denied to us, of not acquiring his first conception at second hand. We read so much about the ancients, in books written about them by moderns, that our notion of antiquity is inevitably coloured by the modern medium" (*IC*, 517–18). What is startling here is the assumption that it is the earlier age, not ours, which is free from perspectival "colouring." We often say that Gibbon's Antonine Romans are, absurdly, eighteenth-century rationalists (with the tacit assumption that *we* have access to the unmodified reality—for while we might have noticed the *difference* between Gibbon's view and ours we could never have detected the *distortion* unless we had access to the truth). The subjective distortions of one's own culture, are, almost by definition, the ones we are unconscious of. But to Pattison it was plain that the Victorians were far guiltier of such tacit modification than Casaubon ever was. Indeed, if one reads, say, a page of commentary by Casaubon and immediately afterwards a page from, say, *Marius the Epicurean,* one suspects that he may have been, simply, right.

Pattison says, not of Casaubon but of another great scholar, Richard Bentley, that his quiet observation in his *Dissertation upon Phalaris* that "Astypalaea of Crete does not once occur in ancient authors" may seem easy, but in fact "a lifetime is behind this negation" (*IC*, 38). Today, in the first years of the twenty-first century, it is not uncommon for older academics, happily arguing about the source of a quotation, to be interrupted by a younger colleague: "I can find this for you within two minutes on the English poetry database." It is indeed obscurely disquieting to reflect how much of Casaubon's peculiar power, his sheer command of detail, has been effortlessly usurped by machines. Casaubon could no more have defeated the computer than the American folk hero in the story could defeat the railway engine.

Pattison sees the absence of any aesthetic and philosophical pre-disposition in Casaubon as locked into — a necessary precondition of — his monumental, cumulative truth-telling: "He never thinks of the Roman Architecture among the objects of a journey to Italy" (*IC*, 286). "He was destitute, if ever man was, of poetic feeling. The erotic and wanton greek muse offended his Huguenot asceticism. He had no metrical skill. He had as little taste for philosophy as for poetry" (*IC*, 221). There is a sense that any such feeling in Casaubon would, for Pattison, have diminished the purity of his enterprise. It is inter-esting that the term "pure" occurs in Rudolf Pfeiffer's essentially Pattisonian summing-up: "Casaubon is the first pure type of a clas-sical scholar destitute of sympathy for human and aesthetic values. He is the best and perhaps greatest example of the ascetic brand of scholar who sacrifices his life for his high purpose."[38] The picture is beginning to harden into a stock caricature. To say that Casaubon, the loving husband and father, was destitute of human values is ab-surd.

But the mere *knowing* of thousands upon thousands of linguistic facts can still seem an arid thing. One immediate answer might have been to stress the fact that Latin was a living language for Casaubon. It is not just that he gave his public lectures in Montpellier in Latin (this was common practice). Du Perron says that he was more fluent, more comfortable in Latin than in his mother tongue. Once when he was asked to turn a Latin petition into Greek he simply did it on the spot, without needing any recourse to dictionary (*IC*, 98). Today many highly intelligent persons devote their lives to Latin, and can-not be said to speak it at all. Latin really is a completely dead lan-guage. I can remember my tutor in 1955 hesitating over a model translation into an ancient language by the nineteenth-century scholar Richard Claverhouse Jebb and saying, "Actually, I wouldn't give this an alpha." But then he added, "But Jebb would have writ-ten this straight down. Today any don attempting it would take a couple of days." This fluency, so lately lost, was a mark of persisting linguistic life. Casaubon's linguistic command, with its vast system of simultaneous, shifting relations, of implication and conversely deliberate dissociation, is radically unmechanical. It is fully human.

But Pattison takes a different line. He is keen to defend his hero from the charge of philological aridity by laying stress on his interest in history. "Casaubon," he writes, "dwelt more fondly on the historical, antiquarian and learned literature of Greece than on the poets and philosophers of the best period" (*IC*, 51). It is true that Casaubon makes a large moral claim for history in his letter to Henri IV prefixed to his *Polybius* and in the Prolegomena to his *Historiae Augustae*, "Est enim historia nihil aliud, nisi philosophia quaedam exemplis utens," "For history is nothing but a kind of philosophy which makes use of examples."[39] He then goes on to say, characteristically dropping into Greek for the key political and ethical terms, that histories of public affairs are politically instructive and the lives of private individuals are morally instructive. The idea is of course commonplace; Justus Lipsius and Sir Henry Savile said very similar things. But the various voices are not quite unanimous; for example, Casaubon thought the period of history covered by Tacitus was so corrupt that it was actually likely to have a damaging moral effect. He writes, "As good examples when they are frequently in sight improve a man, without his observation, so ill examples hurt us, for by little and little they sink into our minds, and have the effect of precepts, being often read or heard."[40] On less formal occasions, Casaubon was capable of showing a still more radical degree of scepticism. He attributed the fall of Robert, earl of Essex—he calls it "the saddest example"—to his putting too much trust in the idea of the *politicus e libro*, "the politician-out-of-a-book."[41] We begin to sense that Pattison is straining slightly when he writes, "Casaubon never reads a grammarian in pursuit of words," and explains that he is bent on historical understanding (*IC*, 356).

While it is true that Casaubon was, as we saw, committed to an investigation of the pagan matrix out of which Christianity developed, it seems bizarre to claim that he never read as a grammarian. Pattison's excitement grows as the great engagement with Baronius comes into view. Here his hero will engage in historical controversy. But all is not entirely as he would have it. It is likely that Pattison would have been best pleased if Casaubon had exposed the manner in which piety occludes proper appreciation of the ancients, in the huge Roman Catholic history. In fact, as Anthony Grafton has pointed out, Casaubon was eager to show that Baronius had been far too generous to the pagans.[42] More importantly, Casaubon did not smite bad history with good history. Rather, he hits back with linguistic scholarship. Baronius knew neither Hebrew nor Greek.[43] The entire situation is uncomfortably reminiscent of the Duplessis-Mornay episode, where Du Perron, despised by Pattison, attacked not the argument but the accuracy of the citations. Casaubon, to be sure, is doing a great deal more than checking his opponent's references. He was in fact able to show how Baronius's ignorance of linguistic usage led him to mistake apocryphal or fabulous accounts for serious history, and so to draw untenable conclusions. Casaubon, as always, hits hard, and while his attack may be that of a grammarian, it has palpable effects that any historian of intellectual honour would have to respect. It remains a work of criticism rather than of creation, a dismantling of history rather than a new counter-history. Of course Casaubon's *Exercitationes* remained unfinished at his death, but one can feel sure that more time would have made no difference to the fundamental character of his work.

I have argued that Pattison projects himself upon Casaubon, or assimilates Casaubon to his own personality. This shows clearly in his overplaying of Casaubon as a potential historian, something which, as we saw, Pattison himself dreamed of becoming. Meanwhile there is the intuition of a labyrinthine enclosed system of erudition. We think of Pattison as one immersed, not just in "a world of books," but in a world of books about books. He, a scholar, wanted to write the life of Scaliger, another scholar. Instead, he wrote about Casaubon (a third scholar!). Casaubon, he finds with the kind of strange relish, turned aside from the great poets and philosophers to the *Deipnosophists* of Athenaeus — a huge quarry of *learned* allusions. Pattison admits that Casaubon in fact found Athenaeus footling, and wanted to escape to better reading (*IC*, 123), but this somehow is entirely congruent with the rest. Pattison, too, enjoyed despising his own labours.

Pattison says nothing about the work Casaubon did on a really great poet, Aeschylus. This survives in the form of notes written in

Casaubon's hand in a copy of Petrus Victorius's edition of Aeschylus published by Stephanus in 1557 and in a manuscript in the Bibliothèque Nationale (MS grec 2791). Pattison probably simply did not know that these notes existed (though they are referred to by various persons in the eighteenth century). When Eduard Fraenkel produced his edition and commentary on the *Agamemnon* of Aeschylus in 1950[44] he went out of his way to set on record his admiration, as a working editor living hundreds of years later, of what Casaubon was able to achieve.

It is not easy to convey the quality of this work to an outsider. Most people think the work of great past writers is simply available, in books. The writers write and the printers print what they write, and that is that. But in fact between the act of composition and the final publication innumerable copyings and miscopyings may intervene. This is especially the case with an ancient author such as Aeschylus. Some intrepid spirits are ready to argue that this miscopying really produces new (subtly modified) works of literature, in response to movements in the circumambient culture and that, because we cannot in any case interpret literature with any other conceptual apparatus than that of our own period, it is idle to pretend that they miscopied version represents any sort of descent. This position will hardly commend itself to anyone who has watched a wall painting slowly lose its outline and colour, through accidental weathering. Not all changes introduced into text are coherent expressions of culturally changing taste. They are, most often, merely accidental. Works of art are organised; gradual decay through error, conversely, is random. Aesthetic loss is therefore inevitable. There may indeed be eddies in the stream. For a time, the weathering may give a superadded charm of antiquity to the decaying fresco. But the ultimate direction of random damage, if followed far enough, is always downwards. The terminus, after all, is no wall painting at all, and this cannot be superior, *qua* work of art, to an existing wall painting. But even when changes are founded on shifts in taste they are so to speak half-accidental and liable to be introduced without regard to the larger design of the whole. Finally, the notion that we are so to speak the prisoners of a cultural solipsism — irremediably enclosed in our immediate given responses — is absurd. Human beings are built, biologically, to learn, to catch on swiftly when presented with unfamiliar systems. We are entirely capable of respecting the otherness of other literatures, though the process of *fully* apprehending this may be indefinitely prolonged. Therefore the need for scholars becomes great. Persons who can arrest and reverse the natural decay of repeated transmission by smelling out the likely "better reading" become the saviours. Casaubon, evidently, could not read a faulty text without scenting at once what might have gone wrong. This "scenting" is only possible to a well-stocked mind. As we saw, Baronius could not tell when he was reading fabulous pseudo-history because he was no scholar. But Casaubon could.

The text of Aeschylus has reached us by a variety of routes. It appears that in the third century A.D., some eight hundred years after Aeschylus's time, the seven plays we know today were selected by Byzantine scholars for study in schools. These were copied and recopied and commentaries attached. The earliest manuscripts we possess are descended from these, but (with one exception) the oldest we have was produced about A.D. 1200, nearly a thousand years after the Byzantine selection of seven plays. The exception, the celebrated "Medicean manuscript," brought from Constantinople to Italy in 1423 by Giovanni Aurispa, is earlier—but only two hundred years earlier—about A.D. 1000. Nevertheless its chronological priority has led some scholars to see it as the answer to all our problems, the archetype from which the copies derive. It is likely that this excited optimism is unfounded. R. D. Dawe has written powerfully against it in his *Collation and Investigation of Manuscripts of Aeschylus*.[45] For the *Agamemnon* our principal manuscripts are, first, the Medicean (if not a panacea still an important source, though it contains lines 1–310 and 1067–1159 only of this play), the "Venetian" manuscript of the thirteenth century, a copy made by Triclinius in the fourteenth century, a manuscript known as "F" in the Laurentian Library in Florence (containing the full text of the *Agamemnon* plus "scholia" or comments, once more, to the fourteenth century), the manuscript called "G" in the Marcian Library in Venice, which contains only a small section of the *Agamemnon* and a small selection of scholia. This last is fifteenth century. Notice how close we are, now, to the time of Casaubon. Remnants of the beginning of the *Agamemnon*, lines 4–

30, are extant in the pre-Byzantine *Oxyrhyncus Papyri*. This last source is far older than anything else available. It belongs to the second century A.D., a mere six hundred years after Aeschylus. Even today, after centuries of patient, skilled repair work, the text of the *Choephoroe* is profoundly baffling, even in the best modern editions. Much is still wrong. It may well be that some of our problems are insoluble.

Casaubon struggled with what he read, but he struggled fruitfully. Fraenkel gives a huge, densely worded list of his suggestions, queries, emendations. We must confine ourselves to a few illustrative examples. The play is about the return of the Greek king Agamemnon after the successful sacking of Troy, to be murdered in his own palace by his wife, Clytemnestra, and her lover, Agamemnon's kinsman, Aegisthus.

Near the beginning of the first great choral ode, we meet in the manuscripts the words

Outh' hupoklaiōn outh' hupoleibōn
oute dakruōn apurōn hierōn
orgas ateneis parathelxei
[ll. 69–71]

Literally, "Neither by a weeping secretly nor by pouring libations beneath, nor by tears will one assuage the unending rages of fireless sacrifices." This, note, makes little sense. The chorus has begun the story of the expedition to Troy and pauses to say that the matter stands as it stands (67–68) and nothing can be done to change it. The general sense, that the gods are not to be conciliated, is clear enough. Here Casaubon made the first crucial move (which has been followed by modern editors). He emended *hupoklaiōn*, "weeping secretly" to *hupokaiōn*, "making burnt sacrifices." This immediately locks into place with the following reference to pouring libation. Private weeping would never have been thought to propitiate gods in the essentially public world of Aeschylean religion. The following *dakruōn* then becomes suspicious. It looks like an attempt to explain the bad reading, *hupoklaiōn*, "weeping secretly," which has somehow found its way into the text, as Fraenkel says.[46] The Oxford text simply excises *dakruōn*, "shedding tears." This makes it possible to

155

take the genitive plural *apurōn hierōn,* "of fireless sacrifices" in a different way. In my translation I took it after *orgas,* "rages" — "rages of fireless sacrifices." This is senseless. Clearly the chorus is thinking of the anger of the gods. It is hard to conceive what the anger of a sacrifice could be. Reference to "fireless sacrifices" ("fireless" would connote such things as fruit and wine, in antithesis to the previous reference to *burnt* offerings) can now be taken as a partitive genitive with *hupoleibōn* (often amended to *apoleibōn,* "from-pouring," or to *epileibōn,* "on-pouring," but the root sense of libation holds in all of these) giving the sense "nor with pouring from un-burnt offerings." The whole passage can now be rendered, "Neither by burnt offerings nor by pouring from unburnt offerings will one assuage the unbending anger." Meaning breaks up on the mind. All this was made possible by Casaubon's piercing ray of initial scepticism when he saw the word *hupoklaiōn,* "weeping secretly."

The pivotal moment of the *Agamemnon* is at line 931. Agamemnon has returned, the conquering hero, to his palace. Clytemnestra, who will soon kill him, seeks to induce him to incur the jealous anger of the gods by a walking into the palace on a costly carpet, the colour of blood. Here every word counts. Agamemnon asks his wife not to treat him as a woman, an Oriental ruler, or a god but as a man. Clytemnestra then says (l. 931), "Kai mēn tod' eipe mē para gnōmēn emoi," "Yes, and tell me this, not *gnōmēn para.*" The last two words are the difficult ones. The minimal meaning is "against opinion." The question is basically whether the opinion is Clytemnestra's or Agamemnon's. A large number of commentators, including John Conington (whom we saw something of in our first chapter), take it to be Clytemnestra's. This immediately implies an aggressive intention behind the words, "Do not flout my opinion!" (they are taken so by the Loeb translator).[47] If instead the opinion is Agamemnon's, the sense becomes, "Tell me this too, not against your opinion," that is, "Tell me, in accordance with your honest opinion." In the dialogue that follows, Clytemnestra gradually induces Agamemnon to concede that in certain circumstances a pious fear might have made him vow to do the very thing he is now being asked to do, to walk on the carpet. The entire sequence makes no sense if Clytemnestra has already declared her opposition. But if we take the second interpretation, "Tell me honestly," with its insinuating tone, finding a foothold *within* the thoughts of Agamemnon, suddenly we have great drama. The second interpretation, since it was driven home by Fraenkel, has commanded general assent.[48] What Fraenkel laboriously corrected in the twentieth century was got right at once by Casaubon. His note reads, "Responde mihi ex animi *tui* sententia," "Answer me from the opinion of *your* mind" (my italics). If only K. P. Schütz, Conington, and the rest had followed him, tracts of misreading might have been avoided.

At lines 258–354 the choral ode, telling the story of Agamemnon's sacrifice of Iphigeneia, to obtain a favourable wind on the way to Troy, draws to a close and ends on a note of anxious uncertainty about the outcome of the war. Clytemnestra then engages in a tense dialogue with the chorus leader, in which she gradually discloses that she has learned, from a message transmitted by beacons, that Troy has fallen. In the text before Casaubon the dialogue was represented as taking place, not between the chorus leader and Clytemnestra, but between an *aggelos,* or messenger, and Clytemnestra. Casaubon's nose told him what was wrong and he put it right. It may be that the "messenger" got into the manuscript and into the appended summaries and lists of persons of the play because of the occurrence of the word *euaggelos,* "messenger bringing good news," at line 264. The chorus has just ended with a respectful request for news from Clytemnestra. She answers, "Euaggelos men, hōsper hē paroimia, / Heōs genoito mētros euphronēs para." That is, translated as literally as I can, "Messenger bringing good news — as the proverb says — may the dawn be, from its kindly mother."

What seems to have happened is this. Someone, somewhere, seized on the word *euaggelos,* which is the Greek for "messenger" plus a prefix indicating that the news is good, and, because of the intervening, disorientated phrase about the proverb breaking the continuity of the sentence, took it as either an address to the last speaker or as descriptive of the last speaker. This turns the last speaker, Clytemnestra's interlocutor in the lines that follow, into a messenger. In fact, as should be clear, Clytemnestra's sentence, if pursued to its grammatical end, identifies the messenger, figuratively, with the dawn. The change introduced by the copyists — the attribution of the chorus leader's lines in the following dialogue to a (totally spurious) messenger figure — turns the passage into puzzling nonsense. Casaubon is here the healer of a wounded poem. He gives back to posterity one of the great exchanges of European tragedy.

Dryden has a fine phrase in his *Religio Laici* (l. 19). Speaking of the blundering atoms of the Epicurean materialist system, he exclaims in wonder at how they "leapt into form." So it is with ancient texts, invaded by randomness, when they come before the eye of Casaubon. Poetry, drama, dialogue leap into form. Fraenkel after describing yet another of his feats of insight, calls him, in passing, "this great and good man."[49] It is unusual to find such a phrase, wholly untouched by irony, in the twentieth century.

The effect of Fraenkel's prolonged analysis of Casaubon's work on Aeschylus is to make us feel that Pattison actually underestimated the scholarly powers of his subject. Fraenkel is forthright on the point: Pattison's book "fails . . . to convey an adequate idea of the true nature of Casaubon's scholarship and of the originality and greatness of his work. There is very little in the book to show that Pattison was sufficiently familiar with even the published editions and commentaries of Casaubon, to say nothing of the wealth of unpublished materials in the Bodleian."[50] The judgement is harsh but it has real force. Pattison was hooked by the *Ephemerides*, and this remains in a curious fashion the alpha and omega of his partial — but brilliant — study. Fraenkel's praise of Casaubon is the more persuasive because it is accompanied by a clear sense that Casaubon had not solved all the problems. He says that the end of his British Academy piece on textual problems in Aeschylus that we will never understand Aeschylus.[51] Casaubon fell short — but then so has everyone else. Fraenkel sees this because he is a real scholar who takes the measure of the material. One may guess that Casaubon, who, unusually among commentators, is never afraid to say, "I don't know," would have got on well with him.

I have suggested that Pattison's picture of Casaubon as untouched by human or aesthetic values falls to pieces, if one pays any attention at all to his relations with his wife and family. Fraenkel observes that one also needs to build into the picture strong religious devotion, which itself produces strong responses of a partly aesthetic character.

This is something of which Pattison is clearly aware, but he, so to speak, wishes it were not the case and averts his mind from it. For example at *Agamemnon*, line 160, the choric hymn to Zeus begins:

> *Zeus, hostis pot' estin, ei tod au-*
> *tō philon keklēmenō,*
> *touto nin prosennepō,*
> *ouk ekhō proseikasai*
> *pant' epistathmōmenos*
> *plēn Dios, ei to matan apo phrontidos akhthos*
> *khrē balein etētumōs*

Literally—it is just intelligible: "Zeus, whoever he may be, if to be invoked by this name is pleasing to him, I so call him. I cannot compare any—weighing all in the balance, except Zeus, if there is need to cast off the futile burden of care, truly."

Here Casaubon wrote, "Egregie dictum: Ad tranquillitatem animi unus patet portus, in Deo acquiescere," "Admirably said: to quietness of spirit one refuge stands open, to rest in God."[52] Casaubon has just read a great passage of religious poetry. He thinks it is about God and is evidently moved. We may wriggle uncomfortably and wish to say that Greek religion is one thing, Christianity another, so that our scholar is losing his historical sense and proper objectivity, but it may also be observed, with still greater force perhaps, that Casaubon's strong, immediately devout response may be substantially nearer that of the Greeks themselves.

Pattison says nothing about Casaubon's work on Aeschylus and almost nothing about the one thing for which Casaubon is famous today, his demonstration of the late date of the *Hermetica*. Pattison irritably remarks that Casaubon's scepticism about the date of the *Hermetica* arises not as a result of critical investigation but from the a priori assumption that God would not have given a fuller apprehension of Revelation to Gentiles than he gave to Jews (*IC*, 376–77). Here, for once, Pattison overplays the devout Christian at the expense of the scholar and does so quite unjustly.

The *Hermetica* — or *Corpus Hermeticum*, or *Hermetic Books* — is a body of writing, philosophical, theosophical, mystical, which was ascribed to Hermes Trismegistus ("Thrice-greatest Hermes"), who, in his turn, was identified with the Egyptian god Thoth. The assumption was that the extant Greek material had been translated from Egyptian. In the sixteenth century these writings were generally believed to belong to the time of Moses or Abraham.[53] Their influence was immense. Casaubon punctured the balloon by showing that they were post-Christian. As Anthony Grafton says, Casaubon had the skill and learning to recognise in these writings the sort of interweaving of scriptural allusions that has to be post-scriptural and is indeed particularly characteristic of the patristic period, the time of the Church Fathers. One section of the *Hermetica*, *Poimandres*, libellus 16, is presented as an epistle from Asclepius, the pupil of Hermes, to King Ammon. In it the writer rhapsodises about the beauty of the original Egyptian text of the *Hermetica* and laments the manner in which this is marred by the Greek translation. Our writings may be thought obscure, he says, but they will seem still more so in the future when the Greeks will translate them into their tongue.[54] The presumption is that the words of Hermes elsewhere and the words of the writer here at the time of composition were Egyptian. This of course fuels the hypothesis of an early date.

Casaubon at once knows, as an informed spectator at once knows Victorian Gothic from medieval, that what he is reading reading cannot be a rendering of Egyptian original. He immediately pronounces it mock gothic, *pseudepigraphon*, "spurious."[55] He is struck by the copious reference to Platonism (Plato lived from about 429 to 347 B.C.). While the date of Moses and the Exodus from Egypt, if it ever happened, has been placed—though of course there are doubts—at 1900/1800 B.C.;[56] Casaubon, who would have been guided by Eusebius's chronology, would have supposed him to have lived about 1500 B.C.;[57] either way, long before Plato. He homes in on developed metaphysical terms like *hulotēs*, not "matter" but "materiality," a secondary abstraction from an original term that is itself a philosopher's term of art, and on *ousiotēs*, "substantiality," "essentiality," another secondary abstraction from a prior term, *ousia*, "substance," "essence," itself technical.[58] "Quis priorum dixit . . . ?" he goes on, "Who, before the birth of Christ used such Hellenisms?" Casaubon suggests that the general character of philosophical thought among the ancient Egyptians can be gleaned from Eusebius.

The *philosophandi ratio,* the method of philosophizing in the *Hermetica* is wholly different in kind ("diversa est genere toto").[59] Walter Scott, the twentieth-century editor of the *Hermetica,* observes that "Casaubon's opinion on this point is confirmed by the results of modern Egyptology."[60] Traces of the influence of indigenous Egyptian thought, if not entirely absent, are rare in the *Hermetica.* One sees the destructive elegance of Casaubon's mind in his comment on *Poimandres,* 9.8, where the Greek reads, "kai eikotōs kosmos keklētai kosmei gar ta panta," "Rightly is it called the Cosmos, for it *cosmizes,* that is, orders all things." "Kosmos et kosmēin voces sunt antiqui sermonis Aegyptici?" "Are *kosmos* and *kosmēin* really terms in the ancient Egyptian language?" he asks, witheringly.[61] He has noticed that the writer is making a point which can be made only in a language that already contains a verb meaning "to order" and a related noun that has taken on the sense "universe." Latin won't do this, nor will English (that is why I was driven, a moment ago, to the desperate shift of introducing the word "cosmizes" into my English translation, to bridge the yawning gap). I am willing to bet, says Casaubon, that ancient Egyptian had no such terms. He wins his bet.

Casaubon was not the first to doubt the early date of the *Hermetica.* Indeed he would probably be surprised at the ignorance of those who today ascribe such absolute priority to him. Scholars such as Beroaldus and Goropius Becanus had raised questions about certain passages.[62] Anthony Grafton is probably right when he argues that there is nothing discreditable in Casaubon's not citing these immediate predecessors. He thought the reader would know! This is clear from the unacknowledged (because obvious) borrowing from his father-in-law, Henri Estienne (Stephanus). Estienne ascribed the Greek poem *Hero and Leander* (previously thought to be the work of the mythical singer of immemorial antiquity, Musaeus, the figure linked to Orpheus by Aristophanes in *The Frogs,* 1023–25) to that other, entirely historical Musaeus, who lived well after the birth of Christ. Incidentally this is another attribution that is now ordinarily accepted as clearly correct.[63] Casaubon does mention Beroaldus on the title page of his copy of the *Corpus Hermeticum* (edited by Adrien Turnèbe). He writes, "De hoc auctore quaedam Beroaldus in *Chro,*

p. 23," "On this author Beroaldus has certain things in *Chro*, p. 23." This turns out to be an accurate reference to Beroaldus's *Chronicae Scripturae sacrae auctoritate constitutum*.[64] Casaubon's working copy of this is in the British Library.[65] Another Becanus, meanwhile, is mentioned in the *Ephemerides*.[66] Here Casaubon says how he gave a few hours (note the usual obsession with time) to books and friends, and the writings of Martinus Becanus fell into his hands; he found him a vivid, bitter disputant (Casaubon read his *De Antichristo reformato* and *De Purgatorio Calvini*).

The antiquity of the *Hermetica* was important to the English Cambridge Platonists. Ralph Cudworth was the most intelligent of them — a philosopher of real, fundamental power, whose critique of materialism continues to command respect.[67] Cudworth was certainly a better metaphysician than Casaubon. At the same time he was prodigiously learned. But his learning is not the essence of his thought (as with Casaubon); rather it impedes his movements like a heavy carapace. Citations and references flow from his pen, but he has no command over them. Nevertheless he mounted the best of the replies to Casaubon on the *Hermetica*.[68] He pointed out that this body of writing was accepted as genuinely ancient during the period when the religious tradition of Persia and Egypt was still a living cultural fact, and proposed that the *Hermetica* as they have come down to later times may well be a mixture of authentic Egyptian philosophy with more recent materials. It is a cunningly modest formulation, not easily falsified, since Cudworth can always say, if confronted with an awkward case, "I didn't say it was all authentic." Oddly enough there actually are signs in the text of later interpolation, though of course these are not intrusions into a text that is itself of immemorial antiquity. The kind of thing that began to emerge at the end of the sixteenth century is altogether more spectacular. For example, at *Poimandres*, 18.4,[69] we have a glaring reference to the sculptor Phidias, who lived in the fifth century B.C. The incompatibility of this with a Mosaic date was pretty inescapable, and was indeed picked up, before Casaubon, by Turnèbe, who notes in the edition Casaubon used, that the phrase must be set aside.[70] Oddly enough Walter Scott, the twentieth-century editor of the *Hermetica*, similarly, excises the reference to Phidias, considering it, in what may be supposed to be a Cudworthian manner, to be an infection from a later period. But Scott is anxious to clarify what he sees as an important reference to the *Timaeus* of Plato in the passage — a reference obscured by the interposition of the name of Phidias. He is not, like Cudworth, arguing for an immemorial antiquity. And indeed, after Casaubon, no one could.

What has happened here? A real knower has exposed pseudo-knowledge. In the first instance it is only the pseudo-knowledge of those who misdate the *Hermetica* that is exposed. But the Hermetic writings themselves do not survive unscathed. Before Casaubon produced his criticism, the hermetic writings were seen as Gnosis, knowledge of the deepest, highest kind. It is ironic that modern science itself arose from the excitement generated by these writings. In the seventeenth century the Hermetic magicians turned gradually into scientists as we understand the term. Bacon, as we saw, sought to eliminate the preposterous secrecy of Hermetical disquisitions but retained a dream of power behind the mask of empirical modesty. In the heady days of the Renaissance the Hermetist Cornelius Agrippa had affirmed the unstoppable potency of the mind: "placed though we are within the world of nature, it comes to us sometimes to exercise dominion over nature and to accomplish feats so marvellous, so sudden, so difficult, by which ghosts may become obedient, the stars be disturbed, the gods compelled, the elements brought into subjection. So men devoted to God and elevated by these theological virtues rule the elements, drive away mists, summon winds, collect clouds into rain, cure diseases, raise the dead."[71] By the mid-eighteenth century, in Johnson's *Rasselas*, all this is recoded as sad megalomania. In comparison with the authoritative pages in the *Exercitationes*, the local insights of earlier sceptics become insignificant. Cudworth, as Grafton notes, could not meet Casaubon's arguments from diction.[72] As elsewhere, he builds his case cumulatively, until it becomes overwhelming. Cudworth, the dazzling dialectician, was in fact completely outclassed. He was confronted by a new species of argumentative strength.

It may be thought that we are forgetting the contrast between humanism and science. English religious radicals after the time of Casaubon attacked the Greco-Latin learning of the universities as an impediment to Christianity. In our time classical studies have come to be seen as, historically, an educational instrument for excluding women. Those who look back at the period of Casaubon through the glass of the seventeenth century can easily think of the humanist scholars as immersed in mere words, playing futile games in which written authorities are evoked instead of empirical facts: scholarship as the (doomed) antithesis of (rising) natural science. But if "fact" is to become a word of power, Casaubon must be seen as a hero. As long as we contrast scholarship *simpliciter* with science, Casaubon will be consigned to the same unregarded shelf as Baronius. It should be clear by now that to do so involves a grotesque misjudgement. Baronius indeed heaped up his authorities in an uncritical spirit. Casaubon's uncompromising sifting of the solid linguistic evidence, in contrast, is thoroughly empirical (languages have actual existence, are an object of real experience). That is why it comes as a mild shock to one who has just been reading a page of commentary by Casaubon to realise that he was a little older than Shakespeare. He feels modern.

Once more there are earlier cases to consider. The most famous is Lorenzo Valla's demonstration that the "Donation of Constantine," the document in which Constantine was thought to have caused power to pass from the emperor to the pope, was a forgery. The poet Dante, hating the effects of the Donation, contested its by metaphysical arguments, saying that Constantine did not have the right to give away an office imposed on him by God. Valla made his case on the basis of the Latinity of the document, by linguistic scholarship. And now it was all over.

This new kind of linguistic scholarship, it emerged, was of a wholly different order from earlier erudition; it could undercut longstanding philosophical disputes. Scaliger said, "Non aliunde dissidia in religione pendent, quam ab ignoratione grammaticae," "Our theological disputes all stem from ignorance of grammar."[73] This, it might be said, is less pre-echoic of the modern scientist than of Ludwig Wittgenstein, the quintessential modern philosopher. For Wittgenstein, famously, loved to look at what he called the fundamental grammar of philosophical positions and to show by arguing, as it were from below, that metaphysical problems could be not so much

solved as resolved — could simply melt away — when proper account
was taken off the different language games being played by different
parties. But to concede this similarity does not damage the case for
the quasi-scientific character of Casaubon's work. When Wittgenstein is intent upon this line it is easy for the reader to feel that he
is not so much continuing the business of philosophy as putting an
end to it.

The natural philosophers of the early modern period shifted attention from purpose to matter. The seemingly simple word "is," as
in "What is this?" turns out to be potentially ambiguous. Where a
medieval, confronted by a plastic ashtray, would say, "This is a re-
ceptacle for small objects of some sort," the seventeenth-century natural philosopher would bang it on the table, scratch it with his knife,
and say, "This appears to be some sort of vitreous substance, but it
is not glass, I'll wager." The slow, cumulative demonstration by the
scientists of something which was not at all obvious at the beginning
of the something century, that breath is a wholly physical thing, no
less physical than than lead, and that the division between it and
"spirit" as used in theological discourse is absolute — this demonstration had enormous, inescapable effects. The theologians were shep-
herded into a smaller enclosure. Similarly, calculations which showed
that even if all the clouds in the sky precipitated their rainfall at
once, the sea level would not rise high enough to submerge all the
mountains, forced a more modestly figurative reading of the story of
Noah upon the clergy. The method of Casaubon, the devout Huguenot, is at its centre materialist. While others drone on in endless
critical dispute he looks at the *stuff* of the dispute, which is language.
This is the fundamental medium in which the sentences form and
reform, as stone is the medium of architecture. Such naturalism can
look at times like mere insensitivity. I once knew a philologist who
had a way of saying, "Gosh that's interesting," after another person
had finished speaking. The first speaker would pause, with an expression of gratified curiosity spreading over his face, and the philologist would continue, "I didn't know that construction was found
south of Nottinghamshire." But, as becomes clearer and clearer, the
linguistic scholar is the man with the gun. To watch Casaubon intervening among disputants is like watching a grown-up entering a

room full of quarrelling children: *"Of course* you can't say that . . . the answer is. . . ."* Pattison, whom so many see as the essence of the Oxford classical education in the nineteenth century, never opposed natural science. Instead, he saw it as real research, the proper cure for half-knowledge and showy, intellectually slack literary debate (*IC,* 492–93).

Where knowledge is wholly disinterested, completely unconcerned with any moral or political programme beyond itself, it can collapse into a kind of private futility. The danger is not that the scholar becomes more interested in his own mind than in the world. Rather, because he is engaged with material that no one else understands, the primary duty (which is a duty, in practice, to posterity) to make public what is happening—to publish—can decay. Gilbert Burnet said of Bishop Lloyd that "he did not lay out his learning with the same diligence that he laid it in." Older universities in England have, still, people of this kind, though modern techniques of monitoring achievement are fast disposing of them. The spectacle of their elimination prompts mixed feelings in the breast of the watching colleague. Such people should exist, and the academy is the right place for them; but one can see why the money-providers are sceptical. The intuition of a dubious privacy falls like a shadow across the picture. Pattison in his memoirs is strangely happy to say that his life has been a life almost entirely of the mind and not of action, and to tell how in his later career, as he distanced himself from the teaching to which he had given so much energy, he simply read and read.[74] Pattison notes that as Casaubon's reading and knowledge grew, in extent and complexity, he began to lose his grip on the practicalities of publication and communication: "He got at last the habit of putting by any topic as he came up, with the remark, "This we have discussed at length elsewhere." The distinction between what he had read, what he had noted down, and what he had printed, became obliterated in his mind."[75] But the confusion of Casaubon, "amazed with matter" as Shakespeare's Cymbeline says, is interestingly different from Pattison's strange quiet exultation in his own withdrawal from the world. Casaubon is grappling with a mass of information far beyond anything Pattison ever essayed. And of course his publications, given to the world, are a huge visible achievement.

Casaubon's epitaph in Westminster Abbey concludes with four lines of verse:

> *Qui nosse vult Casaubonum*
> *Non saxa sed chartas legat*
> *Superfuturas marmori*
> *Et profuturas posteris*

> *He who would know Casaubon*
> *Let him read not tombstones but his pages,*
> *Destined to outlast marble*
> *And to profit generations to come.*

Pattison, as if wishing to draw Casaubon into his own subtly different privacy, acidly observes that, in fact, the marble will outlast the pages — since Casaubon's work is now unread and largely forgotten (*IC*, 470). Here he perhaps scores a trivial debating point. Certainly Casaubon is little read today. But the obvious answer is that, in a more fundamental manner, his work is far from dead. It lives on as the unacknowledged fertilising agent in great areas of modern thought, in the field of classical scholarship and history. One senses that the writer of these verses (probably Thomas Morton, bishop of Durham) saw this rather more clearly than Pattison, for the very last words are about the effect of Casaubon's work on people yet unborn.

But Pattison loved Casaubon and this love we must respect. Our own period rigidly excludes personal emotion from academic studies, and it must be confessed that the example of Casaubon stands behind this very exclusion. In the nineteenth century, however, it was still possible for translators, historians, and biographers to move from academic prose to poetry. At the beginning of the great Victorian translation of the *Iliad* by Andrew Lang, Walter Leaf, and Ernest Myers, the reader will find two sonnets, one by Lang, "The sacred soil of Ilios is rent," one by Myers, "Athwart the sunrise of our Western day." Similarly, Pattison prefixes verses to his book on Casaubon. As an act of piety, he writes, as Casaubon would have wished him to write, in Greek:

> *ton d'out ar kheimōn kruoeis, ouk ombros apeirōn,*
> *ou phlox ēelioio damazetai, ou nosos ainē,*
> *ouk erotis dēmou enarei menos, all'hog'ateirēs*
> *amphi didaskaliē tetatai nuktas te kai ēmar.*

This man neither winter's chill nor endless rain nor the blazing heat of the sun defeats, nor dreadful sickness, nor does popular holiday destroy his drive. Instead he strains by night and by day upon the work of learning.

One can hear in "ou . . . damazetai," "does not defeat," the accent of Pattison's happy memory of his doggedly intense work on the *Catena* in his youth — "I would not be beat." The slightly odd reference to public holidays may be a buried allusion to Casaubon's unwillingness to take time off and to his joke just before his death about being able to withstand anything but holidays — but buried, surely, far too deep for the ordinary reader to disinter! It is interesting to imagine Casaubon reading these lines. Would he have paused, questioning, on the happily metrical word *didaskaliē?* The word, as used by the ancients, means "teaching," not "learning." But here Pattison must intend the sense "learning." Liddell and Scott, however, in their great dictionary allow the sense "interpretation"; this it might be said was indeed something at which Casaubon excelled all other scholars. I fancy however that Pattison simply thought the word meant "learning" and that Casaubon would have marked him — as scrupulously as he marked his fellow Protestant Duplessis-Mornay — wrong.

Yet it remains a touching and beautiful poem. The most touching thing of all about it is as an expected coalescence of the prosaic with — from miserable Pattison of all men — an intuition of the extraordinary inner happiness of such a mind. Just as Mozart, whatever his dreadful practical worries, must have been happy to have that ocean tide of music flowing forever in his head, so Casaubon, Pattison sees, was happy in his progressive, unresting, indomitably successful pursuit of knowledge. For what is not buried from the ordinarily informed reader is the fact that Pattison's hexameters echo

Homer's lines showing the felicity of the gods at *Odyssey* 6.41–46. This is one of the great *topoi* — one of the major constellations of images handed down from writer to writer — in European literature. Homer's description of the innumerable unburied dead recurs in Virgil, Dante, and T. S. Eliot; so this contrary picture of the carefree existence of the gods recurs in Lucretius[76] and Tennyson's version of the Arthurian Paradise, Avilion.[77] Homer sang:

> *Hē men ar'hōs eipous' apebē glaukōpis Athēnē*
> *Oulumpond'hothi phasi theōn hedos asphales aiei*
> *emmenai out anemoisi tinassetai oute pot' ombrō*
> *deuetai oute khiōn epipilnatai, alla mal'aithrē*
> *peptatai anephelos, leukē d'epidedromen aiglē.*
> *tō eni terpontai makares theoi ēmata panta*

So saying, the grey-eyed goddess Athene departed to Olympus, where they say the seat of the gods is safe forever. It is neither shaken by winds nor wet with rain, nor does the snow come near it, but the sky stretches cloudless, and white light has overrun it. Within it the gods are merry, all their days.

Pattison picks up, like one remembering a song, the repeated negations of Homer, "Neither . . . nor . . . nor," and the security from rain and winter weather, but at the end the surprising verb in Homer, *epidedromen* (which I rendered literally as "has overrun," though many commentators suggest "is spread over," thereby losing the energy of the original word) is replaced in Pattison by *tetatai,* literally "is stretched," and the reference is not to the benign circumambient air but to the inner energy of the scholar himself. But the difference from Homer is less important than the great similarity. Pattison looking at Casaubon feels at the last that he is looking at happiness.

The American twentieth century has given us the phrase "Let's live a little." It means, "Let's put the books away, go dancing, hit the town, party." The notion of life here is substantially that of Browning's "Grammarian's Funeral" — the point from which we began. Browning's residual admiration for his scholar figure is real, but he supposes that it must be conceded that the strange, dusty heroism of his subject must stand in antithesis to life: "Actual life comes next . . ." and because "life" is a term that commands profound moral assent from Browning, the grammarian becomes at once philosophically and ethically problematic—and so the proper subject of a Browning poem. We have seen how the opposition of the scholar to sexual vitality, in particular, is at least as old as Shakespeare's Holofernes. For Casaubon, however, life and learning are not opposed but are one thing. A typical entry in the *Ephemerides* reads, "Amici adhuc, libris silentibus. Ita vita perit," "Friends still here, books unread. So life is destroyed."[78] There is one point in the *Ephemerides* where marriage-as-life and books-as-life jostle briefly. Reunited with his family after an absence he writes, "Sine uxore et liberis vita non erat vitalis," "Without wife and children life was lifeless." But then he adds that, now, life without reading is "isothanatos," "the equivalent of death."[79] The incongruity of the two conceptions he clearly sees as, simply, funny (Casaubon is more humorous than one would guess from modern accounts of him). The important thing to note is that the intuition that Mme Casaubon is life does not immediately generate the conclusion "Therefore reading is death." Both wife and books are life in different forms. At the end of a day in which he read from dawn till dusk and then long after, he wrote in his *Ephemerides*—with no sense of paradoxical self-display or of pointscoring, for such things were always foreign to his nature, but in sober joy—"Hodie vixi," "Today I have lived."[80]

Conclusion

The Other Sexuality
and the Morality of Scholarship

Tom Stoppard's *Invention of Love* opened in London on 25 September 1997. It is about A. E. Housman, scholarship, truth, and sex, but not sex as hitherto discussed in this book. It is a work of breathtaking brilliance. The play opens with the dead Housman, whose opposition to Christianity was notorious, finding himself appropriately enough not in a Christian heaven but in the underworld of Virgil, standing in his buttoned-up suit and black boots on the banks of the Styx waiting for Charon, the grim ferryman, to take him across. A pagan afterlife is, as compared with the triumphant fruition of Christian Eternity, a bloodless, reminiscent business. The persons in Dante's *Paradiso* are more fully real than those same persons as they appeared earlier here in the world. The earthly Cacciaguida who fought in the second crusade under the Emperor Conrad III is a mere *umbra*, a shadow of the Cacciaguida who appears like a star in

171

a cloudless evening sky to Dante the pilgrim in the fifteenth canto of the *Paradiso*. The dead in Homer, in contrast, are mere wraiths, crying for blood, thirsty for substance. Virgil in the sixth book of the *Aeneid* seems to glimpse, for a while, the inverted ontology of Dante. It is we, in this world, who are *clausi tenebris et carcere caeco*, "shut up in darkness and a blind prison" (6.734), and those in the next world live under a sky brighter and larger than ours. But before the book is over the old Homeric scheme reasserts itself. These inhabitants of Elysium are not triumphantly at rest in the fruition of final bliss; they are all looking back, we learn, to the life of this world, hungrily interested, above all, in the unfolding history of the real, concrete city, Rome. So here in Stoppard's play the dead Housman is not on his way to some greater good. His underworld becomes at once a place of memory, peopled by figures from his lost life, including a much younger version of himself. Housman, the barren, loving homosexual, finds the nearest thing to a son he can have, himself when young. Gradually the various luminaries of the academic English nineteenth century fill the stage: Ruskin, Jowett of Balliol, Oscar Wilde, Pater, John Percival Postgate, and Mark Pattison, whose first words as he is brought across the Styx by punt near the end of Act I, are marked by the stage direction "complaining bitterly." If the essence of Pattison is to be got into two words one can hardly do better. Incidentally Stoppard knows all about Pattison's great failure: the unwritten history of classical scholarship.[1]

R. P. Graves subtitled his book on Housman (1979) "The Scholar Poet." Stoppard, as he introduces his principal character, sharpens the oxymoron.

CHARON: A poet and a scholar is what I was told.
AEH: I think that must be me.
CHARON: Both of them?
AEH: I'm afraid so.
CHARON: It sounded like two different people.
AEH: I know.

[*IL*, 2]

The contrast Yeats drew between Catullus, tossing on his bed in love's despair, writing poetry to flatter the ignorant ear of beauty, and his dusty editors rises before us, but now Catullus and the editors are strangely combined in a single figure. Housman wrote poetry of love-longing and produced scholarly work marked by an exceptional intellectual austerity. But there is meanwhile a great difference. Catullus may have experienced days and nights of frustration, yet there is a clear presumption that there were other times when he obtained his desires in full. Housman, who never married and indeed did not wish to, never had his heart's desire. The love of his life, Moses Jackson, was himself heterosexual. Even within Housman's poetry, the conventions of English culture crushed the erotic out of its proper shape, so that the homoerotic reappears as a false heartiness, in words like "comrade" and "lads." The poetic side of the equation, then, is a site of repression; the arid scholarly side, by contrast, almost feels more liberated.

Housman was born in 1859, was sixteen when Pattison published his *Isaac Casaubon,* and died in 1936, one year before the birth of the author of this book. He went up to Oxford in 1877, got a first in Classical Moderations in 1879, and then, disastrously, failed outright in the final examination in 1881. The failure has been ascribed to neglect of philosophy and history. It is indeed probable that Housman would have put all his energy into the elucidation of literary materials, but the result remains baffling. One could understand in the circumstances that he might have missed the first, but that a person of his exceptional mental ability should simply have failed remains bizarre. Housman moved to London, got a job as a clerk in the Patent Office and devoted his evenings to unremitting labour in the British Museum. The work bore fruit in a series of learned articles of exceptional quality. At last, in 1892, Alfred Goodwin, professor at University College London, died, and Housman was elected professor of Latin. He held the chair until 1911. His work on Manilius and Juvenal belongs to this period. The years from 1912 to his death were spent as a fellow of Trinity College, Cambridge.

Housman's lectures on Latin poetry were, it seems, grim stuff: highly technical investigations of minute textual and linguistic problems. His ascetic commitment to reason and evidence were countered within his personality by a response to poetry so strong as to manifest itself in physical symptoms. He describes in his Leslie Stephen

Lecture for 1933, "The Name and Nature of Poetry," how he had to be careful when shaving not to think of a line of poetry because if he did his beard would bristle and the razor would cease to act.[2] Matthew Arnold, Housman's favourite literary critic, is famous for transposing religion into literature. Housman himself illustrates the transposition in a curiously surreal, physical manner. That horror or freezing of the scalp that in the ancient world signalled the presence of the supernatural, now suggests the presence of true poetry. That Housman is conscious of the cultural shift is shown by his lightly adding that the same symptoms occurred "in connection with another object" to Eliphaz the Temanite (*Job* 4.15). On just one occasion, in the course of some very dry lectures, he allowed himself to consider ancient poetry as poetry. He chose Horace's ode "Diffugere nives," "The snows are fled away" (4.7). The mere reading aloud of the text caused him to be so overcome with emotion that he was unable to go on with the lecture. The Latin poem, which astoundingly discovers in the coming of spring—in the opening leaves and first warm suns of the year—sheer, terrifying despair, spoke to Housman. His translation of it has passed into English literature as a poem in its own right. It is perhaps the latent bleakness, the quiet irreligion, which found an echo in him. Horace tells his well-born friend Torquatus that once he has died, "nothing can restore his life, not social class, not eloquence, *not even his piety*" ("Non, Torquate, genus, non te facundia, non te / Restituet pietas"). Given the fact that "pious Aeneas" has been referred to nine lines earlier in the poem we can infer that Horace is here expressing a kind of dissent, is saying "no" to Virgil's *Aeneid*, the greatest religious poem of Latin antiquity. In the *Aeneid*, the hero with his exemplary piety conquers death by descending to the underworld and returning to the light, after which he sets in motion the triumphant progress of Roman history, in which he is, as it were, reborn in the form of the Emperor Augustus. When Aeneas comes to the dark river, Charon, like Stoppard's boatman, remembers Theseus and Pirithous, and how they entered the underworld, not in a spirit of submission but violently, meaning to smash the place. The Sibyl, who is conducting Aeneas through the shades, swiftly explains that the Roman visitor in no way resembles the lawless heroes of the older world;

this is "pious Aeneas," who keeps the rules and will give no trouble (6.392–404). In Virgil, piety gets you a long way. In Horace it gets you nowhere. We end in dust and shadow. But all that Horace says, he says from a full, not an empty heart. Horace is quite obviously moved by Virgil's poetry just as he is moved by the coming of spring.

All this is profoundly congenial to Housman. The element of homoerotic grief, which Horace gives us at the end of his poem, must then have clinched the matter. It will be said that Housman's rendering of the passage is weakly evasive: "And Theseus leaves Pirithous in the chains / The love of comrades cannot take away." "Comrades," as I warned, has a false heartiness, but there is perhaps a special pathos in this very falsity. Repression distorts, but at the same time it can strangely intensify poetic utterance. Nineteenth-century scholarship is sometimes seen as a bland period in which the Ancients are too comfortably Victorianised. I suspect that at the time it was all very tense. The readers were almost all male and the environment of reading was virtually celibate. Schoolboys who had been brought up within a code of suffocating sexual propriety were given as culturally authoritative reading matter the extravagant indecencies of Aristophanes and Martial. Horace, who would have been "core curriculum" because of the purity of his Augustan Latin, is far from pure in content. There are many passages where we find Horace extolling Stoic integrity but still more on the Epicurean pleasures, drinking and love, both heterosexual and homosexual. One is sent to the Ancients to be schooled and the schooling they offer turns out to be brilliantly shocking. Nineteenth-century English mores obliged translators of the period to Bowdlerise and sanitise, so that Aristophanes sounds like Gilbert and Sullivan in the metrically exuberant, sexually discreet translation of Benjamin Bickley Rogers. But the under-presence of the ancient freedom, for those with ears to hear, is everywhere. The charge of not-quite-perfectly-concealed homoerotic emotion in Housman's schoolmasterish "love of comrades" is a good example. It might almost be said that the philosophic category of "the aesthetic," conceived by late Victorian decadents as amoral or immoral, is a product of nineteenth-century Hellenism.

Stoppard gives us the love story first. The dead Housman

("AEH") watches his younger self, coming into view in a boat, with his friends Moses Jackson and Alfred William Pollard, chattering happily together. As Jackson appears a single monosyllable, loving yet shattered even after so many years, breaks from the watching AEH: "Mo!" (*IL*, 4). The young men are talking about inflected and uninflected languages, playing with the example "The dog loves Jackson." In English it is clear from the word order alone that "dog" is the subject and "Jackson" the object. In Latin the endings would reveal, regardless of word order, which word was the subject (the one in the nominative case) and which object (the one in the accusative). "Canem amat Jacksonius" mirrors the order of "The dog loves Jackson," but this time, because of the accusative termination of "canem," and the nominative termination of "Jacksonius," it is Jackson who is doing the loving and the dog who is loved. Housman, to illustrate the point about reversing word order having an effect in English, turns it round and says, "Jackson loves the dog." All jolly, emotionally neutral stuff. But already the alert listener knows that the playwright is saying more than the character is saying. In the underlying drama, Jackson is himself indeed, but the dog (devoted, despised, humble) is Housman. Yet at the same time the passage is lightly humorous. Stoppard returns to the man and the dog much later in the play: (Housman speaking) "lost dog loves young man—dog young lost man loves, loves lost young man dog, you can't beat Latin: shuffle the words to suit, the endings tell you which loves what, who's young, who lost, if you can't read Latin go home, you've missed it! You kissed the dog. After that day, everything else seemed futile and ridiculous" (*IL*, 80). AEH, chorus to the scene (but also like Aeneas who wept when he saw his own past depicted ecphrastically on the doors of Juno's temple, *Aeneid* 1.465, 488), says, "I had only to stretch out my hand!—*ripae ulterioris amore!*" (*IL*, 5). Again the reference is to Virgil—6.314, "They were stretching out their hands in love of the further shore." Virgil's *amore* is now eroticised—as unrequited homoerotic desire. AEH says he had only to stretch out his hand, but we know that, if he had, the caress would have been treated with cheerful indifference.

Yet at the same time the passage is lightly humorous. One thinks, irreverently, of the last sentence of Laurence Sterne's *Sentimental*

Journey: "So that, when I stretched out my hand, I caught hold of the *fille de chambre*'s." Stoppard is giving us knockabout comedy laced with intense pathos. AEH now quotes the lines from the end of Horace's "Diffugere nives," telling us how even Theseus could not break the chains of death that held his beloved Pirithous: "Nec Lethaea valet Theseus abrumpere caro / Vincula Pirithoo" (*IL,* 5), and Charon, the ferryman answers, "That's right, I remember him — Theseus — trying to break the chains that held fast his friend, to take him back with him from the Underworld. But it can't be done, sir. It can't be done." The parenthetic "sir" is a touch of comic genius. It instantly transforms Charon into a robust, conventionally deferential Oxford punt-keeper on the Isis.

At the same time Stoppard begins to accustom his audience to what for them is an alien habit of thought — a joyful pernicketiness about linguistic usage. This will become, as we listen, scholarship. The centre of it all is in a way amoral; the love of accuracy is joined to a joyous contempt for the errors of other people. We have seen this before in this book, in the rector of Lincoln. I do not know whether Stoppard was conscious of this connection, but one speech he gives to "AEH" is a concentrated parody of Pattison: "In Greek I am, as it were, an amateur, and know hardly more than the professors: well, a great deal more than Pearson, who knew more than Jowett and Jebb [knew] combined" (*IL,* 3). Self-contempt, succeeded by still greater contempt for the intellectual attainments of his contemporaries, expressed as a series of censorious brief assessments, is pure Pattison.

The ideal is consciously hard. The rosy notion of a classical education producing "a rounded man, fit for the world, a man of taste and moral sense" — "the beautiful the good . . . Culture . . . Virtue" — collapses at once. This is "humbug" (*IL,* 31). Morality will cause the surgeon's hand to shake. Likewise literary sensibility in an editor. "Poetical feelings are a peril to scholarship" (*IL,* 36). Later young Housman says to Pollard, "To be a scholar, the first thing you have to learn is that scholarship is nothing to do with taste" (*IL,* 72). One is reminded of the way Mark Pattison rejoiced at the un-literary, unaesthetic character of Isaac Casaubon's mind. But the steely centre of this philosophy is after all moral — is, indeed, radically moral.

"Knowledge is good. It does not have to look good or sound a good or even do good. It is good just by being knowledge. And the only thing that makes it knowledge is that it is true" (*IL*, 37). Later in the play young Housman, talking to Jackson, concedes that in fact emotion does play a part. Jackson, the scientist, demands usefulness. Housman refuses to go along with this. His work is not useful like the work of a scientist who masters electricity—but "it is exciting, really and truly, to spot something" (*IL*, 57–58). Jowett is given an eloquent speech explaining how the monuments of past civilisation are vulnerable to decay—how the poems of Catullus were almost lost for all time, how corruption and nonsense creep in with each successive copying of a manuscript. Therefore "Textual criticism is the crown and summit of scholarship"—the art of arresting and even reversing this process of decay and loss. Those who can do it must be immensely well read, selflessly engrossed in the frail object before them. Scholarship is "a small redress against the vast unreason of what is taken from us" (*IL*, 74).

At certain points in this book my category of the knower has seemed to split, fatally, into scholars on one hand and scientists, the proper heirs of Faustus, on the other. But there are other times when the two seem to move closer again. I have argued that Isaac Casaubon's demonstration of the late date of the *Hermetica* has the kind of grittiness we associate with science, and that the fact that it is science directed at a body of writing rather than at a rock or a plant is of small consequence. In *The Invention of Love* the sciences are regarded with a contempt that is partly intellectual and partly social. Science is banausic, associated with artisans and with that low thing, utility. Gentlemen usually avoid it. When I was at school from the late 1940s to 1955, it was understood that the brighter boys (there were no girls) did Latin and Greek, while the less bright did "stinks," that is, science. The unconsciously beautiful Moses Jackson, whom Housman loves, is doing the graceless subject, he is a scientist, and Stoppard admirably catches the reversal of hierarchies when we move from the social level to the erotic. Socially Jackson is mildly disadvantaged; erotically, Housman is absolutely disabled. But despite all this gentlemanly disparagement there is a real awareness that beneath the fashionable surface of things, science is the strong thing.

"Knowledge is good" and science — not just etymologically — is knowledge. So young Housman explains to Pollard, "We need science to explain the world, Jackson knows more than Plato. The only reason to consider what Plato meant about anything is if it's relevant to settling the text. Which is classical scholarship, which is a science, the science of textual criticism, Jackson — we will be scientists together" (*IL*, 48). Here young Housman's position is extreme, but he is not betraying his central ideal; rather he is caricaturing it. His remark that Jackson knows more than Plato is a classic topos of the old "Ancients versus Moderns" quarrel. Were the Ancients the wisest people or are we, through the accumulation of knowledge over the centuries, wiser than they? Bacon, who championed the Moderns, argued ingeniously that anyone who reverences antiquity should respect the modern scientist because we are the oldest people who have ever lived — "Antiquitas saeculi juventus mundi," "Ancient times were the youth of the world."[3] When, earlier, I was describing Casaubon's work on the *Hermetica*, I said that he seemed modern, especially if we had admitted to our thoughts the work of Shakespeare, an exact contemporary. The word "modern" betrays much.

What Stoppard then does, having isolated the ideal of minute truthfulness in its hardest form, is to show how, in life, that ideal is in fact not disjoined from passion but everywhere entwined with desire.

The point is first made in an elementary mode by the character Mark Pattison: "A genuine love of learning is one of the two delinquencies which cause blindness and lead a young man to ruin" (*IL*, 9). Remember how Berowne in *Love's Labour's Lost* warned that too much reading can make you go blind. Readers of Robert Baden-Powell's *Scouting for Boys* (first published in parts in 1908) will remember how the same result was promised to those who indulged in the secret vice of masturbation. This was a part of the culture in which Housman grew up. It appears that small boys who masturbated were told not only that they would go blind but also that, as a punishment, they would be emasculated, becoming indeed "dead from the waist down." We have here a constellation of images of cutting, of excising, older than the nineteenth century: the biblical and Miltonic Samson was unmanned when his eyes were put out.

But at the end of the nineteenth century this sexual mythology had every appearance of being the latest medical information — "what the professionals advise."

Inside the general culture there is the small society of the ancient universities, preceded by the public schools. We come now to something that is almost a matter of simple physics. Here were all these young males, with sexual secretions requiring outlet, and no females. *Faute de mieux*, homosexual practices follow. The physics of the situation is of course (for we are dealing with human beings) at once supplemented by its proper metaphysic, by the ramifying mystique of love. A carefully private, incipient response to the beauty of the human body, seen, as it might be, on the rugby field, is in some way strengthened when, against all cultural expectations, the poets and dramatists set before the pupils for academic study sing of male beauty. Aeschylus, the rugged, good old dramatist, who, for Aristophanes in *The Frogs* belongs to the uncorrupted days before Euripides, wrote a play about Achilles' friendship for Patroclus in which the relationship is presented as lushly homosexual (it is not so in Homer's version): "the unblemished thighs I worshipped and the showers of kisses you had from me." We do not have Aeschylus's play. These words are from a surviving fragment. Charon quotes them in *The Invention of Love* (29). Of course to anyone with a sense of comedy there is an incongruity between the "muddied oaf" (Housman's phrase) on the sports field and a marble Antinous. Homosexual E. M. Forster speaks in *The Longest Journey* of a certain young man who had "the figure of a Greek athlete and the face of an English one."[4] But the alliance of imagery is stronger than the local incongruity.

Of course there were various strategies of evasion. Jowett is presented, fairly enough, by Stoppard as the moralising reformer, implicitly cut off from the severe central idea of real scholarship by his prior, essentially Victorian agenda, as toning down the more evidently homoerotic bits in his translation of Plato: "It's required all my ingenuity to re-phrase his depiction of paederastia into the affectionate regard as exists between an Englishman and his wife. Plato would have made the transposition himself if he had had the good fortune to be a Balliol man" (*IL*, 22). The last sentence is funny of course (I solemnly spell it out) because of the world of real difference between a Greek of the fourth century B.C. and a Victorian " 'varsity man." "AEH" himself sees, with a nod to Plato's *Symposium*, a more authentically classical link between the richly emotional literature and morality: "If only an army should be made up of lovers . . . 'although a mere handful, they would overcome the world, for each would rather die a thousand deaths than be seen by his beloved to abandon his post or throw away his arms, the veriest coward would be inspired by love' " (*IL*, 43). This catches very exactly a difference between late Victorian and ancient stereotypes. For the modern the homosexual is womanish, for the ancient he is hyper-male, untainted by involvement with the female. Plato makes this clear at *Symposium* 191E–192A. Having said that I must add that the consciously "hyper-male" can be found, intermittently, in the modern period — most notably in the earlier phases of Nazi ideology in Germany during the 1930s.

Another way to evade the problem is to assume a high-minded tone: sex is one thing, passionate Platonic attachment to one of the same sex, another. The aesthete Walter Pater is clearly by several degrees closer to a confession of the homoerotic component than Jowett, who remonstrates with him in the play for his writing to thank an undergraduate for his sonnets on "the honied mouth and lissome thighs of Ganymede" and signing himself "Yours lovingly" (*IL*, 21). Pater answers, "I am astonished that you should take exception to an obviously Platonic enthusiasm." There is a sinister pre-echo here of Wilde's language at his trial in 1895 for unnatural vice: when asked about a certain phrase in a poem by Lord Alfred Douglas, his great love, Wilde answered, "The 'love that dare not speak its name' in this century is such a great affection of an elder for a younger as Plato made the very basis of his philosophy." The lofty rejection of sexual reference is entirely implausible.

This, before it becomes tragic, is the stuff of comedy and Stoppard is very good at comedy. He ensures that the audience do not lose track of what is really going on by a series of "bumps," collisions of high and low matter:

JOWETT: Nowhere was the ideal of morality, art and social order realised more harmoniously than in Greece in the age of the great philosophers.

RUSKIN: Buggery apart.

JOWETT: Buggery apart.

[*IL,* 17]

We may compare with this a subtler collision, earlier in the play:

HOUSMAN: . . . a hoop, a *trochos,* was a favourite gift given by a Greek man to the boy he, you know, to his favourite boy.

JACKSON: Oh, beastliness, you mean?

[*IL,* 7]

Here Housman, like Horace in the poem to Ligurinus to which we shall come, loses his customary easy command of words as he is momentarily overcome by love, looking at Moses Jackson, and cannot complete his sentence about the ancient love of men for boys. Jackson, in his amiable, unsympathising reply, is given the word "beastliness," an absolutely, exclusively nineteenth-century–early-twentieth-century idiom, which nevertheless succeeds in pinpointing what is really at issue. It is a little like the writerly strategem applied to Jowett, where an obvious Victorianism was suddenly permitted to clash with an alien antiquity, but here the effect is less simply funny, more involved with pain.

The pain is greater because we have moved from the general, cultural intertwining of Hellenism and homoeroticism to the special case of Housman. The essentially local and temporary flowering of homosexual feeling in artificially celibate communities allowed Housman, the lifelong lover of Moses Jackson, a kind of window, a brief opportunity to half-express his real desires. And then, as they leave their youth and Oxford behind, as Housman becomes the professional scholar and Jackson marries, all is repressed again.

The great extended speech which closes act 1 of *The Invention of Love* is a meditation on a poem we have already met, briefly, on Horace's ode (4.1) to Ligurinus. This is the poem in which Horace breaks out in complaint against Venus for moving love in him again, when he is really too old. The speech in Stoppard's play begins in erudite comedy and ends in stark grief:

Intermissa, Venus, diu
rursus bella moves? Parce, precor, precor!
—mercy, I pray, I pray!, or perhaps better: spare me, I beg you, I beg you!—the very words I spoke when I saw that Mr. Fry was determined that *bella* is the adjective and very likely to mean beautiful, and that as eggs go with bacon it goes with Venus.

Intermissa, Venus diu
rursus bella moves?

Beautiful Venus having been interrupted do you move again?, he has Horace enquire in a rare moment of imbecility, and Horace is dead as we will all be dead but while I live I will report his cause aright. It's *war*, Mr. Fry!, and so is *bella*. Venus do you move *war*?, set in motion war, shall we say?, or start up the war, or better: Venus are you calling me to arms, *rursus*, again, *diu*, after a long time, *intermissa*, having been interrupted, or suspended if you like, and what is it that has been suspended? Two centuries ago Bentley read *intermissa* with *bella*, *war* having been suspended, not Venus, Mr. Fry, and—yes— Mr. Carsen—and also Miss Frobisher, good morning, you'll forgive us for starting without you—and now all is clear, is it not? Ten years after announcing in Book Three that he was giving up love, as the poet feels desire stirring once more and begs for mercy: "Venus, are you calling me to arms again after this long time of truce? Spare me, I beg you, I beg you! I am not the man I used to be under the reign of good Cinara," when good Cinara ruled me, *bona Cinara*, an epithet not bestowed lightly by the Augustan poets, so let us say "my dear Cinara," who died young, as we know because Horace tells us so—*proterva Cinara*—naughty, mischievous—who was also *rapax*— greedy, acquisitive—but for Horace amenable even without receiving a gift, or if we recall the collaboration of Mr. Watson and Mr. Wheeler, Cinara who had no gift for amenability. Mr. Watson and Mr. Wheeler blush. Miss Frobisher smiles, with little cause that I know of. If Jesus of Nazareth had had before him the example of Miss Frobisher getting through the Latin degree papers of the London University Examinations Board he would not have had to fall back on camels and the eyes of needles, and Miss Frobisher's name would be a delightful surprise to encounter in Matthew, Chapter 19; as would, even more surprisingly, the London University Examinations Board. Your name is not Miss Frobisher? What is your name? Miss Burton. I'm very sorry. I stand corrected. If Jesus of Nazareth had had before him example of Miss Burton getting through the . . . Oh dear, I hope it is not I who have made you cry. You don't mind? You don't mind when I make you cry? Oh, Miss Burton, you must try to mind a little. Life is in the minding. Here is Horace at the age of fifty pretending not to mind, verse 29, *me nec femina nec puer, iam nec spes animi credula mutui*—where's the verb? anyone? *iuvat*, thank you, it delights me not, what doesn't?—neither woman nor boy, nor the *spes credula*, the credulous hope, *animi mutui*—yes, well, mutual mind is roughly right, shared mind, yes, but he means love requited, you're allowed to notice the context—neither woman nor boy nor trusting hope of love returned, *nec*, nor, that's four *nec*s and a fifth to come before the "but," that's why we call it poetry—*nec certare iuvat mero*—yes, to compete in wine, that'll do for the moment, and *nec*—what?—*nec vincire novis tempora floribus*, rendered by Mr. Howard as to tie new flowers to my head, Tennyson would hang himself—never mind, here is Horace not minding: I take no pleasure in woman or boy, nor the trusting hope of love returned, nor matching drink for drink, nor binding fresh-cut flowers around my brow—*but—sed—cur heu, Ligurine, cur*—

Jackson is seen as a runner running towards us from the dark, getting no closer.

—but why, Ligurinus, alas why this unaccustomed tear trickling down my cheek?—why does my glib tongue stumble to silence as I speak? At night I hold you fast in my dreams, I run after you across the Field of Mars, I follow you into the tumbling waters, and you show no pity.

Blackout.

[*IL,* 49–51]

This is marvellous partly because Horace's poem is marvellous. You can't lose, with material like this. The Latin ends with a superb "nesting" of obduracy within images of flux, which translation into English has to weaken: "per aquas, dure, volubilis," "through the waters, O hard one, as they flow." What happens in the course of this speech is that the scholarly tetchiness, the asthenic jubilation in the detection of error first seen in Holofernes in *Love's Labour's Lost*, gives place to love which disables the very power of language in this clever, knowing, ageing man. We no longer have an absolute opposition of feeling and scholarship. Instead, Housman's very scholarship, his inwardness with Latin poetry, has led him to the perception of an enormous passion which is at last identical with his own. Ligurinus is Moses Jackson. As the clash between feeling and erudition vanishes so does the paper-thin opposition of male love and sexuality. This is sex and it is also love; love without any hope.

That speech ended in soliloquy. Act 2, after the gentle opening, conversation between Housman and his sister, catapults us back into the world of youthful badinage. Jackson enters, flushed with athletic victory:

POLLARD: Ave, Ligurine!
HOUSMAN: Jolly well done, Mo!

[*IL*, 69]

If *The Invention of Love* were to be copied and recopied over hundreds of years by half-comprehending scribes, these lines, one would confidently predict, would be corrupted. For they are, to a person who is not thinking hard enough, "the wrong way round." It should be *Housman* who greets Jackson with the words "Hail, Ligurinus!" and Pollard who stays with the common idiom. "*Ave Ligurine*" is Latin, and Housman is the Latinist of the group. They carry a charge of implied love that is proper to Housman and not to Pollard. Housman's words, by contrast, are asexual, jolly, comradely, as Pollard is to Jackson (and as Jackson is to Housman). But of course Stoppard knows very well what he is doing. Pollard, credibly, happens to remember a Latin tag that he must have heard Housman repeat many times and offers it unthinkingly. It is charged with meaning for the hearer, but the hearer also knows that it is not so charged for either Pollard or—more importantly—for Jackson. One might have expected Housman to answer Pollard, given that Pollard has, so to speak, strayed into Housman's area. But he does not. Instead his voice follows the track of his attention. He is compelled to speak at once to Jackson, man to man, lover to unloving, Horace to Ligurinus. This is urgent, dangerous stuff. The need to disguise it, to make it sound casual, is very great. Instead of allying himself with Pollard's allusion, he swiftly distances himself. The inner warmth of his reaction to the arrival of Jackson is evasively recast as boyish enthusiasm.

The final irony, perhaps, is that in a strange way the heterosexual innocence of Jackson, the great impediment to a full love requital, is an essential element for the lover. Housman loves the heterosexual Jackson as he could never love a Pater or a Wilde, for his simple unreflective maleness, his otherness. Earlier Chamberlain says, apropos of Jackson, "He'll never want what you want" (*IL,* 66). In Forster's short stories we find homosexual wish-fulfilment fantasies about dream-men who suddenly reciprocate erotically and yet are thoroughly heterosexual. At the level of ordinary narrative these moments are simply implausible. The difficulty is a difficulty *in rebus.* There can be few kinds of love more effectively doomed than that of the homosexual not for the fellow homosexual but for the heterosexual.

This gives an extra painfulness to the moving scene in which Housman confesses his love, not in soliloquy, but face to face with Jackson. The exchange opens, heartily, with a handshake:

JACKSON: . . . shake hands?

Jackson puts out his hand. Housman takes it.

HOUSMAN: Gladly.
JACKSON: Still pals?
HOUSMAN: Comrades.
JACKSON: Like whoever they were.
HOUSMAN: Theseus and Pirithous.

[*IL,* 78–79]

Already the tone is beginning to shift. "Comrades," though in some ways an aggressively asexual term, is more serious than Jackson's light word "pals." This time Jackson doesn't remember the Horace and Housman helps him, with Theseus and Pirithous from the end of "The snows are fled away." This carries us, but not the uncomprehending Jackson, into the world of love unto and beyond death. Housman begins warmly to explain the ancient idea of male friendship and then suddenly reverts to a lighter idiom. What is said however, in this lighter idiom, is explosive:

> HOUSMAN: Pollard thinks I'm sweet on you too, though he hardly knows he thinks it. Will you mind if I go to live somewhere close by?
>
> JACKSON: Why? Oh . . .

The expected denial of the absurd suggestion that Housman could be sweet on Jackson never comes. Instead we have the humble, hungry request to be allowed to live somewhere near, and the presentiment is after all confirmed. Even Jackson is baffled for only a second. His puzzled "Why?" is followed once by "Oh . . . ," which connotes understanding. Housman meanwhile is now frightened and abruptly switches back into the asexual idiom: "We'll still be friends, won't we?" But now it is too late. The pretence has gone and Jackson instead of answering with a warm affirmative as he would have done five minutes ago, now responds, again, with "Oh . . ." Housman says, with the courage of despair, "You're half my life."[5]

We think of Forster as, unequivocally, a twentieth-century writer. Yet his life overlaps substantially with that of Housman, as Housman's life overlaps with Pattison's. England was in fact full of living Victorians when Forster wrote *The Longest Journey* (1907). It is his novel about the life of the mind and therefore, in a way, his *Middlemarch*. In George Eliot's novel there is no trace of male homoeroticism, as far as I can see. *The Longest Journey* is, implicitly, full of it. This means that the relation of sex and learning or philosophy, fundamentally antagonistic in *Middlemarch*, is more complex in *The Longest Journey*. The marriage of the character, Rickie, is indeed a kind of deathblow in the book to all that is represented by Cambridge. Rickie's philosopher friend, Stuart Ansell, a figure of pure integrity, says that his objections to Agnes Pembroke, the woman Ricky marries, are: (1) "she is not generous," (2) "she is not truthful" (*Journey*, 82). In other words, she is the antithesis of scholarship. Cambridge meanwhile is an intellectual Arcadia of males who love one another and seek truth. Predictably, the novel is thickly strewn from beginning to end with Hellenist reference — Theocritus on page 5, Pegasus on page 15, Greek constellations on page 16, the Greek idea of a place that is simultaneously laughable and holy (page 18), the Hermes of Praxiteles (to correspond to the Ariadne of George Eliot) on page 33, the "gods of pure flame" on page 39, the conversation with Pembroke, the schoolmaster, about Plato and the Greeks on page 45, Aristophanes on page 47, the *genius loci* on page 58, gods and heroes on page 60, Xanthippe and Euripides on page 82, shepherds and the Doric lay on page 88, Apollo on page 91. There is an implicit positive sexual reference, as against the negative represented by Agnes, running through the book, but it is unconfessed. Where the breast of George Eliot's Ariadne is exposed, voluptuously, the Hermes of Praxiteles in *The Longest Journey* is head and shoulders only, his beautiful body removed from view. This in context is a mildly satirical stroke against the prudery of Mr. Pembroke in whose house the image stands, but it is a jibe too easily retorted upon Forster himself, who nervously reveals only a very small, unoffending part of the real inner meaning of his own novel. Yet when all this is said, the reader cannot miss the strength of Forster's affirmation of a life simultaneously intellectual and irradiated by love; only women excluded.

In Forster's novel women are absolute outsiders. If a woman enters the male Garden, she brings corruption. In the great extended speech which Stoppard gives to "AEH" we glimpse a woman who does not come in from outside. Miss Frobisher — who turns out not to be Miss Frobisher at all but Miss Burton — has been admitted to the society of learning, not as a possible marriage-object (as men's sisters were to other males when they came up to Oxford for the parties in "Eights Week" — the time when the crews of the various colleges competed on the river), but as a fellow student, allowed to attend lectures. She glimmers upon the field of vision of Housman as an incongruous, conceivably comic presence in the room. His very mistaking of her name is an assertion of superiority. His effusive apology is in part a charade, performed, we surmise, to entertain the males who are listening. The casual cruelty of his public commentary on her tears is carried through as if, somehow, she were not there at all. I said earlier that this speech ended in soliloquy, but one should not infer that it began as full, human conversation. Housman here speaks at first as a lecturer, talking *at* a fair-sized audience, rather than as an individual conversing with another. Lecturing is in limbo between conversation and soliloquy. The lecturer's mind is focussed on his subject, not on his auditors. Today lecturers are told to establish "eye contact" with the audience. I would guess that the idea would seem bizarre to Housman. If eye contact happens, it happens by chance. Miss Burton is certainly not welcomed to the society. Housman is not interested in her, as he would be if she were male and good-looking. Nor is he interested in her intellectually. What hope has she of ever beginning to understand the grief of Horace over Ligurinus? Yet at another level Housman seems to re-spect Miss Burton's tears. If she could move *with* her tears, he sug-gests, instead of politely suppressing them, she might after all come closer to the heart of the poem. It is as if, after the studied exclusion of the woman who is there, in the room, Housman discovers at last a kinship with her, in mere tears.

If instead of asking, "Is scholarship opposed to sex?" we ask, "Is scholarship opposed to life?" we may feel that the result of our in-vestigation is that they are, if not opposed, strangely separate. The only kind of sex that seems to join easily with the life of the mind is the kind which is involved essentially with celibate communities, which bears no living, biological children. At the same time we may feel, that the whole question is somehow disappearing.

One sunny morning in, I think, 1966 one of my more enigmatic colleagues said to me, "Whatever happened to scholarship?" I made some nonsensical and uncomprehending reply, for this, like many other remarks by this particular person, really needed mulling over. He had noticed what I, with the musty integuments of a 1950s Ox-ford education still spectrally about me, had not yet seen, namely, that the ideal of scholarship had almost ceased to figure explicitly in the moralising tittle-tattle of English literature academics. The mere incidence of the word, its frequency in intellectual discourse, has dropped, while "intelligent," "brilliant," and "right" have perhaps risen (I had a sense that "learned" in the early seventeenth century began to be ousted in a similar fashion by "ingenious," but the *Oxford English Dictionary* does not support me clearly). The reader may wish to point out that "right," and "correct" are now under attack from metaphysically radical theorists, but I propose to set that aside." Right" is certainly still in vigorous use. I ask myself, do we now say of our peers, "John Carey is a better scholar than Christopher Ricks" (or vice versa)? Or do we all eagerly discuss the level of *scholarship* in Terry Eagleton's *Rape of Clarissa?* As soon as I imagine such an exchange, I find that it has assumed, without my intending it, a faint yet discernible flavour of *period* — of the 1950s, say. It has become almost impossible for a sensitive lecturer to say, "X is unscholarly," with a fine freedom of a Helen Gardner, not only because most of us lack that lady's enviable confidence in such matters. "Scholarly" and "scholarship" are now terms for talking about dons who are in some degree remote from us, who belong to a culture very close to, but not identical with our own.

It may be that "intelligence" and "rightness" have begun to take over from "scholarship" because of an increasingly widespread presumption that scholarship itself, insofar as it is commendable, is already comprehended by those terms. I am reminded here of an argument that is sometimes advanced about loyalty. Loyalty, it is said, is an ethically undeveloped concept. In so far as the practice of loyalty is distinct from virtuous behaviour in general, it is actually immoral. Loyalty means "My country right or wrong," but "My country wrong" is immoral; meanwhile "My country right" is mere virtue, since no special exercise of *loyalty* is involved in supporting a cause which one believes to be right, *on its merits.* So with scholarship: If a writer is intelligent and right about the material, what need have we to discuss the level of scholarship? All that matters has already taken care of. If "scholarly," in any case, means no more than this, why revive a word that is otiose? If, in contrast, it really does carry a meaning beyond "intelligent" and "right," it may continue as a word, but we feel no obligation to notice it, since the whole duty of an intellectual is already comprehended by the other terms, "intelligent" and so on.

This, I suspect, is the tacit logic of the situation. I want to argue that there is something crass and perhaps even disingenuous in the general, easy acceptance of it. I was careful to say earlier that "scholarship" has ceased to figure explicitly in our talk, and I have tried to make it clear that it is the word, rather than the thought, which is now less prominent in gossip about our colleagues. The ideal of scholarship, openly upheld by the educators of my generation, continues to operate at an unacknowledged level — though in varying degrees — even now. Let us return to the question, "What does *scholarly* say, which is not said by *intelligent* and *right?*" The word, I think, connotes a quality of completeness: at the lowest level, complete literacy (never a colon where a comma should be); complete, though not redundant documentation; complete accuracy *even with reference to matters not crucial to the main argument,* and, together with all this, a sense that the writer's knowledge of material at the fringe of the thesis is as sound as his or her knowledge of the core material. This seems to me to be the essence of the matter — that although there may be a strong central thesis which rightly absorbs most of the energies available, the writer nevertheless maintains a broad front of total accuracy, a sort of democracy of fact, in which no atom of truth shall be slighted, however humble in relation to the main theme.

Now this kind of vigilance, this regard for facts even when they are not pet facts, is not natural to human beings. Just as the ordinary person cannot copy a page of eighteenth-century prose without committing about ten errors, so the ordinary person cannot tell a story or advance on argument without mangling and misrepresenting everything at the edge of his or her interest. Of course, people lie and blunder in their main theses too, but at least they are conscious that such behaviour is discreditable. The very concept of trying to get *everything* right involves a queer, abstract *altruism of the intellect* and it took thousands of years to learn.

Some, surveying the intellectual history of humanity, may question whether the effort was worthwhile. So many wonderful people have been quite without scholarship; so many sad bores have possessed it on the highest degree. Shakespeare (natural man writ large, as the bardolaters used to say) has no tincture of scholarship. Everything relevant to his purpose he gets right and the rest is what Virgil called *tibicines* — just props to keep the roof up. On the diction of a courtier, Shakespeare may lavish a linguistic scrupulousness beyond anything we can find in the commentaries of a Frank Kermode or a Harold Jenkins, but on, say, surrounding geographical details (as it might be the sea coast of Bohemia) he will be content with his usual unobtrusive inaccuracy. But Shakespeare, since he is a writer of fictions, may be thought an inappropriate example.

Let us bring the argument nearer home. What, today, is the difference between a scholarly article and one that is not a particularly scholarly but yet such that we admire it? The unscholarly, brilliant article advances and adequately supports a new thesis of great intrinsic interest and explanatory power. At the same time, its author fails to specify which editions are being used, quotes on occasion from two different translations of the same continental work (without noticing the fact that they differ), betrays the fact in passing — though it does not destroy the main thesis — that he or she has not consulted the German original. Note that, as regards the main thesis, all is well. The scholarly article, in contrast, exhibits none of these "vices." It does things "in proper form."

Since the author of the first (the unscholarly) article got right everything which he or she needed to get right, the extra, peripheral accuracy of the second would seem to be, by definition, superfluous. And this implies that scholarship, so defined, = pedantry. Indeed, in the present climate of opinion, it is very easy to make our scholarly writer, doggedly crossing every "t" and dotting every "i," look somewhat foolish. Who needs the sort of thing? Shakespeare we have already mentioned; more examples are easily found. Keats couldn't spell; Plato couldn't quote Homer straight (perhaps didn't even have the *concept* of quoting straight); the great period of ancient scholarship was the Alexandrian, and it was the great period of nothing else, except perhaps astronomy. Jesus (though he gave the doctors in the Temple a bad time) shows no sign of any scholarly distinction whatever. All the really important things — and that includes the really important things of intellect and spirit — can go on without it.

To this it may be replied that scholarship, though never a necessity, has proved at a modest level a very useful assistant to the intellectual life. Aristotle is great, but if he had known how to represent his predecessors in philosophy as something other than lisping Aristotelians, he might have been even greater. My former colleague

Professor Laurence Lerner hates, instinctively and immediately, books with copious footnotes and indexes. I find such things useful and am more often irritated by the absence than by their presence. Scholarly scrupulousness is in the first place useful to other scholars, who may wish to push a given line of enquiry in fresh directions. Getting all your references right becomes, in the context of widespread intellectual endeavour, a sort of good manners, like not slamming doors in people's faces.

But still, my anti-scholar may persist, the scholar's stance has grown more artificial with the years. Accuracy of measurement is necessary to the scientist, but scholarship carefully detached itself, as being "humane," from science some centuries ago, and in consequence its parade of accuracy, when set beside the scrupulousness of a Newton or a Rutherford, appears grotesquely factitious, an affectation rather than an instrument of the intellectual life. This view is given an extra charge by ex-scientist William Empson, who wrote in the preface to his *Milton's God*, "Line references are to the nearest factor of five, because factors of ten are usually given in the margin of the text, and the eye can then find the place without further calculation. The show of scientific accuracy about literary quotations has reached a point which feels odd to anyone who knows how numbers are really used in the sciences."[6]

The question is best judged at the lowest level (it is still my anti-scholar speaking): Why should we insist that our students spell better than Keats? Because a student who cannot spell will write "complaisant" when he or she means "complacent" or, worse still, forget the difference? Such things are drops in the ocean of the intellectual life. Anyone who thinks them more must be, intellectually, in a condition of senile myopia. Even if we admit that scholars do not form a completely closed society — in this differing from say philosophers, who really do spend most of their time wrestling with problems which would not have appeared but for other philosophers — grant, I say, that the effects of scholarly activity permeate the larger intellectual world, is this intellectual world so important? Grant the force of the good manners argument — is the spectacle of so many greybeards bowing and smiling to each other *in the middle of a world of pain* so very admirable? Granted that the meticulous procedures of scholarship have a certain ethical status within the group, what if the group activity is itself only a kind of expensive sport, singularly lacking in spectator interest? The scholars annotate and review and meanwhile babies die and are born.

Here the argument becomes radical and I will confess that in a way I find it insuperable. As long as people are starving and it is in my power to help them, it is wrong to stick to scholarship. I will only add that the same argument disposes of almost every human activity that I can think of. We have all of us, by this just standard, opted for second best; beside Simone Weil, we are all second-rate people. The edge of this argument has been blunted by little, per-haps, by world population problems. But it still cuts. Has the ideal of scholarship no foothold in morality at all? Is there no real virtue in it anywhere?

The most obviously moral component in the scholarly ideal has of course already been mentioned. I mean an altruistic reverence for truth, in all its possible minuteness and complexity. Dorothy L. Say-ers — Tory, Christian, feminist, Dante-scholar, and writer of detective fiction — wrote a novel to glorify this idea: *Gaudy Night* (1935). We now return to Oxford; like Cambridge, a city of learning, and, again like Cambridge, a city which, for hundreds of years, excluded the lower classes. Hardy's stonemason hero in *Jude the Obscure* was en-tranced as a child by the lights of Oxford seen in the distance, but then, years afterwards, was shut out by the great gate of "Biblioll College."[7] As Oxford excluded men of the artisan class so it also excluded women. A book about scholars has to be, in part, a book about the exclusion of women. It was in painful consciousness of this that I made George Eliot the centre of my first case study. George Eliot may have been on good terms socially with the rector of Lincoln College, but really the gates of the Oxford colleges, as educational institutions, were closed upon her no less firmly than they had been upon Jude. Yet George Eliot never begins to hate scholarship in her turn. Hardy's Jude, at a certain level, even loves the city from which he is shut out. We are told how he came to know every inch of the architectural monuments of "Christminster" (Ox-ford) and how the spirit of the place "ate further and further into him" (*Jude*, 2.2:121). In one extended passage that is unusually testing for the modern reader, Hardy says that Jude, walking the streets by night, no longer permitted to enter the quadrangles, senses at every turn the ghosts of Oxford's past and present. This is done allusively, with no proper names, but they are the ghosts of Ben Jonson, Swinburne, Newman, Keble, Pusey, Bolingbroke, Gibbon, Bishop Ken, John Wesley, Peel, Arnold, and Browning (with whom this book began). He evokes in passing, glancingly, the "matrimonial difficulties" (*Jude*, 2.1:116) John Wesley had with Mary Vazeille; we think of Mr. Casaubon, we think of Milton, but still more we think here of course of Jude himself, whose own story will be one of sexual pain entwined with the pursuit of learning. Jude's "matrimonial difficulties" are not with Sue Bridehead only; it is clear that his love affair with Oxford is likewise frustrated, impaired. George Eliot, one senses, was better equipped for the battle of life than Jude. She was strong enough and clever enough not to need Oxford. But it would be a mistake to think of her as unwounded by the exclusion.

Dorothy L. Sayers, however, unlike George Eliot, was admitted to Somerville College, Oxford, and took a First in modern languages in 1915. There is a clear sense in *Gaudy Night* that women are incongruous newcomers on the academic scene, are somehow on the edge of comedy, but in Dorothy L. Sayers, yet again, love of the place is dominant over resentment. *Gaudy Night* is about a ladies' college where the inmates (if that is the right word) are reduced to a state of near terror by a series of obscene notes, drawings, poison-pen letters, wanton destruction, threats, and violence. Lord Peter Wimsey, the great detective, uncovers the source of it all. One of the college servants, Annie, was married, years before, to a young researcher. This man, rather than abandon a treasured thesis, suppressed a fact. One Miss de Vine detected the suppression, and her detection cost the young man his career and perhaps his life. As a result Annie was filled with hatred of the priggish abstractness of Miss de Vine and all she stood for. Annie struggled on in poverty bringing up the children, grieving for the husband she loved. Annie, of course, is the culprit. At the time when the events in the novel take place, Miss de Vine has become research fellow in history at Shrewsbury College, and Annie, in a state of nervous disintegration, has come to detest all female learning and indeed all feminism. She now believes in *Kinder, Kirche, Küche* ("children, church, and cooking") as the proper sphere of women and in this state of mind plans and carries out her campaign against the female Senior Common Room in general and Miss de Vine in particular. The novel mounts to a terrific climax in which Annie, unmasked, verbally lashes the assembled fellows of the college, telling them that they are dried up, frustrated, evil women.

I am told that the book when first published caused great offence in a real Oxford ladies' college (the one which the college in the book was modelled on). Seemingly Annie's barbed arrow went home. Dorothy L. Sayers was not forgiven for what was construed as a terrible insult. But this is odd because Dorothy L. Sayers did not agree with Annie. Every member of the Senior Common Room and the author sides implicitly with Miss de Vine. She could not have done anything else. Miss de Vine herself is distressed that she never took the trouble to make sure afterwards that the young man whose fraud she exposed was personally all right. But on the main question the Common Room and Sayers are adamant. The book is a paean in praise of the absolute obligation of the scholar to truth, even at a terrible human cost.

I suppose the appeal of this severe, intransigent ethic will be greater for some people than for others. Personally, I feel that it has real force. Notice that there is no need to set it up as a simple, autonomous command: "Always tell the truth, not because it will make people happy, but because truth-telling is, in itself, right." The issue is, in practice, muddier than that. Sayers certainly knew that other obligations, such as the obligation of compassion, may also be present, in tension with the obligation to be truthful. Meanwhile, scholarly truth-telling itself may have a utilitarian aspect. Faking can have enormous, if unspectacular consequences. If we cannot place a reasonable degree of trust in our scholars, we cannot trust anyone. The contention of my anti-scholar, that even if habits of scholarly accuracy permeate the intellectual world, this intellectual world is itself negligibly small—this contention after all rests on a rhetorical exaggeration. The area of influence is in fact immense; ideologies spread wider every day; in many populous nations the middle classes now outnumber the proletariat. In the practical details of daily life habitual accuracy is a great oiler of wheels. The output of universities does, by and large, administer the complex institutions of Western society, and, if I ask myself what sort of higher education is likely to instil habitual, small-scale accuracy, I am inclined to think that the old-style scholarly training was better than the present Western vogue for matching ideologies. Of course if you want to train revolutionaries, that is another matter.

One objection I would reject instantly is the claim that scholarship is inherently socially divisive. Certainly it separates the truthful, the dogged, and the patient from the rest, but there is no reason why it must separate the middle and the lower classes. If anything the reverse is the case. It is the free-ranging "idea-mongering" that implicitly favours the middle-class child, while it has been contended that working-class culture prepares people very naturally for tasks involving the steady elimination of error.

But—to return to the immediate consequences of scholarly fraud within the intellectual sphere: morally, the situation of the scholarly faker is like that of the academic pressured to bend the grades of a black American student. An immediate kindness is conferred but a possibly damaging precedent is set up. Currency so given is devalued even as it is passed from hand to hand. I will not attempt to resolve finally the ethical problem of *Gaudy Night*. I use the book only because it isolates with some vividness the principal moral component of the scholarly ideal.

But, of course, ideals are one thing and practice another. "Scholarship" may mean truth-telling and scrupulousness, but scholars are honest and false like other people. Perhaps indeed scholars have a greater capacity for evil mendacity than others just because of the authority they wield. I ask myself whether the ideal in any degree conditions the practice—whether the habit of verification, etc., makes people more truthful in general—and I think that it does, but not in any very marked degree. When I reflect on the characters of scholars I have known, what strikes me immediately is their "dottiness"—eccentricity. This feature of the scholarly character has a long history. The ancient scholar Didymus, who wrote between 3,500 and 4,000 books (ancient books were of course short—this is a mere 300 or so in modern terms), is even at this distance and time, palpably eccentric. Quintilian tells us about the way he forgot in one book what he had written in another,[8] and his nickname, "Brazen Guts," is somehow disquieting. What are we to think of Mavortius, who improvised Virgilian centoes (that is, he could spontaneously emit metrically correct, meaningful Latin poetry entirely composed of re-arranged fragments of Virgil)? The eminent numismatist Richard Payne Knight was deeply — some felt, inordinately — interested in representations of the phallus in antiquity. The great classical scholar Richard Porson once carried a young woman round a room in his teeth,[9] and Friedrich August Wolf, during periods of strenuous study, "would sit up the whole night in a room without a stove, his feet in a pan of cold water, and *one of his eyes bound up to rest the other.*"[10] When I was an undergraduate the most learned philologist I knew once said to an assembled class, "Gentlemen, I shall expect you on Tuesday at eleven," and when one of the pupils said, "But, Mr. Smithers, you are giving a lecture in the schools at eleven on Tuesdays," replied, "Ah yes, but that that is on *Havelok the Dane.* You need not go to that." More worryingly, for all the scholarly ideal of objectivity, I have a distinct impression that real scholars, as compared with the smoother "ideas-men" who have begun to replace them, are characterised by a manic partiality for their own theories. I remember my old tutor Robert Levens telling me how he once met W. S. Barrett, the learned editor of Euripides, and Barrett said something like, "Grube has just come up with a completely new explanation of line 843 — but I'll *shoot it down, I'll shoot it down* somehow." We prate of scholarly objectivity, but does no one remember *odium scholasticum,* "scholastic hatred"?

It is difficult to decide which of these is uppermost in the learned writings of Stoppard's favourite, Housman. Here he is, on Elias Stoeber, who wrote a commentary on Manilius:

> If a man will comprehend the richness and variety of the universe, and inspire his mind with a due measure of wonder and awe, he must contemplate the human intellect not only on its heights of genius but in its abysses of ineptitude; and it might be fruitlessly be debated to the end of time whether Richard Bentley or Elias Stoeber was the more marvellous work of the creator: Elias Stoeber, whose

198

reprint of Bentley's text, with a commentary intended to confute it, saw the light in 1767 at Strasburg, a city still famous for its geese. ... Stoeber's mind, though that is no name to call it by, was one which turned as unswervingly to the false, the meaningless, the unmetrical, and the ungrammatical, as the needle to the pole.[11]

Housman thought little of Franz Buecheler and still less of Siegfried Sudhaus; so he wrote, "I imagine that Mr. Buecheler, when he first perused Mr. Sudhaus's edition of the Aetna, must have felt something like Sin when she gave birth to death."[12] In his 1894 review of G. C. Schulze's edition of Emil Baehrens's Catullus, Housman wrote,

> The first edition of Baehrens' Catullus, which now that the second has appeared will fetch fancy prices, was in the rigour of the term an epoch-making work. But it exhibited a text of the author much corrupted by unprovoked or unlikely or incredible conjecture; so that the task of revision was delicate, and the choice of a reviser was not easy. It was not easy, but scholars who are acquainted with the history of Catullus' text and with the metres he wrote in, who know how to edit a book and how to collate a manuscript, who are capable of coherent reasoning or at all events of consecutive thought, exist; and to such a scholar the task might have been allotted.
>
> It has been allotted to Mr. Schultze.[13]

I fancy that it would take little labour to show that high scholarship is compatible with prejudice and bigotry carried to extremes.

But even if particular scholars may on occasion fail to come up to their own highest standards not only of charity but of ordinary fairness, habits are catching. The habit of truthfulness, though often dishonoured, has spread and had effect. We make jokes in England about the Civil Service, but for all that I believe the Civil Service has some tincture of it. Of course it has now become clear that the question "What can I do, as a scholar, which is morally useful?" is quite different from the question "Should there be scholars?" The answer to the first question is comparatively simple: labour to be accurate; correct the errors of others with charity and honesty, free the minds of young from cant, arm them against sophistry and imposture, teach them to be intellectually just. This duty indeed is made the more pressing by the existence of bad scholars and teachers. As to the second question, "Should there be scholars at all?" I think I do have to say that money spent on university libraries would be better spent on relieving the Third World. But if that is not to be, since man doth not live by bread alone but is an incurable spinner of ideas, we might as well have some who are trained to ask critical questions, to weigh and to test. I myself feel a real disquiet at the thought of, say, even a movement to better the lot of the poor being utterly free from any but a partisan intellectual framework. This means that I am worried by the thought of a total, uncriticised Marxism of mind and spirit. Fortunately this has never happened. Even moral imperatives that seem most absolute, such as that of Marx or, in another age, of Calvin, turn out to need the modest queries of Merry Middle Earth.

I will now interject a thought on teaching. I have a generalised feeling that in some ways recent trends in university education have turned out to be merely an extremely subtle way of making young people wretched. I say "subtle" because of course the superficial indicators point in the opposite direction. Under the old scholarly method one was constantly under correction; one's mental knuckles, so to speak, smarted continuously. Today, by contrast, I suspect that the typical experience of a student in an English university is of a sort of matey neutrality: "Yes, that's very interesting," says the tutor: a dreadful word, that "interesting." Iago would have used it, if it had been available in Shakespeare's time. One of the advantages of being told when you are wrong is that you gradually build up a sense of what it might mean to be right. Progress, when it occurs, is palpable. Meanwhile the matey neutrality of which I spoke a moment ago is often interpreted by students, I would say correctly, as callous indifference.

We do not choose culture. Good or bad, it is ours without our asking. I used the phrase "Man doth not live by bread alone" in a prescriptive manner earlier. I now use it descriptively. It is a fact that human beings ideologise. Although cultures without scholarship can be better than cultures with, other things being equal, a culture laced with scholarship is an inch or two better than one without. In the face of this it seems to be ill-judged to pretend that the life of the mind does not matter, is merely epiphenomenal or less than fully real. The unimpeded exercise of the intellect itself constitutes a good — I think, indeed, one of the terminal goods, though not the most important. It is often said that learning is bad because it is not useful. I have tried in this last part of this book to argue for a modest usefulness. But if intellection is one of the terminal goods, references to further utility have in any case, a secondary status. That is why Aristotle chose to turn the argument round. If all the goods are good only because they promote some other good, we are launched on an infinite regress. Somewhere there must be some thing or things for the sake of which the other goods exist, something not merely useful for a further purpose, but good in itself. And so Aristotle asked, in effect, "What do we do when we are no longer pressed and harried by hunger, enemies, and sickness?" His answer, which is one of several possible, is that we then pursue with unimpeded energy the intellectual life. So that must be good in itself — a terminal good.

History has played a series of strange tricks on Marx. About twenty years ago a friend told me how he crossed from West into East Berlin and how profoundly he was affected by his visit. West Berlin, he said, was a showpiece of capitalism, blazing with pornographic cinemas, the shop windows loaded with *Playboy* magazine goodies, gifts for the man who has everything; meanwhile in East Berlin autumn leaves drifted in a faded street of pale stucco houses, there was a long queue at the opera house, another at the concert hall, and the bookshops were full of classics of German literature. It occurred to me as he spoke that he was moved entirely by the overmastering spiritual value of what he saw, or thought he saw, in East Berlin. Dialectical materialism had turned out to be so much less materialist. Then the Berlin Wall came down and an entirely different set of paradoxes appeared. If the spirit had somehow flourished, economic reality, the professed centre of Marxian thinking, was catastrophic, desperate. And so the countries of the former Warsaw Pact moved convulsively to the free market and also (though there were some exceptions) simultaneously to its presumed necessary correlative: the closure of art galleries and opera houses, the opening of strip clubs. Today in the West we hear little of Moscow and Saint

Petersburg but stories of drug wars and the like — a kind of exaggerated parody of the West. Another friend of mine observed that it was as if one were to think that if one ceased to be a believing Christian one must forthwith become a Satanist.

The monuments of the life of the mind are enormously good in themselves — some of the best things we have. We in England could live without Shakespeare and could not live without the sea, but, for all that, Shakespeare is very like the sea.

This brings me to the last benefit of scholarship, to my mind the most important of all. I once went to a lecture given by F. R. Leavis in which he discussed what a literary education could give to the student. There was a good deal about the capacity for sensitive appreciation of the needs of others, the capacity for fuller life, the development of critical acumen, and so forth. All a bit true and no more. As I left the lecture hall I asked myself what my literary education seemed to be giving me and suddenly the answer blazed in my mind. My teachers had given or were giving me (I refuse to shorten this list): Homer, Aeschylus, Sophocles, Euripides, Theocritus, Virgil, Horace, Chaucer, Langland, Spenser, Shakespeare, Donne, Marvell, Milton, Pope, Sterne, Keats, Wordsworth. And, for good measure, they added Sappho, Catullus, the Gawain poet, Marlowe, Herbert, Vaughan, Crabbe. And then more. Why did no one mention this? I think I had never before noticed what wealth was there. All the clichéd titles of dog-eared anthologies, "The Golden Treasury," "Realms of Gold," and the like, became for the moment soberly meaningful. It will be said that I am describing the literary canon, which has been shown to be an instrument of oppression. I would have had none of that then and I will have none of it now. It was clear to me that I had inherited an endless glittering landscape with hills, dales, and secret woods, "all mine, yet common to my every peer."[14]

There is no doubt in my mind that the scholars gave all this to me. It could be said that I might have read all these books by myself, unaided by scholars. That is simply not true. The ancient authors would have been too hard. *Paradise Lost,* I am pretty sure, I would never have read, for I was instinctively repelled by it at first, though later it altered my consciousness of literature forever. Shakespeare I would certainly have read, but I would have been pusillanimously content with a fraction of his meaning. Mere perusal is not after all enough. These are not tables and chairs but great poets. They are immensely, indefinitely complex objects. Explainers, demonstrators, explorers must always be at work or the thing itself will be lost. More than that, the text we peruse is itself subject to decay. Even more than we need explanatory critics (I have never, by the way, felt the need for "judge-critics") we need editors. Wholly futile essays have been written on the supposedly Yeatsian phrase, "soldier Aristotle." Good editing showed that Yeats wrote not "soldier" but "solider" and the hole was plugged. It is the editors who recover, preserve, and hand down. Scholarship is, at one and the same time, a conservative and an exploratory activity. Even a modern book, carelessly reprinted, deteriorates fast. The hard-pressed printer, true to his principle of *facilior lectio potior,* "rather the easier reading," again and again substitutes the commonplace for the unique and the insensible drift from better to worse begins. The old principle of textual criticism was, of course, the opposite: other things being equal, *difficilior lectio potior,* "rather the more difficult reading." Housman, who has had rather a bad press in these last pages, shows profound editorial skill, in line with this ancient principle, when he tells how, in a printed version of a poem by Walter de la Mare, he read the words "May the rustling harvest hedgerow / Still the traveller's joy entwine." "I knew in a moment," he writes, "that Mr. de la Mare had not written *rustling,* and in another moment I had found the true word."[15] The true reading was the much rarer word *rusting,* meaning "turning brown," the *difficilior lectio.*

Of course as critics we may in the course of doing our job find fault with a line of Hopkins or disparage a Miltonic lyric. But we should not forget that Hopkins's and Milton's writings constitute a good so great as to render such a local discriminations needle-fine in their ultimate effect — a good so large that for most of the time we do not even see it any more than we feel the air in our nostrils. Go to a magistrate's court and listen to the magistrate ordering the burning of books, as I have done, and the fact will break on your mind.

One thing that I am saying may perhaps seem strange, so I will try in conclusion to make its full oddity clear, so that I am at least hung for a sheep, not a lamb. I am saying that Milton and Keats are in a certain sense good in themselves. I am conscious that I say these things at a time when the wind of fashion is blowing stiffly in the opposite direction. When some theorists are willing to argue that the former substances, the poem, the writer, and the reader are all, equally, mere constructions it would seem that *a fortiori* the *value* of a poem is, the more certainly, a social construction rather than a reality-to-be-perceived, yet I am saying just that. Nor is my position here in any way a utilitarian one. I am not just saying that Milton and Keats give better and more lasting pleasure than Jackie Collins and bingo (though I believe that this is true for a large number of people). The hedonistic argument that Donne will be found a better felicific investment than Agatha Christie is often used dishonestly by teachers, I think. The number of those for whom it is true must be small (and many reread Agatha Christie over and over again with the greatest of pleasure). If I examine my own sensibility, I have to say that — not Agatha Christie, whom I can't read, but Arthur Conan Doyle has given me just a little more pleasure than Donne, but it is clear to me that Donne is better than Doyle and the excellence of Donne interests me deeply. If I were to tell a schoolchild that reading the classics would give him or her more pleasure than he or she could get from computer games, I should feel uncertain in my conscience afterwards. But if I were to tell the child that these books were really good, my conscience would be clear. I do not think Milton is good because he gives pleasure. I think he gives pleasure because he is good. If the sustaining of a certain quantum of pleasure were our sole aim in caring for the work of great poets, then there would certainly be occasions when it would be our duty to alter the text, to give not what Blake wrote but what people would like him to have written. The head-counting argument which tells us that the number of those who derive great pleasure from Johnson's *Rasselas* is small would suddenly have great weight. To the scholar it is always the other way round. The poet's authority is first in their minds; it is the poet rather than the sensibility of the present age that is to be followed. Doubtless there will be cases (and it is scholarship that will show us these cases) in which it really does make no sense to look for the individual author. Ballad poetry is a possible example.

But then a parallel principle will still apply: the authority of the culture that produced the work will be set above the present, receiving culture. The celebrated learned drunk Porson, already referred to, said it all when he observed, "I am quite satisfied if, three hundred years hence, it shall be said that one Porson lived toward the close of the eighteenth century who did a good deal for the text of Euripides." Why, so you did, sir (I address his ghost). What would Leavis say in similar circumstances? That he did his bit for D. H. Lawrence? Or that he did something to stop the rot among the English intelligentsia? I suspect that it would be the second. For Leavis was not a scholar. Therefore his head is turned in another direction. Certainly if the sum of readers' happiness was prior to the author's words in the scholar's scheme of values, the task would be easier. The special discipline of compassing thought utterly unlike one's own would gradually fall into disuse. The study of literature would become for all, what it already is for some, a mode of narcissism. No doubt some (notably those who talk most loudly about "relevance") might be pleased to be handed, not Milton, but a Miltonised version of their own features. But to receive ourselves is to receive nothing, and those who provide such stuff are fraudulent. In contrast the real scholars have been generous; the editors, the *editores*, the givers-out-into-the-world; the givers of good things.

Notes

Introduction

1. See Francis Galton, *Inquiries into Human Faculty*, 2d ed. (1907; reprint, London: Everyman, 1928), opp. 8.
2. Hugh Lloyd-Jones, *Blood for the Ghosts: Classical Influences in the Nineteenth and Twentieth Centuries* (London: Duckworth, 1982), 17.
3. John Gower, *Confessio Amantis* 6.1398–1410, 1769–72, in *The Complete Works of John Gower*, ed. G. C. Macaulay, 4 vols. (Oxford: Clarendon Press, 1899–1902), 3:205, 215.
4. See M. T. Clanchy, *Abelard: A Medieval Life* (Oxford: Blackwell, 1997), 115.
5. In *The Works of Francis Bacon*, ed. J. Spedding, R. L. Ellis, and D. D. Heath, 7 vols. (London: Longman, 1857–59), 3:559–60, 532, 584.
6. E. A. Abbott, *Bacon: An Account of His Life and Works* (London: Macmillan, 1885), 370.
7. Francis Bacon, *Novum Organon*, cxxix, in *The Philosophical Works of Francis Bacon*, ed. J. M. Robertson (London: George Routledge, 1905), 300.

8. Ibid.

9. See Leon Battista Alberti, *De Commodis Litterarum atque Incommodis*, ed. Laura Goggi Carotti (Florence: Leo S. Olschki, 1976), 46–47, and Anthony Grafton, *Leon Battista Alberti: Master Builder of the Italian Renaissance* (London: Penguin, 2001), 32.

10. *Robert Browning, The Poems*, Penguin English Poets, ed. John Pettigrew, supplemented and completed by Thomas J. Collins, 2 vols. (Harmondsworth: Penguin, 1981), 1:733.

11. George Eliot, *Middlemarch*, ed. David Carroll (Oxford: Oxford University Press, 1997), 1.4:40, hereafter cited in the text as *Middlemarch*.

12. W. B. Yeats, "The Scholars," in *The Collected Poems of W. B. Yeats* (London: Macmillan, 1935), 158.

13. Francesco Petrarca, *Africa*, ed. Nicola Feste (Florence: G. C. Sansoni, 1926), 278.

14. Lorenzo Valla, "Praefatio" to his *De Elegantiis Latinae Linguae* (written in the 1430s), in Laurentius Valla, *Opera Omnia*, intro. Eugenio Garin, 2 vols. (Turin: Bottega d'Erasmo, 1962; a facsimile of the 1590 Basel ed. of the *Opera*), 1:4.

15. Huldrichus Coccius, "Epistola Nuncupatoria" prefixed to *Io Lodovici Vivis . . . Opera*, 2 vols. (Basel, 1555), 1:2v.

16. Giorgio Vasari, *Le vite de' piu ecellenti pittori scultori e architettori*, 9 vols. (6 text, 3 commentary) (Florence: G. C. Sansoni, 1966–87), 1 (text):31.

17. Sir Thomas More, *Utopia*, in vol. 4 of *The Complete Works of St. Thomas More*, ed. Edward Surtz, S.J., and J. H. Hexter (Yale University Press: New Haven and London, 1965), 50.

18. Quintilian *Institutio Oratoria* 1.7.20; in the Oxford text, ed. M. Winterbottom, 2 vols. (Oxford: Clarendon Press, 1970), 1:57.

19. For a summary of the points of contact with Dickens, see *The Brownings' Correspondence*, ed. Philip Kelley and Ronald Hudson, 14 vols. to date (Winfield, Kans.: Wedgestone, 1984–), 5:368–70.

20. See John Donne's *Letters to severall persons of honour* (London: John Marriot, 1651), 51, and John Keats, "Ode to a Nightingale," l. 18.

21. Robert Burton, *The Anatomy of Melancholy*, 1.2.3.15, ed. Thomas C. Faulkner, Nicolas K. Kiessling, and Rhonda L. Blair, 6 vols. to date (Oxford: Clarendon Press, 1989–), 1:323, 304.

22. Erasmus, *The Praise of Folly*, trans. John Wilson [1668], ed. P. S. Allen (Oxford: Clarendon Press, 1913), 73–74.

23. See Mark Pattison, *Isaac Casaubon* (London: Longmans, Green, 1875), 466–67.

24. Burton, *Anatomy of Melancholy*, 1.3.2.4 (1:418, 417).

25. See Suetonius *Divus Iulius* xlix, ed. H. E. Butler and M. Cary (Oxford: Clarendon Press, 1927), 23.

26. George Monteiro, "A Proposal for Settling the Grammarian's Estate," *Victorian Poetry* 3 (1965): 266–70, 268.

27. Erasmus, *The Praise of Folly,* in *Opera Omnia Desiderii Erasmi Roterodami* (Amsterdam: North-Holland, 1969–), Ordinis 2, Tomus 3 (1979), 140. In John Wilson's translation, edited by Helen Mary Allen (Oxford: Clarendon Press, 1913), 105.

28. J. D. Denniston, *The Greek Particles,* 2d ed. (Oxford: Clarendon Press, 1954), xxxvii.

29. See *Robert Browning, The Poems,* 1:1144.

30. Spinoza, *Ethics,* pt. 5, prop. 23, in *Opera: Werke,* ed. G. Gawlick and F. Niewöhner, 2 vols. (Darmstadt: Wissenschaftliche Buchgesellschaft, 1979–80), 2:536.

31. *Robert Browning, The Poems,* 1:1144.

32. See Laurence Lerner, *The Truthtellers* (London: Chatto and Windus, 1967), 114–17.

33. Martin J. Svaglic, "Browning's Grammarian: Apparent Failure or Real?" *Victorian Poetry* 5 (1967): 93–103, 98–99.

34. Robert C. Schweik, "The Structure of 'A Grammarian's Funeral,'" *College English* 22 (1961): 411–12.

35. Spinoza, pt. 5, prop. 24, in *Opera: Werke,* 2:536.

36. Cicero *Ad Atticum* 1.21.1, in *Cicero: Letters to Atticus,* Loeb Classical Library, trans. E. O. Winstedt, 3 vols. (London: Heinemann, 1912–18), 1: 48.

Chapter 1: Mr. Casaubon in *Middlemarch*

1. Samuel Johnson, *Lives of the English Poets,* ed. G. Birkbeck Hill, 3 vols. (Oxford: Clarendon Press, 1905), 1:145.

2. Ovid *Fasti* 4.221–44; Pausanias *Description of Greece* 7.17.10–12.

3. I take Featherstone (who also dies) to be a substantial *minor* character.

4. Richard Jenkyns, *The Victorians and Ancient Greece* (Oxford: Basil Blackwell, 1980), 127.

5. George Eliot was unwell during her visit to Rome in 1860. She wrote in her journal of "the hideous red drapery in St. Peter's." See *The Journals of George Eliot,* ed. Margaret Harris and Judith Johnson (Cambridge: Cambridge University Press, 1998), 344.

6. *The Life of Saint Teresa of Avila, by Herself,* trans. J. M. Cohen (Harmondsworth: Penguin, 1957), 210.

7. Terence Cave has shown how the idea of the great unfinished work,

central to *Middlemarch*, is one that can be linked to Pascal. The work we know as the *Pensées* is a fragmentary set of notes towards a projected "Apologia" or defence of Christianity. See his "A 'Deep though broken wisdom': George Eliot, Pascal and *Middlemarch*," *Rivista di Letterature moderne e comparate* 51 (1998): 305–19, at 310.

8. "Though Women Strive," 22.3, in *The Complete Works of John Lyly*, ed. R. W. Bond, 3 vols. (Oxford: Clarendon Press, 1902), 3:462.

9. See the letter from Lord Peter's uncle, Paul Austin Delagardie, prefixed to the second edition of Sayers's *Clouds of Witness* (London: Gollancz, 1935).

10. *Effie in Venice: Unpublished Letters of Mrs. John Ruskin Written from Venice Between 1849–1852*, ed. Mary Lutyens (London: John Murray, 1965), 21.

11. The statement is given at length in Mary Lutyens, *Millais and the Ruskins* (London: John Murray, 1967), 188–92.

12. Ibid., 191 n.

13. See *Effie in Venice*, ed. Lutyens, 20.

14. John Batchelor, *John Ruskin: No Wealth but Life* (London: Chatto and Windus, 2000), 135.

15. In a letter to the author.

16. Mark Pattison, *Isaac Casaubon, 1559–1614* (London: Longmans, Green, 1875), 377.

17. George Eliot, Review of Heinrich von Riehl, *The Natural History of the People, or the Foundation of a German Sociopolitical System, Westminster Review* 66 (July 1856): 51–74.

18. See Ernest Jones, *Sigmund Freud: Life and Work*, 3 vols. (London: Hogarth, 1953–57), 1:191.

19. A. D. Nuttall, *Why Does Tragedy Give Pleasure?* (Oxford: Clarendon Press, 1996), 58, 60.

20. James Frazer, *Adonis, Attis, Osiris*, 3d ed., 2 vols. (London: Macmillan, 1914), 1:298. These two volumes form vols. 5 and 6 of *The Golden Bough*, 12 vols. (1911–15).

21. Friedrich Max Müller, *Lectures on the Science of Language*, 2 vols. (1885; facsimile reprint, London: Routledge/Thoemmes Press, 1994), 1:11. See also Frank M. Turner, *The Greek Heritage in Victorian Britain* (New Haven and London: Yale University Press, 1981), 107.

22. Friedrich Max Müller, *History of Ancient Sanskrit Literature* (London: Williams and Norgate, 1859), 3.

23. *The George Eliot Letters*, ed. Gordon S. Haight, 7 vols. (New Haven: Yale University Press, 1954–55), 4:8.

24. See *George Eliot's Middlemarch Notebooks: A Transcription*, ed. John Clark Pratt and Victor A. Neufeldt (Berkeley: University of California Press, 1979), esp. 3, 54, 56, 57–58, 223–24, and Introduction, esp. xlviii–xlix.

25. Edward Pococke, *India in Greece or Truth in Mythology* (London: J. J. Griffin, 1852); Turner, *Greek Heritage in Victorian Britain*, 105. Pococke himself would wish to add the names of James Prinsep, Sir William Jones, and James Tod (41 f.).

26. Karl Otfried Müller, *Prolegomena zu einer wissenschaftlichen Mythologie* (Göttingen: Vandenhoeck and Ruprecht, 1825), trans. John Leitch (London: Longmans, Brown, Green, and Longmans, 1845). The Göttingen edition is available in facsimile (Darmstadt: Wissenschaftichliche Buchgesellschaft, 1970).

27. *Eliot's Middlemarch Notebooks*, ed. Pratt and Neufeldt, xlviii. R. W. Mackay's *Progress of the Intellect* appeared in the *Westminster Review* 54 (January 1851): 353–68.

28. Müller, *Lectures on the Science of Language*, 2:407.

29. R. W. Mackay, *The Powers of the Intellect as Exemplified in the Religious Development of the Greeks and Hebrews*, 2 vols. (London: John Chapman, 1850), 1:215.

30. John Mayor, "Latin-English Lexicography," *Journal of Classical and Sacred Philology* 2 (November 1855): 271.

31. *Eliot's Middlemarch Notebooks*, ed. Pratt and Neufeldt, xlvi.

32. Charles François Dupuis, *Origine de tous les cultes*, 3 vols. (Paris: H. Agasse, 1794), 3:55–64, 114, 115.

33. Pococke, *India in Greece*, 8.

34. Jacob Bryant, *A New System, or, An Analysis of Ancient Mythology*, 3 vols. (London: T. Payne, 1774–76), 3:72.

35. See *Eliot's Middlemarch Notebooks*, ed. Pratt and Neufeldt, xlvii.

36. Ibid.

37. William Hurd, *New Universal History of the Religious Rites, Ceremonies and Customs of the Whole World* (London: Alexander Hogg, 1788), 669.

38. See Stephen Prickett, *Words and the Word* (Cambridge: Cambridge University Press, 1986), esp. 105–13.

39. See Turner, *Greek Heritage in Victorian Britain*, 104, 107.

40. Oscar Wilde, "Phrases and Philosophies for the Use of the Young," first published in the December 1894 (and only) issue of the Oxford student magazine *The Chamelean*.

41. Richard M. Dorson, "Eclipse of Solar Mythology," in Thomas A. Sebeok, *Myth: A Symposium* (Philadelphia: American Folklore Society, 1955), 15–38, at 20, n. 22. Littledale's squib, "The Oxford Solar Myth,"

first appeared in 1870 in the fifth issue of *Kottabos*, a magazine of Trinity College, Dublin.

42. George Eliot, *Middlemarch*, World's Classics, ed. David Carroll, intro. Felicia Bonaparte (Oxford: Oxford University Press, 1997), xl.

43. Frazer, *Adonis, Attis, Osiris*, 1:303–4; Frazer, *Balder the Beautiful*, 2 vols. (London: Macmillan, 1913), 1:22. These two volumes form vols. 10 and 11 of *The Golden Bough*.

44. See *Eliot's Middlemarch Notebooks*, ed. Pratt and Neufeldt, 22, where the Greek is in fact mistranscribed. The phrase is from Hippocrates "On Elegance," 5.

45. The eleventh of the theses on Feuerbach, in Karl Marx and Friedrich Engels, *Collected Works*, 48 vols. (London: Lawrence and Wishart, 1975–2001), 5:8.

46. *George Eliot Letters*, ed. Haight, 5:322.

47. See F. W. H. Myers, "George Eliot," *Century Magazine* 23 (November 1881): 60, and Gordon S. Haight, *George Eliot: A Biography* (Oxford: Clarendon Press, 1968), 450.

Chapter 2: Mark Pattison

1. Letter to Frank Wilson, 20 February 1879, in *The Autobiography and Letters of Mrs. M. O. W. Oliphant*, ed. Mrs. Harry Coghill (Edinburgh: William Blackwood and Sons, 1899), 277.

2. Quoted in John Sparrow, *Mark Pattison and the Idea of a University* (Cambridge: Cambridge University Press, 1967), 14.

3. British Museum Add. MS 49392, ff.138–45. See also John Sparrow's letter in the *Times Literary Supplement*, 16 March 1963.

4. Gordon S. Haight, *George Eliot: A Biography* (Oxford: Clarendon Press, 1968), 449–50, 565.

5. Mark Pattison, *Memoirs* (London: Macmillan, 1885), 11.

6. V. H. H. Green, *Oxford Common Room: A Study of Lincoln College and Mark Pattison* (London: Edward Arnold, 1957), 209.

7. Sparrow, *Mark Pattison and the Idea of a University*, 49.

8. Green, *Oxford Common Room*, 205.

9. Henry Nettleship, *The Academy*, 9 August 1884, cited in Haight, *George Eliot*, 563.

10. Ibid., 449.

11. Ibid.

12. Richard Ellmann, Letter, *Times Literary Supplement*, 30 March 1973.

13. Sparrow, *Mark Pattison and the Idea of a University*, 5.

14. Ibid., 1, 12.

15. Mrs. Humphry Ward, *A Writer's Recollections* (London: W. Collins Sons, 1918), 109–10; quoted in Haight, *George Eliot*, 427–28.

16. Sparrow, *Mark Pattison and the Idea of a University*, 13.

17. Haight, *George Eliot*, 564.

18. Sparrow, *Mark Pattison and the Idea of a University*, 1.

19. Pattison, *Memoirs*, 319–20, hereafter cited in the text as *Memoirs*.

20. Sparrow, in *Times Literary Supplement*, 15 June 1973.

21. Sparrow, *Mark Pattison and the Idea of a University*, 3.

22. In *The Plays of J. M. Barrie* (London: Hodder and Stoughton, 1931), 563.

23. Dante *La Vita Nuova*, 1.

24. Sparrow, *Mark Pattison and the Idea of a University*, 34.

25. See Green, *Oxford Common Room*, 28, 192.

26. See A. O. Lovejoy and G. Boas, *Primitivism and Related Ideas in Antiquity* (Baltimore: Johns Hopkins University Press, 1935), esp. 9–11.

27. Sparrow, *Mark Pattison and the Idea of a University*, 82.

28. Ibid.

29. In M. G. Brock and M. C. Curthoys, eds., *Nineteenth Century Oxford*, vol. 6 of *The History of the University of Oxford* (Oxford: Clarendon Press, 1997), 165.

30. Sparrow, *Mark Pattison and the Idea of a University*, 65–66, 70.

31. Ibid., 70.

32. Brock and Curthoys, eds., *Nineteenth Century Oxford*, 345–47.

33. Sparrow, *Mark Pattison and the Idea of a University*, 66.

34. Brock and Curthoys, eds., *Nineteenth Century Oxford*, 150.

35. Sparrow, *Mark Pattison and the Idea of a University*, 81.

36. Brock and Curthoys, eds., *Nineteenth Century Oxford*, 150.

37. Sparrow, *Mark Pattison and the Idea of a University*, 70.

38. Thomas Hughes, *Tom Brown at Oxford* (London: Macmillan, 1900), ch. 24, 226.

39. Brock and Curthoys, eds., *Nineteenth Century Oxford*, 347.

40. Hughes, *Tom Brown at Oxford*, 224.

41. Ibid., 225.

42. Ibid. Marriage was permitted to those in "halls" as distinct from colleges (large colleges often had halls attached to them). Thus Robert Stephen Hawker, remembered today for the rousing chorus "And shall Trelawny die?" was matriculated at Pembroke College, Oxford, in 1823 and then almost immediately fell in love with and married (when only nineteen) a lady much older than himself. The matter was easily dealt with. He "migrated" to Magdalen Hall and graduated in 1828.

43. Sparrow, *Mark Pattison and the Idea of a University*, 72.

44. Hughes, *Tom Brown at Oxford*, ch. 27, 244.

45. See Sparrow, *Mark Pattison and the Idea of a University*, 61.

46. See Evelyn Abbott, "Jowett, Benjamin," in *The Dictionary of National Biography* (Oxford: Oxford University Press, 1908–37).

47. See Joseph Lightfoot's articles in *Journal of Classical and Sacred Philology* 3 (March 1856): 81–121.

48. *P. Vergilii Maronis Opera*, 2d ed., edited with a commentary by John Conington, 3 vols. (London: Whittaker, 1865), 1:89.

49. François, duc de La Rochefoucauld, *Maximes*, ed. Jacques Truchet (Paris: Garnier France, 1967), 306.

50. Mark Pattison, "Pope and His Editors," first published in the *British Quarterly Review*, 1872; reprinted in *Essays by the Late Mark Pattison*, ed. Henry Nettleship, 2 vols. (Oxford: Clarendon Press, 1889), 2:350–95, at 351.

51. Mark Pattison, "The Present State of Theology in Germany," in *Essays*, ed. Nettleship, 2:243.

52. Green, *Oxford Common Room*, 94–95.

53. See *Memoirs of the Life of Edward Gibbon*, ed. G. Birkbeck Hill (London: Methuen, 1900), 167, and Gibbon, *Decline and Fall of the Roman Empire*, ed. J. B. Bury, 7 vols. (London: Methuen, 1911–21), 7:308.

54. Sparrow, *Mark Pattison and the Idea of a University*, 20.

55. Mark Pattison, "Tendencies of Religious Thought in England, 1688–1750," reprinted in *Essays*, ed. Nettleship, 2:42–108, at 105.

56. Ibid., 2:53.

57. See ibid., 2:46–47.

58. Ibid., 2:48.

59. See Isabel Rivers, *Reason, Grace and Sentiment*, vol. 2: *Shaftesbury to Hume* (Cambridge: Cambridge University Press, 2000), 59.

60. Jonathan Swift, "Thoughts on Religion," in *Irish Tracts, 1720–1723, and Sermons*, ed. Herbert Davis (Oxford: Basil Blackwell, 1948), 262. Note further that it is no longer the devil but God who sows doubts in the mind of the believer.

61. Leslie Stephen, *History of English Thought in the Eighteenth Century*, 2 vols. (1876; reprint, London: Rupert Hart-Davis, 1962), 1:69.

62. Pattison, "Tendencies of Religious Thought in England," 2:55.

63. Ibid.; see Boswell's *Life of Johnson*, ed. R. W. Chapman, new ed., corrected by J. D. Fleeman (London: Oxford University Press, 1970), 189.

64. Pattison, "Tendencies of Religious Thought in England," 2:97.

65. Ibid., 99.

66. Mark Pattison, *Isaac Casaubon* (London: Longmans, Green, 1875), 161–62.

67. Pattison, "Tendencies of Religious Thought in England," 2:50.

68. Ibid.

69. *The George Eliot Letters*, ed. Gordon S. Haight, 7 vols. (New Haven: Yale University Press, 1954–55), 6:202–3; cf. 6:210.

70. See Pattison, "Pope and His Editors," 2:389.

71. Pattison, "Tendencies of Religious Thought in England," 2:70–72.

72. Michael Bauman, *Milton's Arianism* (Frankfurt: Peter Lang, 1987).

73. See David Masson, *Life of John Milton*, 7 vols. (London: Macmillan, 1881–84), 6:823.

74. Mark Pattison, *Milton* (1879; London: Macmillan, 1902), 45, hereafter cited in the text as *Milton*.

75. Milton, *Defensio Secunda*, in *The Prose Works of John Milton*, ed. Charles Symmons, 7 vols. (London: J. Johnson, 1806), 5:230.

76. Ibid.

77. Anthony Grafton, *Joseph Scaliger: A Study in the History of Classical Scholarship*, 2 vols. (Oxford: Clarendon Press, 1983–93), 1:103.

78. W. H. David, *Notes and Queries*, 7th ser. (1889): 366.

79. Samuel Johnson, *Lives of the English Poets*, ed. G. Birkbeck Hill, 3 vols. (Oxford: Clarendon Press, 1905), 1:165–66.

80. See Alexander Gilchrist, *The Life of William Blake, "Pictor Ignotus,"* 2d ed., 2 vols. (London: Macmillan, 1880), 1:112.

81. Quoted in Sparrow, *Mark Pattison and the Idea of a University,* 11–12.

82. Arthur Ransome, *Missee Lee* (London: Jonathan Cape, 1941), 85, 213. The reference is to Cooper's Oxford marmalade, which is indeed very good.

83. *Report of the Commissioners Appointed to Inquire into the State, Discipline, Studies and Revenues of the University and Colleges of Oxford, Together with the Evidence and an Appendix* (London: W. Clowes and Sons, 1852), *Evidence,* 43. This report is vol. 22 of the Sessions and vol. 5 of *Reports from Commissioners.*

84. See Joseph Butler, preface to *Fifteen Sermons*, in *The Works of Joseph Butler*, ed. W. E. Gladstone, 2 vols. (Oxford: Clarendon Press, 1896), 2:24.

85. See, e.g., *Memoirs*, 325.

86. Milton, *Reason of Church Government*, book 2, in *Complete Prose Works of John Milton*, ed. Douglas Bush et al., 8 vols. (New Haven: Yale University Press, 1953–82), 1:810.

87. Green, *Oxford Common Room*, 180.

88. Pattison, "The Present State of Theology in Germany," in *Essays*, ed. Nettleship, 2:214.
89. Ibid., 229.
90. Ibid., 241–43.
91. Ibid., 252.
92. F. H. Bradley, *Ethical Studies* (London: Henry S. King, 1876), 282–84. Matthew Arnold, *Literature and Dogma*, 1.5 (London: Macmillan, 1903), 58.
93. Pattison, "Present State of Theology in Germany," 2:247–48.
94. Bertrand Russell, *History of Western Philosophy* (London: George Allen and Unwin, 1946), 706.
95. Pattison, "Present State of Theology in Germany," 2:248.
96. Mark Pattison, "Joseph Scaliger," first published in the *Quarterly Review*, July 1860; reprinted in *Essays*, ed. Nettleship, 1:132–95, at 136.
97. "Life of Montaigne," in *Essays*, ed. Nettleship, 2:323–49, at 324.
98. Pattison, "Present State of Theology in Germany," 2:232.
99. Ibid.
100. Mark Pattison, "Joseph Scaliger," reprinted in *Essays*, ed. Nettleship, 1:132–95.
101. *Essays*, ed. Nettleship, 1:196–243.
102. Ibid., 1:201, 203.
103. Pattison, "Joseph Scaliger," 1:135.
104. Ibid., 1:148. For Addison on ballads, see *Spectator* no. 70, 21 May 1711, and no. 74, 25 May 1711.
105. Pattison, "Joseph Scaliger," 1:163.
106. Grafton, *Joseph Scaliger*, 1:122.
107. This is Pattison's version of the story. Anthony Grafton points out that Scaliger was ready to believe that Jerome *had* translated both books but that the first had been lost (*Joseph Scaliger*, 2:534).
108. Pattison, "Joseph Scaliger," 1:185–87.

Chapter 3: Isaac Casaubon

1. Mark Pattison, *Isaac Casaubon* (London: Longmans, Green, 1875), hereafter cited in the text as *IC*.
2. *Secunda Scaligerana*, in P. Daismaizeaux, ed., *Scaligerana, Thuana, et Columesiana*, 2 vols. (Amsterdam: Cevens et Mortier, 1740), 2:259.
3. "Mihi nec vacat, nec libet, hoc praesertim tempore: quo allatus mihi tristissimus de obitu—hei mihi!—optimi optimeque de me meriti parentis mihi nuntius, ita me perculit affecitque, ut, prorsus ab istis mansuetioribus Musis abhorrens animus, alias literas requirat, in quibus

acquiescat,ac tanti vulneris medicinam reperiat," *Strabōnos Geōgraphikōn Bibloi 13*, "Isaacus Casaubonus recensuit" (Vignon: Eustathius, 1587), Commentary (separately page-numbered), 84.

4. Isaac Casaubon, *Ephemerides*, ed. J. Russell, 2 vols. (Oxford: Oxford University Press, 1850), 1:250.

5. *Secunda Scaligerana*, ed. Desmaizeaux, 2:259–60.

6. J. E. Sandys, *A History of Classical Scholarship*, 3 vols. (Cambridge: Cambridge University Press, 1903–8), 2:207.

7. Ibid., 2:203.

8. "A.d. Kal. Dec. 1610," letter no. 692 in *Isaaci Casauboni Epistolae* (hereafter cited as *Epistolae*), ed. T. Janson ab Almeloveen (Rotterdam: C. Fritsch and M. Böhm, 1709), 362.

9. "A.d.vii Eid. Februar. 1613," letter no. 864, to Philippe Jacques de Maussac, in ibid., 519.

10. *Isaaci Casauboni ad Frontonem Ducaeum S.J. Theologum epistola* (London: Ioannes Norton, 1611).

11. *The Answere of Master Isaac Casaubon to the Epistle of the Most Illustrious and Most Reverend Cardinall Perron* (London: William Apseley, 1612).

12. For Casaubon's controversy with Fronto and Du Perron and for the king's policy, see W. B. Patterson, *King James VI and I and the Reunion of Christendom* (Cambridge: Cambridge University Press, 2000), 131 f.

13. *Epistolae*, "a.d. vi Eid. Nov. 1612," letter no. 837, in *Epistolae*, 489.

14. "A.d. vi Eid. Januar 1611," letter no. 703, in ibid., 369.

15. *Ephemerides*, ed. Russell, 2:846. See also *IC*, 465.

16. In Casaubon's manuscript *Adversaria* in the Bodleian Library, tom. 28, 125 (Casaubon's numbering repeats itself; this is two leaves from the end).

17. *Anatomy of Melancholy*, ed. Thomas C. Faulkner et al., 3 vols. (Oxford: Clarendon Press, 1989–), 1.2.3.15, 1:308.

18. Nicholson Baker, *Room Temperature* (London: Granta Books, 1998), 74–75.

19. Ibid., 74.

20. John Sparrow, *Mark Pattison and the Idea of a University* (Cambridge: Cambridge University Press, 1967), 53–54.

21. Meric Casaubon, *Pietas contra maledicos patrij nominis, & religionis hostes* (London: Bibliopolarum, 1621), 85.

22. See L. W. B. Brockliss, "Patterns of Attendance at the University of Paris, 1400–1800," *Historical Journal* 21, no. 3 (1978): 503–44, at 511 and 516.

23. M. T. Clanchy, *Abelard: A Medieval Life* (Oxford: Blackwell, 1999), 77.

24. See the English translation of Bayle, *An Historical and Critical Dictionary,* 4 vols. (London: C. Harper et al., 1710), 4:2691–92, s.v. "Scioppius." See also Anthony Grafton, *Joseph Scaliger: A Study in the History of Classical Scholarship,* 2 vols. (Oxford: Clarendon Press, 1983–93), 2:347–48.

25. See S. Schoenbaum, *Shakespeare's Lives* (Oxford: Clarendon Press, 1970), 401.

26. U. von Wilamowitz-Moellendorff, *History of Classical Scholarship,* trans. Alan Harris (London: Gerald Duckworth, 1982), 52.

27. John Aubrey, in *Aubrey's Brief Lives,* ed. Oliver Lawson Dick (London: Mandarin, 1992), 154.

28. Letter to Francesco Vettori, 10 December 1513, in *The Literary Works of Machiavelli,* trans. J. R. Hale (London: Oxford University Press, 1961), 139.

29. *The Letters of John Keats, 1814–1821,* ed. H. E. Rollins, 2 vols. (Cambridge: Cambridge University Press, 1958), 2:186.

30. C. S. Lewis, *A Preface to Paradise Lost* (London: Oxford University Press, 1960), 5.

31. See Bayle's *Dictionnaire historique et critique,* 4 vols. (Rotterdam: Reinier Leers, 1702), 3:2897–98, s.v. "Tiraqueau."

32. "Vi Kal. Mart. 1601"; Russell gives the (very odd) French thus in his edition of *Ephemerides,* 1:335.

33. "Iv, Kal Sept," ibid., 2:101.

34. In ibid., 2:1012.

35. Hugh Lloyd-Jones, *Blood for the Ghosts* (London: Duckworth, 1982), 17.

36. Letter no. 453, to Vertunien, in *Epistolae.* See also Sandys, *History of Classical Scholarship,* 2:205.

37. Calvin himself faces this implication squarely and accepts it at *Institutes* 1.14.17 and 1.16.8.

38. Rudolf Pfeiffer, *A History of Classical Scholarship from 1300 to 1850* (Oxford: Clarendon Press, 1976), 122.

39. On the first page of the Prolegomena to *Historiae Augustae Scriptores Sex* ("Isaacus Casaubonus recensuit").

40. Cited by Degory Wheare in his *De Ratione,* translated by Edmund Bohun as *The Method and Order of Reading Both Civil and Ecclesiastical Histories* (London, 1694), 108.

41. Bodleian Lib. MS Casaubon 28, fol. 127. See also Anthony Grafton, *Commerce with the Classics: Ancient Books and Renaissance Readers* (Ann Arbor: University of Michigan Press, 1997), 205, and Lisa Jardine and Anthony Grafton, "Studied for Action: How Gabriel Harvey Read His Livy," *Past and Present* 129 (1990): 30–77, at 75.

42. Anthony Grafton, "Protestant versus Prophet," *Journal of the Warburg and Courtauld Institutes* 46 (1983): 78–93, at 82.
43. See Sandys, *History of Classical Scholarship*, 2:207.
44. Aeschylus, *Agamemnon*, ed. Eduard Fraenkel, 3 vols. (Oxford: Clarendon Press, 1950). See his Prolegomena, 1:36–38, and Appendix 1, 1:62–78.
45. R. D. Dawe, *The Collation and Investigation of Manuscripts of Aeschylus* (Cambridge: Cambridge University Press, 1964).
46. *Agamemnon*, ed. Fraenkel, 2:42; Denniston and Page agree: Aeschylus, *Agamemnon*, ed. J. D. Denniston and Denys Page (Oxford: Clarendon Press, 1957), 74.
47. *Aeschylus*, with an English translation by Herbert Weir Smyth, 2 vols. (London: Heinemann, 1946), 2:77.
48. *Agamemnon*, ed. Fraenkel, 2:421–24. See, e.g., *Agamemnon*, ed. Denniston and Page, 152.
49. *Agamemnon*, ed. Fraenkel, 1:38.
50. Ibid., 1:75 n. It looks as if Oxford-based Pattison was largely unaware of the editions of classical authors now held in the University Library of Cambridge, with marginal annotations in Casaubon's hand—not only his Aeschylus (Adv. b.3.3) but also his Herodotus (Adv. a.3.2), his Pliny (Adv. a.3.1), his Terence (Adv. e.3.1), his Arrian (Adv. d.3.5), and his Tacitus (Adv. d.3.14). These annotations exhibit astonishing powers of cross-reference and analysis.
51. Eduard Fraenkel, "Aeschylus: New Texts and Old Problems," *Proceedings of the British Academy* 28 (1942): 237–58, at 258.
52. *Agamemnon*, ed. Fraenkel, 1:65.
53. Grafton, "Protestant versus Prophet," 82.
54. In *Hermetica*, ed. with an English translation and notes by Walter Scott, 4 vols. (Oxford: Clarendon Press, 1924–36), 1:262–64.
55. *Isaaci Casauboni De Rebus Sacris et Ecclesiasticis: Exercitationes XVI. Ad Cardinalis Baronii Prolegomena in Annales* (Geneva: J. A. and S. De Tournes, 1655), hereafter cited as *Exercitationes*, Exercit. 1.10, pp. 65, 69, 71. See also *Hermetica*, ed. Scott, 1:41.
56. See Robin Lane Fox, *The Unauthorized Version* (London: Penguin, 1991), 177.
57. See *Exercitationes*, 67, and *Eusebii Pamphili Chronici Canones* (Jerome's version), ed. J. K. Fotheringham (London: H. Milford, 1923), 62.
58. *Exercitationes*, 79.
59. Ibid., 71. See *Hermetica*, ed. Scott, 1:41.
60. *Hermetica*, ed. Scott, 1:41 n.
61. *Exercitationes*, 79.

62. See F. Purnell, Jr., "Francesco Patrizi and the Critics of Hermes Trismegistus," *Journal of Renaissance and Medieval Studies* 6 (1976): 155–88. Goropius Becanus (Jean van Gorp, 1518–72) was a physician, master of many languages, and a writer on exotic curiosities. It is important not to confuse him with the Jesuit Becanus (Martin Bécan, 1563–1624), who published in 1610 a refutation of the "Apologia" of King James.

63. *Isaaci Hortiboni Notae Ad Diogenis Laertii libros de vitis, dictis & decretis principum philosophorum libri x* (Morgiis: J. le Preux, 1583), 3–4. See also Grafton, "Protestant versus Prophet," 80.

64. Beroaldus, *Chronicae Scripturae sacrae auctoritate constitutum* (Geneva, 1575), 23.

65. See Grafton, "Protestant versus Prophet," 86 n.

66. "Xi Kal Nov 1610," *Ephemerides,* ed. Russell, 2:775–76.

67. Ralph Cudworth, *The True Intellectual System of the Universe,* 2d ed. (London: J. Walthoe et al., 1743), 1.5.743.

68. Ibid., 1.4.320–27. See also D. P. Walker, *The Ancient Theology* (London: Duckworth, 1972), 241.

69. *Hermetica,* ed. Scott, 1:276.

70. Casaubon refers to Phidias at *Exercitationes,* 79.

71. *Three Books of Occult Philosophy,* 3.6, in *Henrici Cornelii Agrippae Opera* (Lyons, 1600), facsimile reprint, ed. R. H. Popkin, 2 vols. (Hildesheim: Georg Olms, 1970), 1:256 (my translation).

72. Grafton, "Protestant versus Prophet," 90.

73. *Prima Scaligerana, nusquam antehac edita,* ed. T. Faber (Groningen, 1669), 86.

74. Mark Pattison, *Memoirs* (London: Macmillan, 1885), 331–32.

75. Ibid., 486–87.

76. Lucretius *De Rerum Natura* 3.19–22.

77. Tennyson, "The Passing of Arthur," 427–31. Cf. Tennyson's "Lucretius," 105–10.

78. "Xvii Kal. Oct.," *Ephemerides,* ed. Russell, 1:299.

79. "X Kal. Nov., 1599," ibid., 1:202.

80. "V Kal. Jan., 1599," ibid., 1:215.

Conclusion

1. Tom Stoppard, *The Invention of Love* (London: Faber and Faber, 1997), 28, hereafter cited as *IL.*

2. In A. E. Housman, *Selected Prose,* ed. John Carter (Cambridge: Cambridge University Press, 1961), 193.

3. *The Advancement of Learning,* in *The Philosophical Works of Francis Bacon,* ed. J. M. Robertson (London: George Routledge, 1905), 58.

4. E. M. Forster, *The Longest Journey* (London: Edward Arnold, 1884), 35 (the Abinger edition), hereafter cited as *Journey.* All subsequent references are to this edition.

5. When Virgil set sail for Greece, Horace in the third ode of the first book prayed to Venus to keep the poet of the *Aeneid* safe on the high seas. Here he calls Virgil, his anti-type in poetry, *animae dimidium meae,* "half my life."

6. William Empson, *Milton's God* (London: Chatto and Windus, 1961), vii.

7. Thomas Hardy, *Jude the Obscure* (Ontario: Broadview Press, 1999), 1.3: 57–58. All subsequent references are to this edition.

8. *Institutio Oratoria* 1.7.20, in the Oxford Text, ed. M. Winterbottom, 2 vols. (Oxford: Clarendon Press, 1970), 1:57.

9. Edith Sitwell, *English Eccentrics* (London: Faber and Faber, 1933), 207.

10. J. E. Sandys, *A History of Classical Scholarship,* 3 vols. (Cambridge: Cambridge University Press, 1903–8), 3:51.

11. *M. Manlii Astronomicon Liber Primus,* ed. A. E. Housman (London: Grant Richards, 1903), reprinted in *Selected Prose,* ed. Carter, 31.

12. Ibid., 44.

13. Review of Baehrens's Catullus, *Classical Review* 8 (1894): 251. In *Selected Prose,* ed. Carter, 72.

14. Gerard Manley Hopkins, "To Oxford" ("New-dated from the terms that reappear").

15. In the preface to *M. Manilii Astronomicon Liber Quintus,* ed. A. E. Housman (London: Richards Press, 1930), reprinted in *Selected Prose,* ed. Carter, 52.

Index

Abbott, E. A., 6
Abelard, Peter, 5
Aberdeen University, 84
Abraham, 160
Ackermann, Rudolph, 88
Adam and Eve, 2, 7, 9, 87–88, 111
Addison, Joseph, 121
Aeschylus, 25, 131, 152–58, 180, 202
Agrippa, Cornelius. *See* Cornelius
  Agrippa
Albert, Prince, 78
Alberti, Leon Battista, 8
Andrewes, Lancelot, 128, 132
Antigone, 36
Anti-semitism, 59
Aquinas, Thomas, 5, 42, 98–99
Ariadne, 36, 38, 45, 55, 77–78, 188
Arianism, 107–8
Aristophanes, 85–86, 161, 175, 180
Aristotle, 5, 84, 120, 134, 192, 203

Arminianism, 129–30, 147
Arnold, Matthew, 59, 91, 119, 174,
  195
Asceticism, 40–41
Asclepius, 160
Astypelaea of Crete, 149
Athanasius, 100
Athenaeus, 125, 134–35, 146, 152
Attis, 31
Augustine, 42
Augustus, emperor, 174
Aurispa, Giovanni, 154
Austen, Jane, 50–51
Ayer, A. J., 118

Bacon, Francis, 5–6, 10, 12, 25, 163
Baden-Powell, Robert, 179
Baehrens, Emil, 199
Baker, Nicholson, 132–33
Bancroft, Richard, 128

Baronius (Cesare Baronio), 130–31, 135, 148, 151–52, 154, 164
Baroque, 32, 38
Barrett, W. S., 198
Barrie, J. M., 84
Basilius, 142
Batchelor, John, 49–50
Bauman, Michael, 107
Baur, Ferdinand Christian, 120
Bayle, Pierre, 144
Becanus, Martinus, 162
Bede, Cuthbert, 88
Bellarmine, Robert, 147
Bentley, Richard, 104, 149, 198–99
Berkeley, George, 106
Bernard of Clairvaux, 5
Bernays, Jacob, 120, 123, 138
Bernini, Gian Lorenzo, 38–39
Beroaldus, 161
Bichat, Marie François, 68
Blake, Catherine, 111
Blake, William, 23, 62, 204
Boccaccio, Giovanni, 12
Boehler, Peter, 40
Bolingbroke, Henry St. John, Viscount, 103, 195
Bonaparte, Felicia, 64
Bossuet, Jacques-Bénigne, 42
Boswell, James, 103
Boucher, François, 78
Brabant, Robert Herbert, 74, 82–83
Bradley, F. H., 119
Brontë, Charlotte, 48
Browning, Robert, 9–25, 53–54, 68–69, 108, 121, 131, 146, 195; compared with Aristophanes, 86; on scholarship versus life, 113, 116, 169–70
Bryant, Jacob, 61–62
Buecheler, Franz, 199
Bunsen, Chevalier, 138
Burnet, Gilbert, 166
Burton, Robert, 14, 16–17, 86, 132
Butler, Joseph, 83, 105, 116

Cacciaguida, 171–72
Calvinism, 4, 42, 147, 200

Cambridge, University of, 89, 173, 187, 194
Canaye de Fresne, 126
Carey, John, 190
Carnap, Rudolf, 118
Casaubon, Arnaud, 124–25, 145
Casaubon, Edward (character in *Middlemarch*), 1, 6–10, 23, 25, 26–71, 111, 117, 195; real-life antecedents, 72–83, 106–7; his idea of a "key" rejected by Pattison, 120
Casaubon, Florence (neé Estienne), 125, 133, 144–45, 170
Casaubon, Isaac, 1, 10, 25, 81, 104, 120, 123–70; compared with Browning's "grammarian," 16; his devout Christianity, 56; in relation to his namesake in *Middlemarch*, 73–74, 79, 83; his diary especially fascinates Pattison, 108
Casaubon, John, 133
Casaubon, Meric, 28, 133
Casaubon, Philippa, 143
Catullus, 172–73, 199, 202
Cave, Terence, 209n7
Chaucer, Geoffrey, 32, 34–35, 202
Chekhov, Anton, 29
Chomsky, Noam, 22
Christie, Agatha, 204
Chrysostom, 14, 135
Cicero, 25, 109
Cimabue, 13
Cistercians, 99
Clanchy, M. T., 137–38
Coccius, Huldrichus, 12
Collins, Anthony, 104
Collins, Jackie, 204
Collins, Wilkie, 49
Commelin, Hieronymus, 140
Conan Doyle, Arthur, 204
Conington, John, 96–97, 106, 156–57
Conrad III, emperor, 171
Constantine, 164
Cornelius Agrippa, 6, 163
Cox, George W., 64
Crabbe, George, 202
Creuzer, Georg Friedrich, 60

Cudworth, Ralph, 161–63
Curthoys, M. C., 91, 92

Damarius, 140
Dante, 2–3, 5, 7, 169, 171–72, 194
Darwin, Charles Robert, 68
David, W. H., 109
Davy, Sir Humphrey, 28
Dawe, R. D., 154
Deism, 13, 55, 59, 101–5, 106
De La Mare, Walter, 203
Denniston, J. D., 19, 23
Dickens, Charles, 15, 33, 46, 62, 70, 81
Didymus, Chalcenteros, 14, 197
Dilke, Sir Charles, 73–76, 78
Diodati, Charles, 110
Diogenes Laertius, 134
Dionysius of Halicarnassus, 134
Donation of Constantine, 164
Donne, John, 16, 41, 147, 202, 204
Douglas, Lord Alfred, 181
Dryden, John, 158
Du Maurier, Daphne, 48
Du Perron, Jacques Davy, 126–27, 130–31, 147, 150, 152
Duplessis-Mornay, Philippe, 104, 125–27, 152, 168
Dupuis, Charles François, 60–61

Eagleton, Terry, 190
Ecphrasis, 37, 77
Eden, C. P., 95
Edict of Nantes, 126
Eliot, George, 23, 26–71, 72, 144, 146, 148, 187–88, 194–95
Eliot, T. S., 58, 66–67, 169
Ellman, Richard, 76
Empson, William, 193
Engels, Friedrich, 119
Epicurus, 19, 158
Erasmus, 16, 18, 19–20
Essex, Robert, earl of, 151
Estienne, Henri (Stephanus), 125, 134, 153, 161
Euhemerism, 61
Euripides, 25, 43, 84, 188, 198, 202, 204

Eusebius, 121, 160
Examinations in nineteenth-century Oxford, 92–94

Faustus, 2, 4, 7, 9, 67, 115
Feuerbach, Ludwig Andreas, 52
Flagellation, 40–41
Forster, E. M., 180, 186–88
Fraenkel, Eduard, 153–56, 158
Fragonard, Honoré, 78
Frankfurt, Book Fair, 140
Fraser, George MacDonald, 113
Frazer, Sir James George, 23, 53, 56–59, 66
Freud, Sigmund, 34–35, 39, 42, 57, 58–59, 63
Froben, Hieronymus, 142
Fronton du Duc (Fronto Ducaeus), 130

Galileo, 110
Gallicans, 128
Gallus, Io. Bapt., 128
Galton, Francis, 1–2
Gardner, Helen, 190
Gawain poet, the, 202
Geneva, university of, 136–37, 139
German scholarship, 51–52, 61, 67, 118
Gibbon, Edward, 58, 71, 97, 99–100, 104, 149
Gilbert, W. S., 175
Giotto, 12
Goldsmith, Oliver, 99, 146
Goodwin, Alfred, 173
Goropius Becanus, 161
Goulu, Jerome, 127
Gower, John, 3–4
Grafton, Anthony, 109, 121, 152, 160, 161, 163
Graves, R. P., 172
Gray, Effie Chalmers, 49–50
Gray, Thomas, 99
Green, T. H., 75, 76, 101, 105
Green, V. H. H., 74, 118
Gregorius Thaumaturgus, 135
Greuze, Jean-Baptiste, 77–78

Grote, George, 61
Gwynne, Stephen, 76

Haight, Gordon S., 74, 75, 76, 79–80, 82
Hall, S. P., 94
Halliwell-Phillips, J. O., 140
Hardy, Thomas, 22, 35, 87, 112, 194–95
Harrison, Jane, 56
Hawker, Robert Stephen, 213n42
Hazlitt, William, 50
Hegel, G. W. F., 96, 119
Heinsius, Daniel, 131, 138–39
Hellenism, 36, 61, 100, 160, 175, 182, 188
Henri IV, 125, 128, 130, 151
Herbert, George, 202
Hercules, 31
Hermes Trismegistus, 4, 56, 159
Hermetism, and the *Hermetica*, 4–7, 12, 13, 56, 135, 159–64, 178
Heywood, Jane, 91
Hippocrates, 4; quoted, 67
Hippolytus, 43
Hitler, Adolf, 127
Hobbes, Thomas, 141
Hodson, Frodsham, 84, 85
Homer, 2–3, 25, 167–69, 172, 180, 192, 202
Hooker, Richard, 40
Hopkins, Gerard Manley, 47, 202, 203
Horace, 174–75, 177, 182–84, 186–87, 202
Housman, A. E., 87, 171–87, 198–99, 203
Hughes, Thomas, 91, 93–95
Hume, David, 71, 75, 99, 103, 105
Hurd, William, 62–63

Ibsen, Henrik, 47

Jackson, Moses, 173, 176–79, 182–87
Jacobson, William, 92
James I, 128–31, 139, 147
Jansenism, 40

Jebb, Richard Claverhouse, 150, 177
Jenkins, Harold, 192
Jenkyns, Richard, 36
Jenne, Francis, 92
Jerome, 121
Jesuits, 40, 122, 130, 138
Jesus, 192
John of the Cross, Saint, 44
Johnson, Samuel, 30, 97–98, 109–10, 132, 163, 204
Jowett, Benjamin, 96, 113, 172, 177, 180, 182
Juvenal, 173

Kant, Immanuel, 75, 100–101
Keats, John, 16, 37, 45, 142, 192, 193, 202, 204
Kermode, Frank, 192
Kettlewell, J. L. R., 82
Knight, Richard Payne, 198

Labyrinth, 54–55
Lang, Andrew, 167
Langland, William, 202
La Rochefoucauld, François, duc de, 97
Lavoisier, Antoine, 67
Lawrence, D. H., 204
Leaf, Walter, 167
Leavis, F. R., 202, 204
Lee, Sidney, 76
Leibniz, Gottfried Wilhelm, 57, 105
Leighton, Frederic, Lord, 13
Lerner, Laurence, 193
Levens, Robert, 198
Lewes, George Henry, 77–78
Lewis, C. S., 144
Lightfoot, Joseph, 96
Linacre, Thomas, 18
Lipsius, Justus, 151
Lloyd, William, 166
Lloyd-Jones, Hugh, 2, 146
Locke, John, 29, 32, 42, 101–2
Lowth, Robert, 63
Lucan, 13
Lucretius, 19, 169

Luther, Martin, 139
Lutyens, Marty, 49–50

Machiavelli, Niccolo, 142
Mackay, R. W., 60
Maine, Henry James Sumner, 61
Mallett, David, 103
Manilius, 173, 198
Mantegna, Andrea, 13
Marcilius, 141
Marlowe, Christopher, 4, 7–9, 137, 202
Marsh, Herbert, 104
Martial, 175
Marvell, Andrew, 10–12, 202
Marx, Karl, 68, 119, 200, 201
Masson, David, 107–8
Mavor, John, 90
Mavortius, 198
Mayor, John, 60
Medcalf, Stephen, 121
Methodism, 40
Mill, J. S., 101
Milton, John, 15, 57, 90, 105, 179, 195, 202–4; on knowledge, 4–5; referred to in *Middlemarch*, 30–31, 38, 42, 44, 107; as seen by Mark Pattison, 107–13, 116–17; on superiority of Hebrew poetry, 143–44
Moberley, George, 92
Montaigne, Michel Eyguem de, 120
Monteiro, George, 18
Montpellier, 125, 139, 150
Moravians, 40
More, Thomas, 13
Morton, Thomas, 167
Moses, 56, 61, 160
Mosheim, J. L., 63, 118
Mozart, Wolfgang Amadeus, 168
Mozley, Thomas, 141
Muggletonians, 62
Müller, Friedrich Max, 59–60, 63–64
Müller, Karl Otfried, 60
Murray, Gilbert, 56
Musaeus, 161
Myers, Ernest, 167

Napoleon Bonaparte, 119, 127
Nettleship, Henry, 75, 120
Neufeldt, Victor A., 60
Newman, John Henry, 98–100, 105, 117–18, 121
Newton, Isaac, 139, 193
Noah, 165
Nominalism, 100

Odysseus, 2–4
Oliphant, Margaret, 72–73
Ophite Gnosticism, 62
Origen, 135
Ovid, 123
Oxford, 113, 115, 117, 131, 138, 141, 173, 194–96; in the nineteenth century, 83–97

Paley, William, 91
Paracelsus, 6
Paris, University of, 125, 137–38, 143
Pascal, Blaise, 40, 42
Pater, Walter, 75, 172, 181, 186
Patmore, Coventry, 144
Pattison, Francis. See Strong, Emilia Francis
Pattison, Mark, 1, 25, 72–122, 151–53, 173, 177, 187; his awareness of German pre-eminence in scholarship, 52; as possible model for Mr. Casaubon, 72–83; his non-election to the rectorship of Lincoln College, 81–82; his sense of affinity to Casaubon, 139–42, 146–49; underestimates Casaubon's scholarship, 158–59; not opposed to natural science, 166; writes verses in praise of Casaubon, 167–70; as character in Tom Stoppard's play, 172, 179
Pattison, Mark James, (Mark Pattison's father), 84–90, 105
Paul, Saint, 96
Peacock, Thomas Love, 135
Perronneau, Jean-Baptiste, 77
Persius, 97, 135
Petrarch, 12

Petrus Victorius, 153
Pfeiffer, Rudolf, 150
Phaedra, 43
Phidias, 162–63
Pithou, Pierre, 128
Plato, 4, 22, 86, 96, 109, 120, 160,
  163, 180–81, 188, 192
Pliny, 134
Pocock, Edward, 59, 61
Pollard, Alfred William, 176, 185–87
Polyaenus, 134
Polybius, 135, 141, 144, 151
Pope, Alexander, 57, 97, 104–5, 141,
  202
Popper, Karl, 67
Porson, Richard, 67, 198, 204
Postgate, John Percival, 172
Poussin, Nicolas, 90
Powell, Mary, 111–12
Pratt, John Clark, 60
Praxiteles, 188
Prideaux, Henry, 103
Prior, James, 99
Prolyot, Marie, 124
Ptolemy, 4
Pusey, Edward Bouverie, 98, 105,
  118
Pythagoras, 4

Quintilian, 198

Racine, Jean, 43
Ransome, Arthur, 113–15
Ricks, Christopher, 190
Riehl, Heinrich von, 56
Rogers, Benjamin Bickley, 175
Rome, 33–34, 37–39, 41, 48, 73, 78,
  150, 172
Rosebery, Lord (Archibald Philip
  Primrose), 77, 112
Rothe, Richard, 119
Ruskin, John, 49–50, 172
Russell, Bertrand, 119
Rutherford, Ernest, 193

Salmasius, Claudius (Claude de Saumaise), 108, 117, 131
Samson, 31

Sandford, D. K., 93
Sandys, J. E., 128
Sappho, 202
Savile, Sir Henry, 136, 148, 151
Sayers, Dorothy L., 48, 194–97
Scaliger, Joseph Justus, 12, 79, 119–
  24, 127, 131, 138–41, 148, 152; on
  grammar replacing theology, 164
Scaliger, Julius Caesar, 120
Schleiermacher, Friedrich, 118
Schulze, G. C., 199
Schütze, K. P., 157
Schweik, Robert C., 22
Science and magic, 2–8, 67, 163
Scioppius, Gaspar, 138–39
Scott, Walter, 129
Scott, Walter (editor of the Herme-
  tica), 161, 162–63
Seneca, 142
Shakespeare, William, 71, 131, 191–
  92, 202; Love's Labour's Lost, 8–10,
  13, 17, 86, 170, 179, 185; Merchant
  of Venice, 15; Othello, 22, 100; Henry
  IV, part 2, 28–29; Measure for Mea-
  sure, 41, 48; As You Like It, 44; An-
  tony and Cleopatra, 45; Hamlet, 51;
  Tempest, 65–66; King Lear, 69; Mac-
  beth, 143; Cymbeline, 166
Sharpe, C. K., 92
Shelley, Percy Bysshe, 66
Sidney, Sir Philip, 125
Sigonius, Carolus, 109
Sleath, John, 96
Smith, Adam, 29
Smithers, G. V., 198
Socrates, 85–86
Solar myth, 64–67
Sophists, 86
Sophocles, 25, 30, 71, 202
Southey, Robert, 29–30
Sparrow, John, 74, 75, 76, 79, 82–
  83, 89, 92, 138
Spenser, Edmund, 202
Spinoza, Benedict de, 19–20, 23
Stanley, A. P., 118
Stephen, Leslie, 102–3
Sterne, Laurence, 62, 176–77, 202
Stewart, Dugald, 105

Stoeber, Elias, 198–99
Stoppard, Tom, 171–87, 198
Strabo, 124, 134, 144
Strauss, David Friedrich, 52, 120
Strong, Emilia Francis, 72, 85
Sudhaus, Siegfried, 199
Suetonius, 134
Sullivan, Arthur, 175
Svaglic, Martin J., 22
Swift, Jonathan, 102
Swinburne, A. C., 76, 195
Syncellus, 121

Taylor, Jeremy, 40
Temple, Frederick, 93
Tennyson, Alfred, Lord, 12, 97, 169
Theocritus, 111, 125, 134, 188, 202
Theophrastus, 133, 134
Theresa, Saint, 36–39, 43, 68, 70
Thomson, Richard, 147
Thou, Jean Auguste de (Thuanus), 125, 127–28, 144
Tiraquellus (Andrée Tiraqueau), 144
Toland, John, 102
Tractarians, 89, 98–100, 102, 105–6
Triclinius, 154
Turnèbe, Adrien, 161, 162
Turner, Frank M., 59
Tutorial system, 93–95

Ultramontanism, 128
Ulysses, 2–5
Ussher, James, 117
Uytenbogaert, John, 147

Valla, Lorenzo, 12, 164
Vasari, Georgio, 12
Vaughan, Henry, 202
Vazeille, Mary, 195
Victoria, Queen, 78
Virgil, 18, 96–97, 114, 169, 172, 191, 198, 202; as seen by Horace, 174–76
Vives, Juan, 12
Voltaire (François Marie Arouet), 118

Wagner, Richard, 10
Walton, Izaak, 135
Warburton, William, 103
Ward, Mrs. Humphry, 52–53, 75, 77–78
Waugh, Evelyn, 90, 138
Weil, Simone, 194
Wells, H. G., 62
Wesley, John, 40, 195
Wilamowitz, Ulrich von, 140
Wilde, Oscar, 64, 172, 181, 186
Wilson, Bernard, 127
Wittgenstein, Ludwig, 169–70
Wolf, Friedrich August, 198
Wordsworth, William, 28, 89, 105–6, 139, 202
Wotton, Sir Henry, 140
Wycliffites, 101

Yeats, W. B., 9–10, 62, 172–73, 203